THE

SERENDIPITY
MINDSET

THE

SERENDIPITY
MINDSET

The Art *and* Science
of Creating Good Luck

—

CHRISTIAN BUSCH, PhD

RIVERHEAD BOOKS
New York
2020

RIVERHEAD BOOKS
An imprint of Penguin Random House LLC
penguinrandomhouse.com

Images courtesy of Penguin Random House Ltd.
Image on page 48 courtesy of Leith Sharp.

Riverhead and the R colophon are registered trademarks of Penguin Random House LLC

Library of Congress Cataloging-in-Publication Data
Names: Busch, Christian (Professor of business), author.
Title: The serendipity mindset: the art and science of creating good luck / Christian Busch, PhD.
Description: New York: Riverhead Books, 2020. | Includes bibliographical references and index.
Identifiers: LCCN 2020008801 (print) | LCCN 2020008802 (ebook) |
ISBN 9780593086025 (hardcover) | ISBN 9780593086049 (ebook)
Subjects: LCSH: Serendipity. | Success. | Success in business. | Fortune.
Classification: LCC BF637.S8 B795 2020 (print) |
LCC BF637.S8 (ebook) | DDC 158.1—dc23
LC record available at https://lccn.loc.gov/2020008801
LC ebook record available at https://lccn.loc.gov/2020008802

Printed in the United States of America
1   3   5   7   9   10   8   6   4   2

Book design by Cassandra Garruzzo

For my dear parents, Ulla and Rainer,
whose love, kindness, and resilient optimism have been
an inspiration to me throughout my life.

CONTENTS

―

THE

SERENDIPITY
MINDSET

INTRODUCTION

—

*I'm always surprised when I see people who have been
successful . . . and they're absolutely convinced that it's all because
they were so smart. And I'm always saying, well, I worked hard,
and I've got some talent, but there are a lot of hardworking,
talented people out there. . . . There was this element of chance to
it . . . of serendipity . . . [and] you want to see if you can maybe
figure out how to sprinkle that stardust on other people.*

BARACK OBAMA, 44TH PRESIDENT
OF THE UNITED STATES OF AMERICA

W̲e all like to feel like we are masters of our own destiny—to feel in
control of our future, to know how we will reach our goals and
ambitions. In short, we all like to have a plan.

This seemingly innate human desire to map out our future is reflected in
almost every aspect of modern life. Organizations, governments, and every
one of us all structure our activities around plans, strategies, and targets
that we make. We construct routines, rules, and processes—from setting
the alarm clock to organizing national elections—to ensure that those
plans come to fruition.

But are we really in control of our lives? Or is this just an illusion? Despite all of our planning, modeling, and strategizing, there appears to be
another factor at work: the unexpected.

We all recognize that unforeseen events, chance meetings, or seeming
coincidences are often not just minor distractions or specks of grit in the

machines of our well-oiled lives. The unexpected is often the force that makes the greatest difference to our lives and our futures. It is the critical factor.

Perhaps you found your spouse "by coincidence"? Or came across your new job or apartment "by accident"? Did you meet your future cofounder or investor "by chance"? Or did you "randomly" pick up a magazine just to find exactly what you needed to know to solve a problem?

How did such moments, big or small, change your life? How could your life have played out had everything just gone according to plan?

Wars are won or lost, companies thrive or collapse, and love is found or lost all on the turn of the unexpected. Whatever our ambitions are in life—finding business success, love, joy, or spiritual meaning—we are prone to coincidental encounters. The most mundane moment, like running into someone in the gym, can change your life.

Even in the rigorous world of scientific research, the power of the unexpected is (almost) always at play. Studies suggest that around 30 to 50 percent of major scientific breakthroughs emerge as the result of accidents or coincidences. One chemical spills into another, cells combine in dirty petri dishes, or there is a chance encounter between experts whose incidental conversation sparks new insights. The greatest opportunities, for individuals and organizations alike, are often a matter of serendipity.[1]

So does most success boil down to blind luck, to success or failure brought simply by chance rather than through our own actions? No; intuitively we sense that this isn't true either. While we recognize that the greatest turning points and transformative opportunities in our lives often seem to occur by chance, some people just seem to have more luck, and subsequently more success and joy, than others.

This isn't just a modern phenomenon, either: The chemist and biologist Louis Pasteur thought that chance favors the prepared mind. The military leader and emperor Napoléon Bonaparte said he would rather have lucky generals than good ones. And the Roman writer and statesman Seneca argued that luck is a matter of preparation meeting opportunity.

Their beliefs all reflect the idea that while chance is a real force in our lives and in the world, there is more to life than blind luck. Indeed, the word "fortune" can refer to both success and luck. Even commonplace phrases such as "You make your own luck" or "He's a man with an eye for the main chance" all point to the idea that success in life depends on an interaction—a *synthesis*—between pure chance and human effort.

What is really going on here? Are some people able to create the conditions for positive coincidences to happen more often than others? Are they better able to spot and grasp these moments and turn them into positive outcomes? Can our education and approach to work and life equip us with the most important skill of all—the ability to navigate the unexpected and make our own "smart" luck?

This is a book about the interactions of coincidence, human ambition, and imagination. It is a book about *serendipity*—this unexpected good luck resulting from unplanned moments in which proactive decisions lead to positive outcomes. Serendipity is the hidden force in the world, and it is present all around us, from the smallest day-to-day events, to life-changing, and sometimes world-changing, breakthroughs.

However, only few of us—including many of the people you will meet in this book—have deciphered this code and developed the mindset needed to turn the unexpected into a success and a force for good.

Once we realize that serendipity is not just about a coincidence that happens *to* us but is actually a process of *spotting and connecting the dots* do we start to see bridges where others see gaps.[2] Only then does serendipity start happening all the time in our lives.

Then, the unexpected changes from being a threat to a constant source of joy, of wonder, of meaning—and of sustained success. In a world that has been running on a fight-or-flight lizard brain, in which fear-mongering, populism, and uncertainty have taken over, the mindsets and contexts that we are used to are simply not working anymore. Developing a serendipity mindset and shaping the related conditions becomes the essential life skill and capability for ourselves, our children, and our organizations.

Imagine a world driven by curiosity, opportunity, and a sense of connection, rather than by fear, scarcity, and jealousy. What would it look like? A world in which enormous challenges like climate change and social inequalities are being tackled by solutions that are bold and up to the task.

In a fast-changing world in which many of the emerging problems are complex and where much of our future will be driven by the unexpected, developing a serendipity mindset becomes an evolutionary necessity as well as an opportunity to identify what is most important to us so that we can develop a true enthusiasm for life.

Serendipity is a popular subject—but we know surprisingly little about what specific, science-based methods we can adopt to create conditions for serendipity in our lives. And we know little about how this plays out in different contexts.

The Serendipity Mindset fills this gap. It stands on the shoulders of giants, on science that explains how serendipity can unfold and on anecdotal accounts of how we can nurture serendipity for ourselves and others. Building on those stories and on research in the natural and social sciences, as well as highlighting inspiring examples from around the globe, this book offers a framework and exercises to help you make fortunate surprises more likely to happen in life—and with better outcomes.

This active perspective on serendipity—"smart luck," if you will—is thus different from the "luck of the draw," the "plain" or "blind" luck that just happens to us without effort.

If you aim to shape your own future and the future of people around you—even if that future is impossible to predict—then this book is for you. It gives a holistic, science-based insight into how lucky (and unlucky) coincidences can be facilitated, leveraged, and sustained—but never really emulated. It is the first comprehensive science-based methodology and framework on how to develop a serendipity mindset and the related conditions.

A serendipity mindset is both a philosophy of life that many of the world's most successful and joyful people have turned to in order to create meaningful lives and a capability that each of us can develop.

Along with conversations with individuals I call "serendipitors," this book draws on my decade-long experience as a researcher, business consultant, university lecturer, codirector at the London School of Economics Innovation Lab and at New York University's Global Economy Program, and my fifteen years of cultivating serendipity in my own life. This is an interest I have pursued as the cofounder of both the Sandbox Network, a community of inspiring young people that is active in over twenty countries, and Leaders on Purpose, a global organization that brings together high-impact executives and policy makers. My advisory work with a broad range of organizations and individuals—from one of China's largest companies to small community organizations around the world—has given me access to a diverse range of people, and the opportunity to witness serendipity in a wide range of situations and settings. Living in a variety of places, from Moscow to Mexico City, has imbued in me a deep appreciation for contextual nuances, which this book will explore.

The Serendipity Mindset combines my own research with colleagues at the London School of Economics, Harvard University, the World Economic Forum, Strathmore Business School, and The World Bank with the latest studies in neuroscience, psychology, management, the arts, physics, and chemistry. Based on hundreds of academic papers and over two hundred interviews and conversations with a diverse range of people from all corners of the world, it offers inspiring firsthand stories and experiences from individuals in all walks of life—from former-drug-addicts-turned-teachers in the impoverished Cape Flats in Cape Town to the filmmaker in New York to the entrepreneur in Kenya to the waiter in

London to the student in Houston to over a dozen of the world's most successful CEOs.[3] While each of these stories of embracing and leveraging the unexpected is very different, as we will witness, their patterns are very similar.

A Collision with Fate

While I can now discuss serendipity from different standpoints, my journey to it and its power began with a personal incident in which juvenile hubris met bad luck.

As an eighteen-year-old in Germany, I crashed my car into several parked cars at a speed of more than 50 mph. Miraculously, I survived, but the cars I hit were severely damaged, as was my own. Until then I had never really believed stories about near-death experiences. But my life really did flash before my eyes in the split second before that collision, when my car was spinning out of control and I felt absolutely powerless, certain that I would die.

In the days that followed I asked myself questions. Many questions. "If I had died, who would have come to my funeral?" "Who would have actually cared?" "Was it all worth it?" I realized that I had been neglecting some of the most important parts of life, like treasuring deep and lasting relationships and being proud of doing something relevant and meaningful.

My narrow escape made me consider what my death would have meant in terms of lost opportunities: the people I would not have met, the ideas and dreams that I would never have explored, the (serendipitous) events and encounters that would have been missed.

The accident and the realizations that came from it set me on a journey to search for what life was really about.

I grew up in Heidelberg, a historic and romantic city in southern Germany that, while beautiful, is a bit sleepy when you are a teenager set on exploring what life is all about.

Ever since I can remember, I had always felt that I did not belong. My family moved several times when I was young, so I was often "the new kid" in school, and on the soccer club I was "the incomer." The skin problems I suffered back then were the icing on the cake.

My retreat was the coffee shop where I started to work when I was sixteen. It was there that I began to feel I had found my tribe. Working there as a waiter taught me a lot about human behavior and group dynamics, such as how people treat you if they assume that you're "just a waiter," and the value of physical work, of working from 8 a.m. to 9 p.m. without a real break.

My boss at the coffee shop was an entrepreneur, and it wasn't long before I was helping him on different projects, from selling imported T-shirts to driving cake deliveries as soon as I turned eighteen. About that time I also started working part-time for a market research company, asking people in Heidelberg's main street which size of sausages they would prefer to buy, and why. Would they be open to buy salami instead of pastrami if it was cheaper?

I had lots of energy but I was never sure what to do with it. I tried to create excitement wherever possible, and I tested all kinds of boundaries in order to channel my energy. I veered between extremes: spending time with a group of left-wing activists (during my French/German-reggae phase) and going to clubs, while starting to invest my work money in the stock market—my parents having given, with hesitation, the bank authorization to deal with a minor. (To this day, I have deep admiration for my parents, who handled my rebellious streaks with grace and understanding.) I started to spend more time on the telephone in my school's basement to buy and sell stocks than I did in the classroom.

I always enjoyed tapping in and out of these very different worlds—I enjoyed them but never really felt at home. Naturally, these various explorations did not help my grades. I was a terrible student—I was in the 5 percent of the class that made the top 95 percent possible. I had to repeat a year and was "offered the opportunity to change schools"—a nice way of saying that I was expelled. The next school I attended fortunately proved to be more understanding about my rebellious streaks.

When I turned eighteen, I got my first car. It was exciting and I transferred my hedonistic and overoptimistic attitude into my driving style. I probably broke the city records in the number of parking tickets one driver can accrue in a week and the number of trash cans someone can knock over on the way to school.

Still, I felt in total control of life, of my destiny.

And then, one day, I pushed too far. The car accident shuttered my confidence and sense of control.

The liberation that I had felt earlier on that sunny day when I was hanging out with two close friends on Heidelberg's Neckarwiese turned into both shock at what I had done and relief that I had managed to avoid becoming an accident statistic. My friends and I had planned to get some food. We had taken two cars, and I was behind my friend's car in which he and my other friend were driving. In my adolescent hubris, I tried to overtake the car. I still remember looking over at my friend as I passed him in the opposite lane, and him frantically waving at me and pointing to the traffic island in the middle of the road ahead that I hadn't seen. It's a vivid memory: To avoid hitting the island I turned the wheel fast, the car spun around a couple of times, and I crashed into a line of parked cars.

My Volvo's double-secured doors saved my life. The passenger side was completely destroyed. I later learned that any other angle of collision would probably have killed me. My friend who was a passenger in the other car had initially wanted to ride with me but he'd remembered he had left his jacket in the other car and so changed his mind at quite literally the last second. If he hadn't, he would have been in that passenger seat.

I remember getting out of the car, amazed that I was still able to walk. My friends and I exchanged a few words of disbelief as we tried to grasp what had happened. What would we tell the police? My parents?

While we waited for the police to arrive, I sat back in the wrecked car, dizzy and exhausted. The police officer who arrived at the scene and surveyed the wreckage was amazed I was still alive, with no major injuries apart from light whiplash.

I wandered through the city that night in a strange state of bitter-sweetness, not wanting to go home. I had survived, but I couldn't stop thinking about what could have happened. If I had died, would I have made my family's life a living hell? If my friend had ridden with me, would I have killed him? How on earth could this happen? How did I let it happen?

The old proverb that "death is life's greatest motivator" started to make a lot of sense to me. When you face death, you don't worry about how much money you have in the bank, how many cars you have in the garage, how great last night's clubbing experience was. This all becomes meaningless and you try to understand what's really important, what life really is about.

Perhaps you've had a similar experience like this in your life. Or another inflection point, incremental or radical, that changed your perspective. Perhaps a toxic relationship that you needed to break out from, an illness, or a job you wanted to leave?

The accident helped me start to turn my life around, and it gave me a sense of direction. I applied to dozens of universities (given my miserable school record, out of more than forty applications only four universities accepted me). I started to channel my energy into my studies, my relationships, and my work. I went on to cofound several communities and organizations focused on enabling people to live meaningful lives.

These ventures were themselves often the result of serendipitous encounters. The more active I became, the more I started seeing the patterns in my and other people's lives, and later in my research.

When I started out with my PhD research at the London School of Economics in 2009, I assumed it would be relatively separate from the cultivating of serendipitous experiences in my personal life. The research focused on how individuals and organizations can grow and increase their social impact and meaning, which appeared quite unconnected to serendipity at first. But to my surprise and delight, the concept popped up over and over again. Many of the most successful and joyful people I interviewed for my research appeared intuitively to cultivate a force field—a "serendipity field"—that allowed them to have more positive life outcomes than others who started under similar conditions.

Connecting the dots—in this case, in hindsight—made me realize that a way to combine these streams and passions would be to write this book: a book that encompasses what I deeply believe in as a life philosophy and a more realistic model of how life really unfolds.

Today, nothing makes me happier than to see the spark that comes from two ideas or people who unexpectedly click—the joy of serendipity. I have experienced it as a beautiful way to support someone as they unleash their real potential, of exploring what's possible in a world in which we could adopt many different personas and live many different lives. This is what cultivating serendipity is all about—supporting people in their journey of discovering and exploring who they are and who they can become.

The Serendipity Mindset is about recognizing that we can open ourselves to the unexpected. And it is about being prepared and free from the preconceptions that can stop us being the victims or beneficiaries of luck (bad or good). We can nurture it, shape it, and make it a tool for life. In the science of serendipity, luck can be caught, coached, and created.[4] This means that we can direct our learning, skills, education, and training programs toward influencing and mastering that process.

In part this involves removing barriers to serendipity, in our own thinking process and in our lives and workplaces. We all know instinctively about these practical barriers and how they kill enthusiasm: senseless meetings, email overload, pointless memos to be written or read. But it is just as much about developing a mindset that allows us to use our skills and available resources to turn unexpected discoveries into outcomes with real value.

This is not about developing a particular competence but about nourishing a constantly evolving capability. It is about shifting from being a passive recipient to becoming an active agent of our own smart luck, about setting ourselves up to make unexpected change an opportunity for success, and finding meaning and joy. The next step is to develop the conditions—in our families, our communities, our organizations—that allow serendipity to be nurtured and used to create opportunities and value. This allows us to grow and harness our serendipity field—all the dots that can potentially be connected.

This book guides you through the process of deciphering, creating, and cultivating serendipity, step by step. It also tackles the elephant in the room: If serendipity is inherently random, how can we influence it?

Thus . . .

In this day and age, being successful and joyful is not about trying to plan everything. In a world where we often cannot predict what will happen tomorrow, the best we can do is to embrace unexpected conditions and make the most out of the randomness of life.

The Serendipity Mindset is about what we can control: namely, how to cultivate serendipity for ourselves and others. This powerful mechanism for unleashing human potential demonstrates not only that (smart) luck favors the prepared but also that there are ways in which we can accelerate, nurture, and harness the positive coincidences in our lives.

We can never abolish the importance of randomness, chance, and coincidence in life or in business, but this book will help you transform those things from being uncontrollable forces into tools you can leverage for personal or greater good. Then you will start to see and create serendipity everywhere.

Naturally, we are all busy, and few of us have the time to change our lives completely all at once—which is why the book is peppered with examples of small, immediate adjustments that will directly make a difference in your day-to-day experiences, allowing you to live a more meaningful, joyful, inspiring, and successful life.

CHAPTER 1

SERENDIPITY

More Than Blind Luck

⟵

Humiliating to human pride as it may be, we must recognize that the advance and even the preservation of civilization are dependent upon a maximum of opportunity for accidents to happen.

FRIEDRICH HAYEK, WINNER OF THE 1974
NOBEL PRIZE IN ECONOMICS

Serendipity: A Brief History

When King Giaffer, ruler of the ancient country of Serendip (an Old Persian name for Sri Lanka) became concerned that his three sons were too sheltered, privileged, and unprepared for the challenges of ruling the kingdom, he decided to send them on a journey on which they would learn some important life lessons.

In one tale, the princes come across a merchant who has lost a camel. From observations they have made during their journey they describe the camel so well that the merchant believes they must have stolen it.

The merchant takes them to the emperor, who asks how they could possibly have given such a clear description of the camel if they had never seen it. They explain that they knew the camel was lame because they observed tracks showing the prints of three feet and a fourth being dragged, and that they knew it was carrying butter on one side and honey on the other because flies had been attracted to the butter on one side of the road and ants to the honey on the other side of the road, and so on. Suspicions that the princes might have stolen the camel—given their detailed description of it—are rebutted when another traveler enters to say he has found a camel.

The princes did not yet know that a lame, honey-bearing camel was missing when they made their observations. But when they learned that one was missing, they connected this information to what they had observed earlier—they *connected the dots*.

In 1754, the British writer and politician Horace Walpole wrote to a friend about an unexpected discovery, which he compared to the story of the three princes. In doing so, he coined the word *serendipity*, describing the princes as people who "were always making discoveries, by accidents and sagacity, of things they were not in quest of."

Thus, the word entered the English language, and while it has been reduced by many to mean simply "good luck," it is clear that Walpole had spotted its subtler meaning.

There are other definitions of serendipity, but most demarcate the phenomenon as chance interacting with human action, leading to a usually positive outcome—which is the definition I use here.[1] This action-focused perspective allows us to understand how to develop a space that we can control in which serendipity can happen—a serendipity field.

By definition, serendipity is not controllable, let alone predictable. However, there are tangible, achievable ways to develop the conditions in which serendipity can happen, and to ensure that when such potentially transformational coincidences occur, we can recognize them and grab them with both hands. Serendipity is about seeing what others don't, about noticing unexpected observations and turning them into opportunities. It demands a conscious effort to prompt and leverage those moments when apparently unconnected ideas or events come together in front of you to form a new pattern. Put more plainly, it is about connecting the dots.

From Volcanoes to World Champions

On a sunny Saturday in April 2010, an erupting Icelandic volcano with an unpronounceable name (Eyjafjallajökull) entered popular culture after its resulting ash cloud had grounded thousands of flights across most of Europe. That same morning, an unknown number popped up on my phone. On the line was a stranger, who started speaking self-confidently:

"Hi, Christian. We don't know each other yet, but a mutual friend gave me your number. I'd like to ask you for a favor."

Sitting at brunch after a long night out, I was still a little bit sleepy, but nonetheless intrigued.

"Ahm, tell me more," I replied.

This is how Nathaniel Whittemore, an entrepreneur and blogger, entered my life. Nathaniel explained that his flight from London to Southern California had just been canceled and that he was stuck in London along with many of the attendees of the Skoll World Forum, a major annual conference for social entrepreneurs and thought leaders held at Oxford University. Most of them did not know many people in London, and had their schedules clear. "So why not organize an event to bring them all together and make the best out of the situation?" he asked. By then, Nathaniel had already written an email along those lines to the TED team, whom he had briefly met a few years earlier.

To my amazement, within thirty-six hours, Nathaniel organized the first ever—and probably last—"TEDxVolcano" conference, a spontaneous version of the popular TED conference. With absolutely no budget, over a weekend, and with few direct contacts in London, Nathaniel turned a challenging situation into an event with two hundred top attendees, hundreds more on the waiting list, speakers including eBay's first president, Jeff Skoll, and a recorded livestream that was watched by more than ten thousand people.

While this was amazing in its own right, two questions occurred to me: How did he do this? And what can we learn from it?

Nathaniel, like all of us, had encountered something random and unexpected in his life—in this case, an unforeseen and unplanned-for period of time in London. But he had the sagacity—the perceptiveness, the creativity, and the energy—to turn it into something positive. Most of us may not have seen the potential trigger for serendipity in such a situation. Nathaniel realized not only that exceptional people were stuck in London, but also that their experiences could be great stories to tell in the context of TED. And where many may have been deterred by the lack of resources, he used his enthusiasm and negotiation skills to convince a local coworking office to donate space for the event, used the innovation community Sandbox to recruit volunteers, and enlisted top people like Larry Brilliant, the former executive director of Google.org (Google's charitable arm), to give extemporaneous talks. Nathaniel's ability to connect the dots produced a world-class event with no budget within a day and a half, in a city where he previously had a limited network. This precis is only half of the story, to which I shall return later in this book, but the important point to make here is that encounters such as these happen more often than we realize.

For example, Dr. Nico Rose, a German organizational psychologist, was on a business trip in 2018 when he ran into former world heavyweight champion boxer Wladimir Klitschko in the gym of a Boston hotel. Though he was jetlagged and had gone to the gym to battle it, Nico nevertheless immediately recognized Klitschko, one of his idols. He hurried back to his hotel room to fetch his cell phone, planning to ask for a selfie if he could do so without disturbing Klitschko's training routine.

The ideal moment arose when Klitschko's manager entered the gym and spoke to the boxer in German. Nico gathered that the pair did not know where breakfast was served in the hotel. He took the opportunity to explain to them in German where it was. The resulting chat led to a selfie, and off they went to do their separate workouts. When they had finished, Klitschko was looking for the elevator—so Nico walked with him and they chatted further. At the end of their time together, Klitschko asked Nico to introduce him to the corporate university where he worked for speaking opportunities. In turn, Nico told him about his upcoming book, for which Klitschko ended up agreeing to write the foreword.

Did Nathaniel expect to encounter a volcano that spewed an ash cloud across Europe? Did Nico expect to bump into his idol in a hotel gym? Did they expect they would ever organize a global event in London or find a writer for their book's foreword from one of the world's foremost sportsmen in Boston?

Certainly not. But both of them had laid the foundations for them to happen well in advance.

Does Success Really Come Down to Luck?

A lot of life makes sense only when you look at events in the rearview mirror; we tend to connect the dots in hindsight. When we do so, we often turn random life choices and chance happenings into a convincing and logical story that we tell others.

Which one of us hasn't presented their CV as if their life was, in fact, a coherent, rationally organized plan? In truth, we might not have had a clear plan for our careers at all. The reality was almost certainly different, often driven by coincidences and accidents, by an unexpected idea, encounter, or conversation.

But what if we can learn to start to connect the dots, not only with hindsight but also with foresight? What if we could prepare the ground to take advantage of these coincidences, creating a field where they could germinate and thrive? What if we knew how to nourish and cultivate them? And most important, what if we could make sure they flourished into better outcomes?

While few of us can engineer a seismic event or running into Wladimir Klitschko, we can, by being attuned to opportunity, shape an outcome that develops and takes advantage of serendipitous conditions.

What we often fail to realize is that successful people have often not just "been lucky," even when it appears that a chance event has played an important role in their achievements. In fact, successful people have often, either consciously or subconsciously, done the necessary groundwork to create the conditions that have brought them such "luck."

Not only is it the Oprah Winfreys, Arianna Huffingtons, Richard Bransons, and Bill Gateses of the world who are lucky and who can set up equally lucky environments for others—all of us can be part of nurturing serendipity for ourselves and for others.

Serendipity Is Everywhere

It's true. Inventions such as nylon, Velcro, Viagra, Post-it Notes, X-rays, penicillin, rubber, and microwave ovens all involved serendipity. Presidents, superstars, professors, businesspeople—including many of the world's leading CEOs—credit a big part of their success to serendipity.

But serendipity isn't just a guiding force in great scientific discoveries, business achievements, or diplomatic breakthroughs. It is present in our everyday lives, in the smallest moments and the greatest life-changing events.

Imagine that your neighbor rents an industrial-sized ladder to climb in order to cut down some overhanging branches in her garden. You spot her working away and suddenly remember the loose tile on your own roof. It's not serious so you weren't going to bother fixing it, but hey . . .

You pop outside, start chatting with her, and help her drag away the branches. You invite her in for a beer, and then she's holding the ladder while you fix your loose tile. (Before you've drunk the beer, of course!) What's more, while you are up on your roof, you realize the guttering is loose and about to fall off. It's too big a job for you, but now you know you need to hire some professionals to fix it—which might well have saved someone in your family from an injury had it fallen at the wrong time.

Perhaps you had a similar situation recently yourself?

It's the kind of situation that happens all the time. We might not recognize it as serendipity, but it has all the characteristics: A chance event appears, we pay attention to it, and link it to an unrelated fact that we're also aware of. We connect the two and then follow through with a bit of determination, leading to a solution to a problem that often we didn't even know we had.

Even love may be said to be the child of serendipity. I met almost all my romantic partners in coffee shops or airports, often because of a spilled coffee or a laptop that needed to be watched, sparking a conversation that unveiled common interests. Many of the most famous love stories—including that of Michelle and Barack Obama, who met when a young and impossibly tardy Barack joined Michelle's law firm and was allocated to her as a mentee—were born out of the unexpected. (And as we will see later, tenacity is often crucial in turning potential serendipity into a positive outcome: When Michelle kept Barack at bay by suggesting that, as his adviser, she was not supposed to date him, he suggested he would be ready to quit—there was some back and forth and the rest is history.)

If you're in a relationship, how did you meet your partner? Even if you met them "randomly," it probably was not blind luck. That would imply you had no role in it at all. It may have sprung from a chance encounter but you spotted a powerful connection, an empathy, or a shared outlook, and crucially you worked at it. You nurtured the connections and found ways in which you complemented and inspired each other.

That was not just luck. It was serendipity.

Types of Serendipity

Every case of serendipity is unique, but research has identified three core types.[2] All involve an initial serendipity trigger (something unexpected), but they differ depending on the initial intent and on the outcome. It comes down to two basic questions:

> *Were you looking for something already?*
> And
> *Did you find what you were looking for, or did you find something entirely unexpected?*

What are these three types of serendipity?

1. Archimedes Serendipity

Archimedes serendipity occurs when a known problem or challenge—a broken bathtub, or trying to get a dream job—is solved, but the solution comes from an unexpected place. You have a destination in mind, but the way you get there changes. Take the story of when King Hiero II of Syracuse asks the Greek mathematician Archimedes to find out whether a sneaky goldsmith had substituted silver for some of the gold meant for the king's crown. The crown weighs the right amount, but how can anyone tell whether it was made of pure gold?

Unable to find a way to solve the problem, a flummoxed Archimedes heads for the public baths to relax and idly watches the water level rise and pour over the side as he lowers himself into the tub. And then—Eureka!— he realizes that a crown mixed with silver, which is lighter than gold, would have to be bulkier to weigh the same. Therefore, when submerged in water, it would displace more water than a pure gold crown of the same weight.

This type of serendipity is common in our personal lives as well as in organizations of all sizes. What is natural for entrepreneurs—they often change course based on random encounters or unexpected user feedback— also occurs in the biggest of companies. David Taylor, CEO of the multi-national consumer goods company Procter & Gamble, told me in an interview that he likes it when an approach changes, because it opens up possibilities that his team did not envision before. In his words: "It still solves the problem we wanted to solve, but it does it in a different way than we thought of. You can't plan all that, but you need to have an idea of what you want to try to solve. There is a magic in this, and it often happens when you have access to different sets of experiences, of people who fall in love with the problem and are open to the unexpected."

One of the first serendipitors we will meet in this book is Waqas Bag-gia, now a sales consultant at Mercedes-Benz Canada. Canadian by birth, he had moved to the UK with his wife, who was studying law there. After she received her degree, they moved back to Canada, and he worked in a retail shop until he found something in his field, having previously worked in the UK at Jaguar Land Rover as a technical recruitment consultant. He had applied and progressed through half a dozen interviews at different companies but hadn't made the final cut at any of them. His friends kept asking him why he worked so hard at his job: "It's just retail!" they said. But Waqas's principle is that whatever he does, he does it properly or not at all.

One day he helped a customer with the same professionalism and en-thusiasm he always brought to the job, and the customer was impressed. He asked more about Waqas and his background, and Waqas told him that he was working at the store until he could transition into luxury automotive sales. When Waqas asked the customer what line of work he was in, the customer replied, "Luxury automotive!" He was the general manager of a Mercedes-Benz dealership, and he gave Waqas his cell phone number. After several interviews, Waqas became the first sales consultant the dealership hired without specific automotive sales experience—and they created a training program specifically for him. Waqas's strong work ethos and enthusiasm paired with the customer's lateral thinking led to this unexpected advancement of Waqas's career.

2. Post-it Note Serendipity

Post-it Note serendipity occurs when you examine a particular problem but stumble across a solution to an entirely different or even previously unrecognized problem. Your journey goes off into a completely different direction but still gets you to a destination that you like. Take the example of Post-its: In the late 1970s, Dr. Spencer Silver, a researcher at 3M, the consumer goods company, was trying to discover a stronger glue. What he actually got was the opposite—a substance that didn't stick particularly well. But this weak glue was perfect for a new product that 3M produced that sprung from Silver's discovery: *Post-it Notes*.[3]

Another example comes from a multinational nutrition and chemicals group that was struggling to sell a coating for picture-frame glass that pushes the light through the glass—thus preventing it from reflecting. The product worked well, but the company couldn't find a market for it. The project manager was about to abandon the idea when a chance interaction with a colleague from another division sparked the notion that the technology could be highly effective on solar panels, which need to absorb as much light as possible. This unexpected new solution to a different problem than initially imagined fueled the solar business unit at the company.

We will see later why its CEO was right when he said, "Someone else will say: 'This is pure luck.' But that's serendipity."

In our openness to unexpected solutions that solve emerging problems, we often end up in places we could have hardly predicted. Peter Agnefjall, IKEA's CEO between 2012 and 2017, told our Leaders on Purpose team in an interview how he would have laughed at us had we told him five years ago that IKEA would own wind farms and solar power installations. "But when I look back, that's what we do now, right?"[4]

3. Thunderbolt Serendipity

Thunderbolt serendipity happens when no search or deliberate problem solving is underway. It follows something entirely unexpected, like a thunderbolt in the sky, and sparks a new opportunity or solves a previously unknown problem. We often fall in love this way, and many new ideas and approaches emerge from this type of serendipity.

When Olivia Twist (not her real name) was young, she moved into her first apartment and found a strange object in a kitchen drawer. She showed it to one of her friends, who realized that it was a radiator key, used to let out unnecessary air from the apartment's radiator, so keeping it running efficiently. Olivia had no idea there was such a problem or that such a thing as a radiator key was necessary. But when the weather started to turn and it got cold in her apartment, she put her radiator key in its slot and her apartment got warmer. The chance discovery of an unexpected object, together with the curiosity and will to learn what it was and how it worked, led her to the solution of a problem she did not even know she had.

Or take the invention of Sofar Sounds, a global movement that reimagines live music events. When Rafe Offer, Rocky Start, and singer-songwriter Dave Alexander went to see indie rock band Friendly Fires live, they were annoyed by other concertgoers nearby who talked over the music and stared at their smartphones. Struck by the realization that the days when people attending a show focused solely on the music were long gone, in 2009 they decided to organize an intimate gig in Rocky's front room, in North London, with Dave performing his songs to a small, hand-picked audience.

They repeated the living room experience in other parts of London as well as Paris, New York, and other cities, and received requests from people around the world who wanted to host similar events. Sofar (an acronym of "songs from a room") Sounds was born. By 2018, Sofar Sounds had hosted more than four thousand intimate gigs in peoples' homes in more than four hundred cities around the world, partnering with companies as varied as Airbnb and Virgin Group.

What had started as a conversation prompted by an annoying encounter had evolved into a magical experience—combining the intimacy of a living room with the intensity of a live concert.

But Not Everything Fits a Category

Any effort to categorize serendipity will always be slightly subjective, and some examples will combine elements of one or more of the three types described above. If you have a serendipitous moment, don't waste time trying to work out which type it was. Indeed, the temptation to try to put everything in simple categories is one of the things that can kill serendipity stone dead.

So while the core of active serendipity is constant—connecting the dots between unexpected or apparently unrelated events or facts—a lot of serendipitous events defy such efforts at categorization, including some of the greatest known examples.

One such case—and one that transformed the world for the better—was Alexander Fleming's discovery of penicillin. The story is well known and is taught to schoolchildren as a model of a medical and scientific break-through, but here's a brief reminder.

Fleming was researching the bacterium Staphylococcus—various forms of which can cause a huge range of human infections, some of which can be fatal. One morning in 1928, he returned to his laboratory in the base-ment of St Mary's Hospital in London and found that one of his petri dishes containing samples of the bacteria had been left uncovered on a windowsill. But something unexpected had happened—a blue-green mold was growing in the dish. Even odder, in the space around the mold the original Staphylococcus bacteria had disappeared.

The mold was *penicillium chrysogenum*. Thus was penicillin discovered as an agent that would kill certain bacteria. From this discovery emerged the entire science of antibiotics, which has saved millions upon millions of lives. (Serendipitously, the mold that in the end allowed the dramatic upscaling of penicillin production was discovered by Mary Hunt, a laboratory assistant at the U.S. Northern Regional Research Laboratory, who came across a "golden mold" that yielded dozens of times more penicillin than Fleming's).

The key features of serendipity are all here in this story.[5] An accidental contamination leads to a mold, which turns out to be a lifesaving drug. But which type of serendipity is this? The answer depends on what we think Fleming was trying to achieve. In one sense any medical research scientist is looking, if only indirectly, for medical treatments, and Fleming found one. On the other hand, he almost certainly wasn't looking for antibiotics—no one had conceived of such an idea.

Whatever type of serendipity this was, it began with a trigger (the ac-cidental contamination of a petri dish), but the critical moment is Flem-ing's reaction. Rather than curse his own sloppiness for leaving the dish exposed and throwing it in the bin, he was curious. He showed the dish to colleagues and carried out further research. Others followed over many years—and so began the process that turned an accident into life-changing medicine.

While penicillin was discovered by accident, it would be wrong to dismiss Fleming as "just lucky" and argue that human agency had no role in this breakthrough. Crucially, Fleming made the key decision to connect the dots—what's known as "bisociation." It may have taken years to reach fulfillment, but had Fleming not had the right mindset to make that association, the green mold contaminating his petri dish would have remained just another forgotten laboratory mishap. In fact, the antagonism between mold and germs had been observed decades earlier, but nobody had paid proper attention to it. Could millions of lives have been saved had serendipity played out earlier?[6]

Leverage the Unexpected

Serendipity is not just something that *happens to us*—it is a phenomenon with distinct features, and each of those features can be nurtured in our lives. For us to really understand serendipity and to be able to see it not as an external force but as a magical tool we can use, we need to look more closely.

To do this, based on existing research we can identify three interrelated core characteristics of serendipity:[7]

1. A person encounters something unexpected or unusual. This could be a physical phenomenon, something that comes up in conversation, or one of countless other eventualities. This is the serendipity **trigger**.

2. The individual links this trigger to something previously unrelated. She *connects the dots*, and so realizes the potential value in this apparently chance event or meeting. This linking of two previously unrelated facts or events may be called the **bisociation**.

3. Crucially, the value realized—the insights, the innovation, the new way of doing something, or the new solution to a problem—is not at all what is expected, and not what someone was looking for, or at least not in the form it appeared. It is **unanticipated**.

While surprise and chance are important, they are only the beginning steps. What's also needed is someone who is capable of understanding and using that chance finding. That means creatively recombining events, observations, or fragments of information based on the (unexpected) recognition of a meaningful link. Often contributions come from connecting two utterly unconnected ideas that were previously regarded as "strangers to each other."[8]

Serendipity is about the ability to recognize and leverage the value in unexpected encounters and information.[9] Thus, it can be learned and facilitated at every step. We can develop a serendipity mindset—the capacity to identify, grasp, and wield this powerful force.

While a particular chance encounter is an event, serendipity is a process. Surprise and chance are important—but only as a first step. The essential second step comes from being able to understand and leverage the unexpected observation. We need to see links or bridges where others see gaps. And it often takes sagacity—being able to filter and see the value—and the tenacity to see it through.[10]

If we do not see the serendipity trigger or its potential connections, then we can miss serendipity, and there are many potential coincidences that could have happened but never did. We might encounter a potential prompt (such as running into Wladimir Klitschko or meeting a potential love interest), but if we don't connect the dots, it will be *serendipity missed*.

Imagine all the possible times—the missed hits—where serendipity might have happened, but we were too blind to see them (or saw them but did not act)! Perhaps you had a situation in your life recently where it would just have needed a small nudge to do something but you didn't—and felt afterward that there "could have been something"? This is why it's crucial to develop our serendipity mindset.

We can also influence the conditions for serendipity by restructuring our organizations, networks, and physical spaces. A serendipity mindset together with nurturing conditions provides the fertile soil for a serendipity field that we can grow and harness.

The figure here illustrates the process and the emerging serendipity field. (Please note that this is a simplification; often the trigger and connecting the dots happens simultaneously, and there are "feedback loops"— as we explore later, initial outcomes can amplify the occurrence of more, or less, serendipity.)

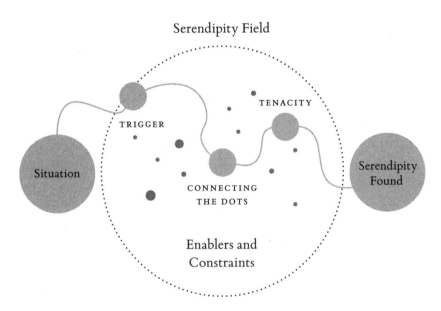

From Chance and Randomness to Serendipity

In my work as a researcher, community builder, and entrepreneur, I often hear people say things like, "Wow, it was such a coincidence that such-

and-such happened!" But once you start connecting the dots in hindsight, it becomes clear that this is not strictly true. These lucky accidents often occurred because someone or something had laid the groundwork. As we have just seen, although science and luck would seem to be odd bedfellows, serendipity itself is at the very heart of much scientific research.

Take the field of combinatorial chemistry, where manufacturing coincidences is at the core: Tens of thousands of chemical compounds are created simultaneously and then sifted for valuable new uses. In essence, combinatorial chemistry involves creating thousands of "accidents" and being ready for any one of them to be a breakthrough opportunity. The chemists who identify new drugs are really good at setting up these experiments, and by getting the right approaches and people in place they make it more probable that "coincidental" discoveries happen—and that when they do, they are being spotted and grasped. By definition they cannot know the outcome, or when exactly it will happen—but they can be relatively certain that *something* will happen.

Qualitative research methods such as *grounded theory* similarly look not for statistical patterns but for the surprising or unexpected insight.[11] In that respect, researchers do have a lot in common with Sherlock Holmes.

With the many political, social, and environmental changes the world is currently facing, the unexpected shapes much of our future. Among other things, it threatens the survival of organizations. Companies such as Haier, the world's leading white goods company, deal with this by "disrupting ourselves before we get disrupted," in the words of its CEO Zhang Ruimin. The company built an appreciation of the unexpected into the core of its organization. Who would have thought that Chinese farmers would use Haier's washing machines to clean their potatoes?*

This mirrors the experiences of one of the world's leading financial

---

* When Haier's representatives learned that farmers used their washing machines in other ways than they had envisioned, they quickly adapted and adjusted the machines to be able to cope with the additional dirt that the potatoes produced (and that had overwhelmed the normal machines).

service companies, whose CEO shared with me his approach of sensing his way through the future: "Don't for a minute go away thinking that this is all some master plan. It just kept happening along the way, and we seized it." He and his team simply provided a vision, the culture, and the practices that helped give a sense of direction to the company and allowed opportunity to emerge, often in unexpected places and in unexpected ways. They helped develop a serendipity field for the people they work with.

In my research into what makes individuals and organizations fit for the future, one insight has come up again and again: It turns out that many of the world's leading minds have developed an (often unconscious) capacity to cope with the unexpected. For Tom Linebarger, CEO of Fortune 500 company Cummins, cultivating serendipity is at the core of what he does—he considers it an active rather than passive approach to leading during uncertainty.

Some will ask, and I have asked myself: Is serendipity still serendipity once we take a more active role in it?

The answer is a resounding yes, because that is the precise difference between serendipity and just plain, blind luck. Cultivating serendipity is first and foremost about looking at the world with open eyes and connecting the dots. It is not just about being in the right place at the right time and having something happen *to* us—but rather a quality or process in which we can be actively involved.

Thus . . .

Serendipity is active, "smart" luck that depends on our ability to spot and connect the dots. The three types of serendipity I outlined above are all based on a serendipity trigger. Developing a serendipity mindset helps us see the trigger, connect the dots, and develop the tenacity necessary to focus on and influence valuable outcomes.

We can also influence the different enablers and constraints of serendipity, such as communities and companies. In combination, this allows us to create what I call a serendipity field—all the dots that could potentially be connected by ourselves or by others. To create more meaningful accidents—and to make more accidents meaningful. But where do we start?

CHAPTER 2

BECOMING ATTUNED

Breaking Down the Barriers to Serendipity

⸺

Life is what happens to us while we are making other plans.
ALLEN SAUNDERS, AMERICAN WRITER,
JOURNALIST, AND CARTOONIST

Today is your birthday. To your dismay, you have to attend a work event. Around sixty people from across your industry are coming together for broad-ranging conversations. At the event you listen to a number of talks, many of which turn out to be not as exciting as you had hoped they would be. You think, "I can't believe I'm spending my birthday at work—I'm the only one here who has to spend their birthday at this place." But what if you aren't?

Each term, as part of my teaching I play a game with my incoming students. I ask them, "What do you think is the probability that you have the same birthday as at least one other person in this room of sixty people?"

Usually, the students estimate anywhere between 5 and 20 percent. That makes sense—there are around 365 days in the year, and so logically, our tendency is to divide 60 (people) by 365 (days). So essentially, this reasoning offers a very low probability that there are two people in the room that have the same birthday.

I then ask each student to briefly state the day and month of their birthday. I ask the other students to shout out "here!" whenever they hear their own birthday. Students usually are shocked when after approximately ten or so students having announced their birthday to the class, the first "here!" daringly comes out of a corner.

Then another one, and another one. In most sessions of around sixty students, I've been surprised to find that three to six birthday pairs emerge.

How is this possible? Is it magic? No, it's pure statistics. It is an exponential rather than linear problem: Each time a student mentions their birthday, there are many potential "pairs" that could happen. Student No. 1, for example, has fifty-nine other people who could potentially have the same birthday as they do; student No. 2 still has fifty-eight potential people with the same birthday (assuming the first one had a different birthday), and so on. And when we add together all of these potential pairs that could happen, we end up with what's known as the *birthday paradox* (see figure below).

The paradox states that at twenty-three people there is already a 50 percent (!) chance that two people in a random sample have the same birthday (as there are 253 "chances" or potential pairs).[1] Even more aston-

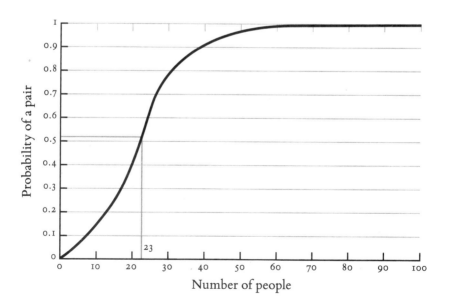

ishing, already at seventy people it is almost certain (a 99.9 percent probability) that two people have the same birthday. (As someone who had to repeat a year in high school because of my suboptimal mathematical prowess, it did take me a while to grasp this. But it's true.)

What does this insight tell us—apart from the fact that you will most probably not be the only birthday celebrant at that industry conference?

It's proof that we often underestimate the unexpected because we think linearly—often "according to plan"—rather than exponentially (or in contingencies). But the unexpected happens all the time, even if we are either surprised when we see it, or if we don't see it at all.

Everything from the most life-changing turnaround experiences to the small improvements in life is possible once we realize that every day, every second, serendipity could happen.

As I discuss below, our natural and learned ways of thinking tend to obscure serendipity, making it harder to spot and even harder to harness. The biggest barriers to serendipity are our preconceptions of the world, the biases that often unconsciously direct our thinking and close down the possibility of serendipity. And if you don't think you have any, well that might well be your biggest preconception.

Our biases can blind us to serendipitous moments when they occur, and they can even make us misinterpret serendipity that has already happened.

When asked to explain their success, many people will describe their hard work and careful planning—the long-term vision and strategy that inexorably led to glory. Sometimes this is accurate, but often it is not. The key turning points in life often are moments of serendipity (or sometimes even just blind luck) that were reinterpreted after the fact, like when you present your CV to a potential employer as a very clear journey from A to B.

These biases are often useful and have evolved for sound reasons—it is impossible to function in a world that we perceive only as random chaos. And it is impossible to capture all the complexity that defines social interactions. But our ability to step outside these biases and preconceptions is what has allowed our species to make its greatest leaps forward, and it is what allows individuals or organizations to take their own giant steps.

These biases come in many forms, but there are four basic ones that are major obstacles to serendipity and that we need to overcome—or at least recognize—to be able to effectively cultivate serendipity. Their names are a little bit technical, but what they signify is fascinating: *underestimating the unexpected; conforming to the majority; post-rationalization;* and *functional fixedness.*

We Underestimate the Unexpected

A friend at school used to be fond of saying, "It's very probable that something improbable will happen." It sounded mysterious at the time, and only over the years have I started to truly understand what he meant.

The unexpected, the unlikely, and indeed the downright extraordinary happen all the time. What matters is whether we spot them and whether we grasp them and nurture them when they can be useful.

I have taught a negotiation class in which one of the exercises involves the owner of an independent gas station aiming to sell it to a large oil company. The negotiation is set up in such a way that if the two parties stick with their initial position, there is no deal possible. The company can pay up to $500,000 for the station but the brief states the owner's minimum demand is $580,000. Theoretically, there is no bargaining zone, no potential outcome that both parties could accept if they stick to their positions.

I then ask students—both those playing the station owner, and those playing the company representative—to let go of their positions and to be open to capturing the real underlying needs and interests.

Once the oil company representative starts asking questions about *why* the owner feels they need $580,000, something unexpected often happens: The station owner mentions that their dream is to retire and go sailing with their partner, and that this is the amount that they think they will need to do that.

At this point students often say something along the lines of, "Oh, I didn't expect that. We could provide you with gas for your journey and put our name on your sails. We actually wanted to do more sponsorships like this!"—or other potential unexpected ideas that are cheap to the company but valuable to the owner.

Once you see the underlying interests come to the fore, unexpected ways emerge on how you can resolve the situation. (This comes more intuitively to students who are in a win-win mindset, and thus assume that there might be solutions that could benefit both sides; students who start with the mindset of "I win, you lose" often take longer to identify that there are ways of "increasing the pie" that benefit both. The ones with a win-win mindset are often able to build trust and exchange information about the actual underlying interests, and they can prioritize more effectively than those that assume that a benefit for one means a loss for the other.)

There are many implications here for improving one's negotiation strategy, but what is important to recognize is that many of us will not "see" the unexpected because we don't realize it's there. What was an artificial—and expensive—price tag that the station owner asked for (and that we might take for granted), obscured their real underlying interest—and other, even more exciting possibilities emerged once their real interests were articulated.

This insight is particularly important in areas such as business negotiations: an employee negotiating for a new job or a prospective home-owner trying to buy their first house. In these situations, often unexpected dots need to be connected in order to find a mutually agreeable solution. But it goes far beyond that, and once we start to connect the dots in hindsight, we can see that the unexpected shaped much of our life, from how our career evolved to how we met our life partner.

Each of us has structured a biased view of the world that we consider "typical," the kinds of things that we expect to happen. As a result of this bias, "the expected" is what we tend to see. But what if we could broaden the range of what we expect? Then, increasingly we will see the connections and come to understand that unlikely things are happening all around us, just waiting for us to take advantage of them.[2] This is a central part of developing our serendipity mindset.

If you think about it, you will realize that we all actually do look out for the unexpected every day, but generally only as a defense mechanism. When we use a pedestrian crossing on a busy road, we expect the cars to stop at a red light. But most of us do not take that entirely for granted. Even when the light turns red and we step out into the road, we turn half an eye to the traffic, because we also know that occasionally a driver will not stop at a red light. In a situation like this, our field of vision is broader than usual and we are looking out for the unexpected, because we know that missing it could be fatal.

Imagine if we applied the same approach to the positive—keeping a broader field of vision and being alert to the unexpectedly good or useful things that might happen.

British psychology professor Richard Wiseman conducted a fascinating experiment about self-perception: He found people who identify as either "extremely lucky" or "extremely unlucky," and he tested how they perceive the world.[3] In one experiment, he selected two participants: Martin, who considers himself lucky, and Brenda, who considers herself unlucky (for example, she had the feeling that often bad things happen to her).

The research team asked both participants to walk down a street toward a coffee shop (separately from each other), go into the coffee shop, buy a cup of coffee, and sit down. Hidden cameras in the street leading up to the coffee shop as well as in the coffee shop itself filmed them.

The researchers placed a five-pound note on the pavement directly outside the entrance to the coffee shop, so that the participants would need to step over it. They also rearranged the coffee shop to only have four large tables, placing one person at each of these four tables: Three of them were actors, and one of them a successful businessman. The successful businessman was sitting close to the coffee counter. The four individuals were briefed to interact the same way with both participants.

Can you guess the outcome?

Martin—the lucky person—walked up the street, recognized the five-pound note, picked it up, and went inside. He ordered a coffee and sat down next to the businessman. He started a conversation and made friends with him.

Unlucky Brenda, on the other hand, failed to spot the five-pound note. She, too, sat down next to the successful businessman, but remained silent until the end of the experiment.

When Wiseman's team asked the two later how their day had been, they received two very different responses: Martin described how it had been a great day, that he found a five-pound note and got into a great conversation with a successful businessman (it's unclear if there was a follow-up positive outcome—but if there was, that wouldn't be unexpected at all). Brenda, unsurprisingly, said it had been a completely uneventful morning.

Both participants were presented with exactly the same potential opportunities, but only one of them "saw" them.

Openness to the unexpected is key to being lucky—and to experiencing serendipity. People like Martin are lucky all or most of the time for a number of reasons, but among the most important ones is their ability to recognize the unexpected. This makes the unexpected more likely to be harvested—not necessarily because it happens more often, but because we start seeing it once we start expecting to see it. It can make us luckier even if we face exactly the same situation that others do.

Haven't we all had serendipitous happenings in our lives that we remember? Perhaps when we met our partners, when we got this unexpected job, when we came up with that random idea, or when we got that investment? But what about all the occasions on which we might have overlooked serendipity, or narrowly missed out on it?

Think back to that person in the coffee shop who accidentally spilled coffee on your pant leg. On second thought, they were kind of cute, weren't they? Maybe they were interested, too . . . but no one acted on that spark. No contact details were exchanged to "send over the dry-cleaning bill." A lot could have happened there, but in the end nothing did. (Later in this book we will return to the question of what we can learn from *counterfactuals*, the potential "alternative life stories" that could have unfolded instead.)

The figure illustrates how we can miss serendipity if we don't appreciate the serendipity trigger, don't connect the dots, and don't have the tenacity to follow through.[4]

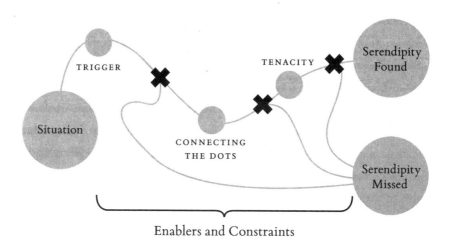

Enablers and Constraints

How can we avoid missing serendipity? There are a number of strategies you can use (which we will explore later). For now, let us take a look at an office furniture producer based in Salt Lake City that aimed to use serendipity to its advantage. Researchers Nancy Napier and Quan-Hoang Vuong assessed the results.

When an executive at the company first put forward the proposal to look at serendipity as something to be cultivated, it was met with skepticism. But despite the doubts, the company's executives agreed to spend thirty minutes every two weeks trying to identify unexpected information they had encountered, discussing how they had noticed and evaluated it, and then deciding what could be done to take advantage of it.

During the first two months of the study, the researchers found at least six major examples of "serendipity gained" at the company. The researchers concluded that as the executives "have begun to calculate the economic impact [of spotting serendipity], their skepticism about the rather fuzzy notion has dissipated."[5] This experiment trained the executives to be more alert to unexpected information, and they began to find and grasp information that they might have previously dismissed or simply not spotted at all. For example, the company was launching a new product, and as usual had some market analysis carried out. In the process, the executives discovered unexpected information suggesting that their approach to setting the price might be inaccurate. Missing—or ignoring—this information could have been a costly mistake.

People who are aware of the unexpected—like the executives in the examples of this furniture producer and Haier—are open to serendipity because they are already in the state of mind of looking out for the hidden value in unexpected data and events. Consequently, senior leaders such as Anand Mahindra, the CEO of one of India's largest companies, Mahindra Group, ponder about installing "serendipity spotters" across the organization.

An industry dinner is coming up. What do you expect? The same as usual? To be sat next to a boring individual, half listening to his dull conversation while wondering how early you can leave without offending anyone? If that is all you expect, it is more likely that that is all you will get.

Are You Self-Censoring?

There are good reasons many of us may have a tendency to conform to the majority. Consensus is safety. And large numbers of individuals can make surprisingly accurate decisions—often better than the smartest people among them would. Daniel Martin Katz and his colleagues used the data of FantasySCOTUS—where since 2011 over five thousand everyday people have made over six hundred thousand predictions about the results of over four hundred decisions of the U.S. Supreme Court—to show that the "wisdom of the crowd" can robustly and accurately predict decisions of the nation's highest court.[6]

Or take forecasts. Forecasts for complex systems, from the weather to the economy, are often wrong and are almost always wrong in the detail. But a crowd of forecasters is often more likely to be right than one individual.[7]

But what about the maverick, the genius—the forecaster who correctly predicts an extraordinary event that everyone else missed? Well, people who successfully foresee one unusual event tend to have a poor record of success when all of their forecasts are considered. In other words, one terrific forecast does not a seer make.

Research by behavioral scientists Jerker Denrell and Christina Fang shows that those whose predictions were most in line with conventional wisdom were the ones who were most accurate overall: Consensus is indeed more likely to be right. It is a rash person who dismisses the wisdom of crowds and follows the maverick unthinkingly. However, the pressure to conform to the majority view can kill serendipity, especially if it makes us ignore or look down on life's unexpected encounters, or if politics or unhealthy group dynamics take over.[8]

In fact, the insight that groups tend to make better decisions changes when individuals are not acting independently, but influence each other strongly (like in many company boardrooms)—then, decisions tend to become worse than those of independent individuals. This herd mentality can kill serendipity. So ignoring the majority carries some risk, but we should always question the majority view. Many of us *self-censor*, dismissing or burying thoughts or ideas, because we fear that our idea or discovery might not fit the respective context or existing beliefs.

Whenever I visit a new company or community for a consulting project, I do what I call the "watercooler test." I sit down somewhere where people talk openly—be it the cafeteria, the kitchen area, the coffee shop, or the actual watercooler—and pretend to work on my laptop. What I'm actually doing is listening in on people's conversations.

On occasion, conversations will go something like this: "Lilly brought up this strange idea again. I don't think she understands what's going on. We've always done things this way so why should we change anything?"

Often, after listening to a few conversations, a pattern emerges: People tend to talk about what went wrong in a given situation. In these work cultures it is more difficult to share an idea or insight as tomorrow, you might be the one being talked about.

But even when we do share our insights or ideas, we may be afraid to admit that they came to us in an unconventional way. Many valuable discoveries are later made to appear as if they were purposeful and rational from the beginning so as to not rock the boat or open ourselves up to the criticism that we might not have gone through a rigorous substantiation process.[9]

This brings us to the next of our obstacles to serendipity: post-rationalization.

The Gift (and Perils) of Hindsight

How do we make sense of something after it's happened? We employ what experts call "post-rationalization." Post-rationalization is about how we think about the past. To understand its power and risks, let's start by looking at how we think about the future.

Forecasts for complex systems are often wrong, at least in the detail. But sensible forecasters are well aware of the limitations of their work, and the degree to which forecasts differ from actual outcomes. Forecasts for the sales of fast-moving consumer goods such as beverages or toiletries, film box-office revenues, and company growth often have error rates of 50 to 70 percent, and so are off by millions of dollars.[10]

The reasons for this are apparent: Most systems and situations are too complex to model every detail accurately. To make matters worse, we cannot hope to understand the butterfly effect—small changes that over time have larger consequences.

Plans are, in effect, forecasts. They outline what we will do, the targets of achievement we expect to hit, and the consequences and actions that we will take. Add to that the social dynamics of a workplace, the honest mistakes people make, and unexpected events, and the actual outcomes often turn out very differently from those that were expected.[11]

And just as with forecasting, research shows that plans such as business plans rarely explain success. Seminal work in management and economics has shown that up to 50 percent of success is what experts call "unexplained variance"—in other words, it simply cannot be explained by the factors that management and economics textbooks traditionally focus on.[12]

So how does all of this relate to the past, to post-rationalization?

The point is that when we construct our story of past events, we do what forecasters do: We create a model and ignore the details and the random events. Forecasters have a good excuse for doing this with the future: They cannot model every detail, and, by definition, cannot foresee unpredictable events. But what is our excuse for doing this with the past?

Post-rationalization is closely linked to what's known as "hindsight bias"—the common tendency for people to perceive events as having been more predictable than they actually were. We downplay or exclude the unpredictable events from our version of the past because random events that happened are no longer unpredictable. In fact, in hindsight they can start to look like they were inevitable. We then use information that wasn't available to us at the time, and construct narratives that conveniently explain everything, including how each piece of the story logically connects with the rest of the story.[13]

In our need for control, we tend to look at the world as more explainable than it is. We want to see patterns in everything. Have you ever seen the Man in the Moon? Well, others have seen the Virgin Mary in grilled cheese sandwiches.

Our minds respond to a stimulus—such as a sound or an image—by looking for a familiar pattern or for an identity we know. Often we find one when none is there—a phenomenon known as "pareidolia." People have heard indistinct voices in the whir of fans or air conditioners, they have interpreted hidden messages in music played backward or at lower-than-normal speeds, and some see faces of animals in cloud formations.[14]

From an evolutionary perspective, this makes sense: Our unconscious processing accelerates the process of recognition and decision making to give us an edge, the opportunity to attack preemptively, or escape more immediately.

We all recognize this tendency in ourselves when it comes to visual images. But, in fact, it goes deeper. The larger phenomenon behind this is called "apophenia," our tendency to attribute meaning to patterns or perceived connections that are unrelated.[15]

One of the most intriguing examples of this comes from an experiment carried out by behavioral psychologist B. F. Skinner. In Skinner's experiment, a hungry pigeon was placed inside a box. Then food pellets were released into the box at entirely random intervals. Obviously, the pigeon had no way of predicting when the pellets dropped, and no way of causing it.

But the pigeon began to behave as if it could. If it received a food pellet while performing some kind of action (e.g., walking in a circle, turning its head to one side), it then started repeating that action it had performed before, until the next pellet appeared.

The pattern in which pellets were falling was entirely random, but the pigeon began acting as if it was a predictable event over which it could exercise some control.

This matters for serendipity because our tendency to seek recognizable patterns or identities can obscure the significance of random events. It can even lead us to creating rigid formulas for success when there is no real underlying mechanism to support them.

Put bluntly, if we airbrush serendipity out of our history, we make it far harder to spot when it happens again. This is particularly important given that serendipity is a process rather than a singular event, and it often has a long incubation period. We might not always be willing or able to track it back to the moment where it "started." Instead, we try to make sense out of what just happened and usually tell only half of the story. Or often even a completely different story.

Creating a story can be constructive as it helps provide a focus for future progress, but if we are to learn from it, it has to be an honest one, interrogated properly, and open to reassessment.

That also plays a role in how organizations operate. Take senior executives, who often narrate milestones or decisions as if they were all planned from the beginning in order to satisfy expectations. The CEO of one of the world's most successful companies told me how this has a lot to do with investors and employees, who might not appreciate him saying, "Well, this was luck, or this was unplanned"—because it feels dependent and coincidental.

It makes him and his colleagues feel that they should say something along the lines of "Well, of course, this was our goal, we had this in mind already, all the time." Why? "Because that story sells, that is the story investors want to hear. I'm pushed to the so-called 'official story,' because it feels like you are totally in control. But I'm almost ten years CEO, and I can tell you I'm not always in control. It doesn't always feel good to say, but I'm not always in control."

We are often trained to tell a linear story, portraying how we were in control at all times. We might retrospectively adapt the storyline to what suits best. Because this narrative is not the reality, the chance of learning what really allowed an outcome to happen is missed—along with the true learning that might allow similar insights to happen again in the future.

Which is why random anecdotes can do more harm than good. Picture the hero entrepreneur speaking at a conference about how he came up with his idea at his kitchen table, or the top CEO giving a master class on how she made her business a success. Sometimes they might even believe that the story they tell is the truth and "the full story," but each was embedded in a very specific context and set of conditions, which are almost certainly not the same for the respective listener.

Just copying a hero story such as J. K. Rowling's ascent to becoming the world's most successful writer—which almost certainly will leave out many of the initial conditions, or parts of the journey—can even be harmful given that it might lead us in the wrong direction. But a good story is often more unlikely than a less satisfactory one, and we can instead learn by trying to understand the actual underlying patterns. (In this book, I use stories to substantiate systematic patterns that have emerged—but only if those patterns emerged from different places, and if they appeared to ring true as actual experience rather than official narrative.)

What are the patterns when it comes to the reality of how things actually happen? Looking at more than a thousand purpose-driven ideas and their development, my Leaders on Purpose colleague Leith Sharp, the founder of Harvard's Executive Education for Sustainability Leadership program, in her two-decades-long teaching and research at Harvard has shown that once we are honest about it, what is supposed to be a linear story—our original plan—often becomes a "squiggle story." But then, we again tell the story as if the unexpected didn't happen (see figure).

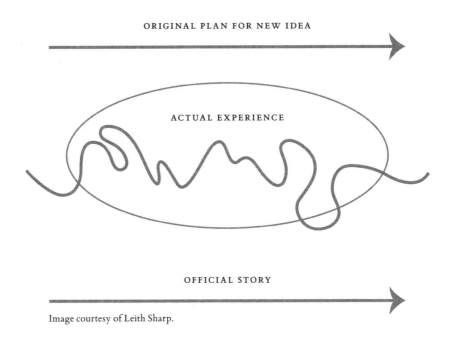

ORIGINAL PLAN FOR NEW IDEA

ACTUAL EXPERIENCE

OFFICIAL STORY

Image courtesy of Leith Sharp.

We often are more comfortable telling it as a "planning" story, even though it might have been an "emergence" story—with many turns.

Pearson's CEO, John Fallon, succinctly summarized it in our Leaders on Purpose 2018 CEO study: "Trying to get the original plan and the official story more aligned with actual experience is a very liberating and empowering thing to do. Hard, though, but it's the right approach."[16]

This applies to other areas as well, including writing books. Seasoned novelists, such as Deborah Levy, in her words, "map out a book and then let go."[17] They allow storylines and characters to emerge over time; they plan and adapt. They often get surprised by where a story leads them—but few people (like Deborah) are open about telling it as it is, rather than pretending that they mapped it all out from the beginning.

Do You See Nails Everywhere?

Knowledge and expertise are both a blessing and a curse when it comes to serendipity.

Expert knowledge tends to be well-organized and highly accessible in our minds, and so having a deep knowledge of a particular domain makes it more likely that you will spot bisociations or connections that others might miss. But deep domain-specific knowledge can also lead to "functional fixedness."

Functional fixedness refers to the way people who use a tool in their everyday lives, or see it used regularly in familiar ways, are often blocked mentally from seeing or using that same tool in a novel way.[18] The old phrase "if you have a hammer then you see everything as a nail" rings true here—and the mental agility or openness to see that tool in a new way is essential if we are to build our serendipity mindset.

The popular portrayal of this ability is a well-known trope of action movies. The hero—usually a James Bond, Lara Croft, or Jason Bourne-esque character—is outnumbered or outgunned, but thanks to her or his quick thinking manages to turn an everyday object like a library card or a set of curling tongs into a deadly weapon.

Yes, it's a Hollywood cliché, but we all recognize how remarkable this talent would be, and it applies not just to objects, but to all ways of thinking and problem solving.

Research has shown that individuals who are familiar with particular problem-solving strategies are unlikely to devise simpler ones when appropriate.[19] Many of us recognize in ourselves a tendency at times to "do something the hard way"—because that is the way we know.

But creativity is born when we are forced to abandon the physical and mental tools that we are familiar with and find new ways to work or think. People usually display the highest degree of creativity when they use problem-solving approaches that they do not routinely use.[20]

Companies and individuals are often rightly proud of their "core competencies"—the deep proficiency in something that enables them to create value—but we must beware that they don't turn into core rigidities.

Just like the Hollywood superspy, we do not need to be born with the ability to overcome functional fixedness—we can practice it, and train ourselves for it. Unusual situations and new experiences are excellent training grounds. They enhance our cognitive flexibility and help us overcome this functional fixedness.[21]

One example is the work of the nonprofit organization Ojos que Sienten (which means "eyes that feel" in Spanish). Founded by Mexican social entrepreneur Gina Badenoch, it aims to transform the lives and role in society of the visually impaired. It does so by placing the emphasis not on their disability, but on their abilities. It also invites those who are not visually impaired to consider their own abilities, which only come to the fore when their ability to see is put into question.

The best-known Ojos que Sienten initiative is its "dining in the dark" experience, which is exactly what it sounds like. In a dark room, blind waiters guide guests to their seat at the table and the participants sit next to people they have never met before.

Because the diners cannot see each other, their conversation is different from what non–visually impaired people are used to: Being together in the dark can help to develop a connection without our usual judgments based on factors such as physical appearance. The diners have to use other tools, principally their ears, to do the work that previously they would have done with their eyes. Without facial expression cues, people become more attuned to vocal tones and inflections, and in turn they're more expressive in their own speech in order to be sure they are understood correctly.

I have had some of my deepest and most meaningful conversations in these settings, because the focus is on the conversation (and the food), and nothing else. At one of these dinners during the Performance Theatre—an annual immersive leadership conference—I sat next to a man called Yves. We "went deep" and discovered a lot of common ground in our lives and thinking—some of it expected, some unexpected—which I suspect would not have emerged in a traditional dinner in the light. Yves turned out to be the director-general of the International Committee of the Red Cross (ICRC), an organization that has won three Nobel Peace Prizes and commands fifteen thousand staff around the globe. Would we have immediately connected on such a personal level if we had seen or "known of" each other? I wonder.

Even more directly, functional fixedness disappears altogether if you have no idea what a given tool is for. If you have no idea about a particular solution, method, or system, you do not have to "unlearn" preconceptions and you are free to innovate without the constraints of fixed thinking.[22]

At the same time, of course, functional fixedness never arises at all if there is no tool to begin with. Imagine someone presents you with a nail and tells you that you must drive the sharp end into a block of wood. You or I might immediately start searching for a hammer, cursing that the tools are never where you last left them.

But what if you had never heard of a hammer, never seen one, and certainly never watched someone use one to bang in a nail? You won't search for a hammer, and you won't even realize that you are missing the obvious tool. You will simply reach for the first suitable heavy object.

The absence of complex tools can even be seen to accelerate change and innovation, such as in some developing economies that are missing certain tools that developed economies take for granted—such as ATMs in almost every village. As a result, they often have not been trapped in preconceptions about how things should be, and so have often been quicker to adopt newer technologies and solutions.

Imagine a friend asked to borrow $20 from you, and on the way to her apartment you intend to withdraw that money from a nearby ATM. But what if the ATM is out of cash, or out of order, or has even been closed down? You'd be focusing on how the system you've relied on has let you down. You might call the bank to complain, and the bank might try to devise a better-working machine.

But when you've never had an ATM nearby or live in a world where there isn't such a thing, you don't fixate on the machine itself. Instead you think about the underlying question: How do I get $20 to my friend?

Enter MPesa, a money transfer system in Kenya that is a thriving example of banking via cell phone. In a rapidly developing society that has never had a reliable nationwide ATM network, MPesa has thrived and is used by millions of Kenyans.

As the economy in Kenya has developed and grown, more people have begun taking part in financial transactions. But the national network of ATMs is relatively weak and physical bank branches are scarce in more rural communities. Kenya instead moved straight to mobile banking.

When it comes to mobile banking, Kenya's developing economy is now more advanced than many so-called developed economies. The fact that we have thousands of ATMs and banks across the industrialized West—and many related regulations—might actually have been an obstacle to faster development of new and more effective banking solutions.

The point is not that we must close every ATM and bank branch to accelerate the acceptance of mobile banking (though some may suspect that is what banks are actually doing). The point is broader: If we are not fixated on an existing set of tools for a certain job, there is no functional fixedness, so the space is open for a quite different set of tools to be adopted.

That's why Netflix shows such as *The Final Table*—where top chefs compete against each other—are so different from traditional TV shows such as Gordon Ramsay's *Ramsay's Best Restaurants*. Cooking shows like Ramsay's followed the reality TV model and simply applied it to food. Content, plot, and indeed the food are relatively plain. In contrast, *Chef's Table*—which inspired *The Final Table*—was driven by the philosophy and approach of people with feature-filmmaking backgrounds. And it shows: The show's producers didn't have to unlearn the focus on narrative sequences, but they did introduce their ethos and approach of slower, more deliberate high-resolution narration, in the process turning simple mushrooms into mouth-watering art.

If you ask the show's creators, they will tell you that this shift originally came from "a place of ignorance," of inexperience.[23] They weren't functionally fixed. If there's no hammer, you don't see everything as a nail.

One way to not be trapped in mental models that place restrictions on what we regard as possible or likely is to hold multiple models in our minds. Charlie Munger, vice chairman of Berkshire Hathaway and Warren Buffett's ideas sparring partner, is renowned for his sharpness. His belief is that remembering isolated facts often does not help. Instead, we need a "latticework of theory" to connect facts and make sense out of them. This avoids solving problems from only the basis of what we know already—our *availability heuristics*.

As Munger points out, the mind works a bit like a sperm and egg: The first idea gets in and then the mind shuts. But our tendency to settle on first conclusions leads us to accept many erroneous results and to stop asking questions. Thus, Munger suggests that we are well advised to look at the world while holding different—and potentially competing—models in our head. Munger estimates that with fifty or so models at our disposal we can be a "worldly wise person."[24]

This approach of holding different and potentially competing models in our minds has many parallels with one that I've been intrigued by since I was a teenager and walked by its inventor's house in my home city of Heidelberg: Hegel's process of dialectics.

Georg Wilhelm Friedrich Hegel was a German philosopher who conceived of the progress of ideas as a dialectic, meaning that we start with a perspective (a *thesis*), which we then find out is flawed. We then counter this thesis with an alternative perspective (an *antithesis*), which has flaws of its own. But from this confluence of opposites we emerge with a new perspective (a *synthesis*) that creates a fresh perspective by integrating the best elements of both the thesis and the antithesis. The synthesis then becomes the new thesis against which emerges a new antithesis, and the process continues.

Such a process would break down if ever we became rigid in our thesis and we refused to consider the antithesis. But, obviously, for a period before the synthesis emerges, we may have to somehow hold both contradictory perspectives in our head at the same time, to look at things as not mutually exclusive. This runs counter to the way many of us think about the world. But in fact, many of the most successful people in our studies indeed hold conflicting ideas all the time.

Frameworks can act in two ways—they can be a barrier to serendipity if they blind us to anomalies or if they lead us to discredit or simply miss altogether those unexpected things that do not fit. This often shows in limiting beliefs that can hold us back. But they can also allow us to organize knowledge and information and to make sense of it. Similar to muscle memory, we have patterns that we need to unlearn in order to be able to truly move forward. What's important is that each of us should be able to use frameworks, rather than allowing them to use us.*

---

* There are a number of systems that can help to break out of functional fixedness and the related limiting beliefs. I discuss these in later chapters. But often, it's the simple things, such as changing perspective: In Russian Formalism, a core idea was to learn to re-familiarize ourselves with everyday things that we take for granted. Tolstoy, for example, used the technique across his works—in *Kholstomer*, a horse is the narrator, looking at the world from the horse's point of view (Crawford, 1984; Shklovsky, 2016). Another example is TRIZ, a tool kit developed by Russian inventor Genrich Altshuller. Based on the study of countless previous inventions, ideas, and breakthroughs, the core idea is that basic types of problems and solutions are repeated across sciences and industries. Often the problem seems intractable because making a change in one aspect of a system requires a compromise in another. It does not seem to matter which lever you pull, the problem either doesn't go away, or is replaced by another

Writing this book turned out to be an excuse for me to reflect on my own functional fixedness, what I take for granted in my own life. In the early stages of my writing, I met my good friend and ex-girlfriend Sophie for a coffee. I had just come from a great meeting with my publisher, who mentioned that it'd be good to integrate more personal stories into the book. So I asked Sophie if she knew about beautiful love stories based on serendipity.

"Ours!" she exclaimed.

I laughed and said, "But we're not together anymore!"

What she said next changed my perception of how I gauge the positive outcome of what makes something successful, whether it's a love story or a new business venture.

Sophie had always considered herself an introvert hidden inside a person who seemed like an extrovert. Although she was a keen risk-taker in her personal life, she was more risk-averse in a working environment. When Sophie moved to London, it wasn't long before she wondered whether she had made a mistake. Her plan was to get a master's degree in global mental health at one of the schools there, and she had been advised to move to the city before she applied.

One day, when she was feeling especially lost, she went to a local Starbucks to apply for a job. She ended up, in her words, "next to a guy [me] who would become my boyfriend for more than a year, and who introduced me to a completely new world—the world of social entrepreneurs."

Though we dated, it eventually became clear that Sophie and I were not meant to be a couple but friends. But when she and I talked about it later, it occurred to Sophie that had she not gone to that exact Starbucks on that day, she and I would not have met and her life would have gone in

---

problem. TRIZ provides a system for problem solvers to systematically "try out" possibilities that they might otherwise not have considered—solutions that don't just involve pulling the existing levers. In other words, it pushes users to consider the approaches and possibilities that their existing knowledge of the system might otherwise lead them to ignore or not even imagine.

a very different direction. As she put it, "You introduced me to The Hub [a local coworking space in London], where people were driven and passionate about social issues. I realized that even though I'm not an entrepreneur, I do have an entrepreneurial spirit, and I got to meet and talk to people who understood the power of taking personal risks, who sacrifice comfort and security for passion and dreams. Without our serendipitous meeting, I know that I would never have found this community."

In the shared workspace in which Sophie found her next job, she also met her next partner, who helped her find a new self-confidence and is now one of the most important people in her life, although they decided to continue their journeys separately.

With this new confidence, Sophie began to have a number of serendipitous encounters. More important, though, is that Sophie started to let go of social norms, such as that she needed to find a partner before the age of thirty. Today Sophie lives a life in which she is surrounded by interesting people and opportunities for development—all because she took a chance.

"Where would I be today if it hadn't been for that Starbucks meeting?" she asked. "I must admit I don't know. But a love story can have a happy ending even if the two people don't stay together!"

What Sophie said made my day. And as someone who considers himself to be open-minded, it made me reflect more deeply on my own biases.

And it made me realize that I as well was put on a very different track due to the chance meeting with Sophie, which I treasure still.

Where Does This Leave Us?

These biases and types of preconceived thinking are impossible to escape altogether, and many of them have developed for good reasons. While we can't remove them completely, we can moderate them and make a conscious effort to make room for something else.

Resisting our innate biases and thinking beyond the usual models and tools does not mean leaving everything to chaos and blind luck. Once we let go of simple narratives and pseudo-patterns and examine the real journeys of people and ideas (and the actual underlying patterns), we can see that serendipity plays a huge role. What is more, far from being about chaos or blind luck, serendipity itself has a form and a structure—it is a process that we can influence.

Looking at my own and my colleagues' research and experience, combined with advances in chemistry, library science, neuroscience, sociology, psychology, philosophy of science, economics, management science, and even the arts, it becomes clear that there are several clear patterns behind the cultivation of serendipity.

Throughout the next chapters, we explore these real patterns, and how the serendipity mindset can become a practical philosophy for life and for business. Then, we stop regarding luck as something that "happens *to* us," and become an agent of our own and others' (smart) luck.

Thus . . .

In this chapter, we encountered major biases that have the potential to impede serendipity, including underestimating the unexpected and post-rationalizing events. We can attempt to overcome these biases by opening our eyes to the unexpected, by capturing and legitimizing how decisions actually unfold—and by adding additional tools to our mental toolbox.

Being aware of and taming our innate biases and our propensity to live with preconceptions prepares the ground. The next step will explore how we can open up our mind.

But before we get to it, let's focus on a short exercise to clear the clutter and start to overcome our biases—and build our serendipity muscle.[25]

SERENDIPITY WORKOUT: DECLUTTER YOUR MIND

To start you off, I will ask you to start keeping a **serendipity journal**, and to write down what comes to you when reflecting on the workout below and in subsequent chapters.

1. Think carefully about the last six months of your life. What were three important moments of serendipity you experienced within that time? What did they have in common? Is there something you can learn from them?

2. Write down the serendipitous encounters and related ideas that excited you but you never followed up on. Once you have completed the list (it might take some time—no need to hurry), contact a trusted person to act as "filter" to discuss which ones might be interesting for you to consider further. Pick your favorite one, and then sleep on it. If in the morning the idea or thought still excites you, reach out to a key person in that field and discuss how to make the idea happen. Don't be afraid to make the effort here—it will pay off.

3. Reflect on your daily routine activities, especially meetings. Which meetings are truly necessary? Do they really need the amount of time they are allocated? If they are under your control, can you restructure them?

4. Start detailing your important decisions: the reasons for them and the related information that you had at the point you made them. Ask yourself: "Based on which assumption or belief do I make this decision?" and "What would influence me to make this decision differently?" and write down your answers. Review the entry whenever you have buyer's

remorse at the decision you made or when you (after the fact) think you knew something all along.

Serendipitous tips:

- When giving advice to someone, don't focus on what worked for you—no two situations or people are the same. Instead, start by asking the person asking for advice: "What is your intuition about it?" or "What do you think might solve your problem?" Often, the best advice you could give is already present within the person and their situation.
- When someone tells you a story that involves two potential courses of action—or when you tell such a story—ask yourself: "What could have happened instead if the other option had been taken?" and "What if the action had been performed differently?" Thinking about different scenarios will help you understand the actual situation and how likely or unlikely it was to happen.
- For important outcomes, ask yourself: "How did we get here?" Try to reconstruct the real story based on reflections of the people involved, looking back at emails or other notes. Then try to understand what you can learn from them. Was there a particular trigger point? Did someone connect the dots who wasn't rewarded for it?[26]

CHAPTER 3

THE OPEN MIND

Reframing Thoughts and Learning to Be Alert

—

Chance favors only the prepared mind.
Louis Pasteur

P eople with a serendipity mindset are not born luckier than others. They cultivate it in a number of ways—including the way they frame the world.

Serendipity Alert

When British researchers Peter Dunn, Albert Wood, Andrew Bell, David Brown, and Nicholas Terrett started their research on how to cure heart problems such as angina, they did not expect to be greeted by a prominent bulge as they inspected their patient's current condition. The drug sildenafil was supposed to help cure angina, but male patents encountered something else: a penile erection. The researchers were surprised.

What would most people in their situation do? Perhaps just accept it as an embarrassing side effect of the treatment? Or simply ignore it? Or develop another way to cure angina that avoids this unintended by-product? The three researchers did none of these things. Instead, they saw the opportunity to develop a drug that might cure erectile dysfunction. Viagra was born. Their connecting the dots led to one of the most successful inventions of all time.

Louis Pasteur famously quipped that "chance favors only the prepared mind." He might not have been far off. Research in the cognitive sciences and management has shown that *alertness* is at the core of noticing unexpected events. It is about noticing something without searching for it—and in the process identifying previously overlooked opportunities.[1] Take the chocolate-chip cookie: it was invented by a homemaker, Ruth Graves Wakefield, when she accidentally made these cookies instead of regular ones and started a million-dollar industry.

Being observant—or alert—can change the whole way we see and experience the world. This is as true for the invention of chocolate-chip cookies as it is for our daily operations.

Isabelle Franklin (not her real name) lives in Freiburg, Germany, and told me about her husband, a pharmacist. In the laboratory he was trained to look out for details that don't fit in. As a result, she said, "he looks at the world with the eyes of a child—or more like a detective. Lots of serendipitous things happen to him!" When I asked how often serendipity happens in her life, Isabelle said that "the last time I had serendipity in my life was when I met my husband." How can two people who have the same life have such different experiences with serendipity?

How we look at and make sense of the world—the way we frame it—is a critical feature of our ability to spot and connect the dots. We need to be alert to a potentially meaningful serendipity trigger, and to be prepared to make sense out of it.[2] An unprepared mind discards unusual encounters, and often overlooks serendipity.

If we are not alert, if our minds are not prepared to notice the valuable anomaly or insight, we are not merely missing potential serendipity, we are actually changing the whole way we perceive the world around us for the worse.

Do you look at the world as a series of barriers or of opportunities? Do you use constraints to justify why things just don't work out for you? Or are you alert to the potential serendipity around you that can bring so much joy, excitement, and success into our lives, even under the most challenging of circumstances?

We've All Been Framed

Over the last decade, colleagues and I carried out a number of studies into resource-constrained environments—settings in which there is a lack of financial resources and formal skills. In our research we came across many people who despite the evident limitations of their environment were actively creating their own luck. (These people have surprisingly much in common with successful people around the globe.)

One such individual is Yusuf Ssessanga, who was born and raised in Uganda and moved to Tanzania, a country in which the majority of the population lives under the poverty line, in his late teens. Arguably, the odds were stacked against him: By the standards of Western developed economies, he was in a tough spot with regard to material resources and life prospects.

Well-meaning (and usually white) people from the industrialized West would visit his community and ask what they "needed" and how they could "help" him. This automatically framed his community as potential beneficiaries, or even more negatively, as passive and powerless victims of their circumstances. This curbed local entrepreneurial spirit and incentivized a handout culture—an approach that unfortunately some Western nongovernmental organizations are still fostering.

But this approach to *framing* was dramatically changed by the South African social enterprise Reconstructed Living Labs (RLabs). The people at RLabs questioned those perceived resource limitations and instead focused on previously unrecognized or undervalued resources—such as the resourcefulness of former drug dealers—and enlisted them to redefine opportunities from something that might happen *to* local people to something that they could be part of creating themselves.[3] Through a number of meetings and training sessions, online and offline, the approach was spread.

As a result, Yusuf and his team now look at local assets and partners that are around and not used, and how they might be leveraged—for example, using abandoned garages as training centers. What stuck with me was how much this was not only about a pragmatic approach but about a new way of life.

In Yusuf's eyes, the problem with most outside partners was that they wanted to know the locals' "needs," and once he started to tell them about a community's assets, they wouldn't give funding. This led to people painting a picture of a needy community instead, and once that narrative became commonplace, those in the community began to "believe it themselves." Yusuf and his team are learning from RLabs, and stopped doing it that way. Looking at it from this perspective, to Yusuf the world looks very different.

Adopting the mindset that resource limitations are in part socially constructed, Yusuf became an agent of his own fate by taking his luck in his own hands. He now experiences serendipity regularly—as he puts it, "all the time." He now finds himself running into new people that work cooperatively with him on his projects.

How did RLabs get him there? RLabs began in Bridgetown, part of Cape Town's Cape Flats district. The area was characterized by run-down houses and high crime rates. To identify the community's needs for emotional support, a team of Bridgetown residents under the leadership of RLabs' founder Marlon Parker developed a network using cell phones to connect people who needed counseling with other local people. Over time, RLabs increasingly helped the community to work with the few existing resources available to them, and developed simple training modules that allowed them to teach one another to use social media in positive ways, to share their stories with online audiences and to connect with like-minded people around the world.

RLabs' headquarters now consists of a training center that provides affordable courses on how best to use social media and related subjects, an enterprise incubator that helps to start up and support new companies, and a consulting arm that focuses on advising companies and governments on issues such as how to engage local communities. Often, organizations complement their own services with components of RLabs' approach and integrate them into their respective locations—they form a new "hub." RLabs' simple education and training model now operates in over twenty locations around the world, educating tens of thousands of people. The organization uses recombining material resources (e.g., using abandoned garages as training centers) and talent (e.g., integrating people who were formerly regarded as unskilled) to empower locals.

Marlon Parker grew up in Cape Town during the apartheid era, when gang membership and crime were on the rise owing to his community's high unemployment rates and the social inequality they faced. Raised by a single parent, and with a younger brother who was involved in a local gang, he was inspired to study information technology in college to improve his life. Marlon started teaching fellow students about computers as soon as he learned how to use one himself, and used the money he made to support his family. Marlon realized both that community members in the Bridgetown area had lost hope that life could be turned around, and that those people already possessed the solutions to many of their problems but did not know it.

RLabs started with the idea that if you can change one person's life by sharing a story of hope, and then inspire others, it can make a real difference. The organization itself sprang from experimentation and chance. When Marlon's father-in-law, a local pastor, asked him to start giving computer lessons, he realized that digital tools could be an effective way for people to tell their stories. This quickly spiraled into people developing their competences around social media, and even companies that advised others on how to use such platforms.

The core idea was to make the best out of whatever and whoever was at hand. In this way, people who were previously considered unemployable became valuable contributors—and turned their lives around. Making the best use of whatever diverse materials are at hand—*bricolage*—can apply not just to objects but to skills and people as well. Examples in the Cape Flats are former drug addicts and dealers who became useful and joyful members of the community by telling their stories of hope and recovery and teaching others.

The result was a paradigm shift in the community, from focusing on what was missing (money or formal skills) to what resources were available—and making the best out of every situation. A former drug addict can now picture herself as a teacher, having seen others with a similar background enter the profession and having a space in which to do it. She is no longer perceived as a liability but rather as a valued member of society. She is now someone who has the agency to create her own luck. Serendipity is within her grasp.

An RLabs partner summarized to me her realization that they can make things happen themselves, giving them inspiration and dignity. To them, it is the opposite of being in need, of being a victim.

Shifting toward this opportunity-focused mindset enables previously unseen possibilities. Taking whatever is at hand, looking at it afresh, and recombining it with other objects, skills, people, or ideas frequently leads to yet more previously unimagined ideas and insights and, as the example of RLabs demonstrates, a profound change in outlook.

Serendipity at RLabs now happens all the time, and the related approaches are now being used by companies and governments around the world. A large South African bank that was planning to cut its workforce and sell office space now looks at former cashiers as potential financial trainers, and the office space as potential training centers. What were liabilities became assets.

In my research I have encountered many people such as Yusuf and Marlon. Some of them have faced severe structural constraints and challenges that seem impossible to overcome. (And sometimes they are, and we can never blame someone for their circumstances—as we will see in later chapters, working on changing structural constraints related to poverty, socioeconomic class, race, and gender is paramount). However, many individuals and organizations, such as Yusuf in Tanzania and RLabs in South Africa, started creating their own luck by being alert to the possibilities around them. In this way, their entire situation was reframed from one of passivity and powerlessness to one of activity and opportunity.

Reframe or Perish

I may have made this sound too easy, but the mindset that is alert to serendipity is difficult to develop, particularly if we feel our thinking might be off-base, or if our environment is hostile to new ideas. Yet, despite the difficulties, there are clear steps we can take to foster this serendipity-enhancing approach and reshape our minds to be open and prepared.

In a multiyear-long research project, we found that RLabs developed a number of simple practices that successfully shaped mindsets, and enabled serendipity to blossom.[4] By providing simple rules of thumb that empowered partners to *make do* in their respective contexts, RLabs was able to function with a small team while growing the reach of the organization.

Its budgeting approach for new projects is guided by questions such as, "Is this item essential?" If the answer is yes, then does someone here have access to the item without having to buy it? If no, do you know someone who might have access to it? If not, is there an alternative that is less expensive? Only after you answer these questions should an item be bought. This approach is driven by the idea that often we look for new resources even though we might have alternatives at hand that might work just as well.

In Yusuf's case, the RLabs team used personal interactions via Skype and in person, storytelling, and the transfer of simple, inexpensive practices and tool kits, including a simple guide to social media, to shift mindsets and nurture his local activities.

RLabs might appear to be a rare example, but our research shows that similar patterns hold true, whether it's a waiter in London or the painter in midcentury Europe or a Fortune 500 CEO in the United States. The lessons can be extended into almost any sphere, be it our own lives, apprenticeship schemes, business support programs, enterprise incubators, or, indeed, whole companies.

Once we stop obsessing about our lack of resources and look to enable individuals and give them dignity, we find that instead of beneficiaries looking for our help or employees worried about budgets, we have stimulated people who start creating their own luck.

Reframing helps to create serendipity by enabling people to see potential events and situations and feel they have the capacity to act on those— to spot the triggers and connect the dots. At the core of this are changes in thought and practice. Once we stop waiting for an opportunity to loudly declare itself, we realize that opportunity is all around us if we keep our mind open and release it from closed templates and frames.

When we do not take structures and constraints for granted, we look at the world with different eyes. We start to see bridges where others see gaps.

How can we train ourselves to do this in our day-to-day lives?

Nudging Toward Serendipity

It often starts with small changes in behavior—such as by viewing every situation not as a problem but rather as a learning opportunity. Many of us—including myself—have had tough situations in our lives that felt like a crisis in the moment but that became a key pillar of who we are today. They presented us with the challenge of focusing on the possibility to do something with them rather than framing them as a negative that would hold us back.

If we see a car accident as purely bad luck, it stays just that—bad luck. If we consider a bad decision as defining us, it will define us forever.

I still vividly remember what I consider to be one of my worst decisions in life: to accept an additional investment into one of the organizations that I cofounded, against the views of some of my cofounders. At the time, my head told me to go ahead, as on paper it looked like the only really sustainable option in a financially and strategically tense situation. Yet my gut told me not to.

After an initially positive period it indeed turned out that the expectations between the investors and the cofounders/management were not completely aligned, which led to a painful breakup. It was particularly painful for those cofounders who felt all along that it was not the right path.

For some time I let myself be defined by that decision, that mistake I made. I wouldn't talk about it with colleagues, as I couldn't make sense out of the cognitive dissonance that I felt.

It is still something that I am not proud of, and if I could do it over, I probably would have decided differently (hindsight bias aside). However, I also realized that this was one of the few situations in my life that made me painfully experience what I now treasure most in life: that I want to do what "feels" right rather than what looks better on a spreadsheet.

What felt like an existential situation—individually and organizationally—turned out to be a fascinating learning opportunity. It helped me become more empathic toward people who faced similar decisions and helped me realize that there are no black or white decisions. It helped me *frame* the world differently. When I face crises today, I think back to that situation, try to collect all the information I can, and then trust what I've come to think of as my "informed gut feeling." This makes me calmer based on the feeling that things will work out somehow even if it doesn't feel that way in the moment. It also made me understand more clearly what drives my decisions, and that if I'm not clear with myself about my fears and desires, I'm easier to manipulate.

As Richard Wiseman might put it, if bad things happen, take the long view. Having realized that often the most challenging situations can be the real treasures of life, I now ask myself for each situation that seems to be challenging: "Will this really matter ten years from now? If not, why do you worry? If yes, how can you already now help shape it in a way so that it becomes a valuable learning opportunity?"

Grace Gould, founder of the School of the Digital Age (SODA), used to cheer me up with her own take on John Lennon's famous quote: "Things tend to work out in the end—and if they haven't, it's not yet the end!"

A related approach that Wiseman suggests is to look at the counterfactual, or what could have happened (we will return to this in chapter 9). The car crash could have left me paralyzed, or it could have left me dead. If the additional investment hadn't happened, we might have ended up in financial disarray from early on. And so on.

Wiseman reports on an interesting experiment. His research team presented people who consider themselves "lucky" and "unlucky" with the following scenario: Imagine you are in a bank when an armed robber enters and shoots you in the shoulder. You escape with a flesh wound.

People who self-identify as "unlucky" will frame this situation as something that *tends to happen* in their life. This would be one more bad experience in a line of them. "Lucky" people will frame it as a situation that could have been worse, such as "the bullet could have killed me," or "I could have been shot in the head."

What is happening here?

Lucky people tend to frame counterfactuals along the lines of what could have been worse, while unlucky people frame them as what could have been better, or even more pronouncedly, as "the story of my life."

Lucky people also tend to compare themselves with others who have had less luck (that is, with the person who was killed during the robbery), while unlucky people tend to compare themselves with those who had more luck (the person who didn't get hurt at all).

This becomes either a vicious or virtuous cycle: The unlucky person talks himself into misery by comparing himself with those who ended up better off, while the lucky one tends to compare herself with those who ended up worse—softening her bad luck. Guess who will probably experience more serendipity in their life?

We Are What We Say (and How We Talk)

Wiseman's experiments also show that unlucky people tend to rely on ineffective ways to alter bad luck, like superstition and going to fortune tellers.[5] Lucky people, in turn, tend to take control and often aim to understand the root cause of a problem, so to be able to learn from the situation. This approach manifests in our language: If we say something like "x happened *to* me," we frame it as a passive endeavor. We become a passive recipient of fate. But once we start focusing on the elements that we can control, we start becoming agents of our own luck.

It's worth emphasizing that the base level of serendipity will be very different for a child born into a privileged family in the industrialized world than that of a child born into a family in the impoverished Cape Flats. However, as our and others' research shows, while the initial level is different and while structural constraints such as power dynamics are often a very real concern (sometimes completely shutting down potential serendipity), individuals across all contexts, from a former drug dealer in South Africa to the world's foremost leaders, have been shown to create their own serendipity. They are not smarter than other people, but they approach life differently, and by doing so they tend to make better decisions and experience more serendipity.

Thus, the way we frame a situation—especially situations that might appear to us as if they are bad luck—is crucial. There are many ways to develop the foundations for this, both emotionally and cognitively. This can include approaches such as meditation, turning an abstract challenge or fear into concrete action steps,[6] or focusing on the positive elements of a situation while mitigating the risks of the bad ones. Fascinating experiments have shown that self-fulfilling prophecies particularly apply to the way we frame the world: If we think things will turn out well, they turn out well more often—and the opposite is true as well. We quite literally "manifest" and "speak into existence."

Serendipity Is Abundant—If We Want It to Be

Starting to see every situation—and particularly, every conversation—as an opportunity to experience serendipity is an active decision. When listening to people, we can think about how what they're saying relates to our or someone else's area of interest, even if it seems far-flung. Building on others' ideas, rather than trying to "compete" with them, trains us in connecting the dots, for ourselves and for others (see chapter 5).

Take Shaa Wasmund, MBE, a successful businesswoman and bestselling author. Born in California, she went on to study at the London School of Economics, and during her studies won a magazine contest to interview Chris Eubank, a UK-based boxing world champion.

During the interview, the two got along so well that to Wasmund's surprise, Eubank unexpectedly offered her the job of managing his public relations. She accepted, and over time created a hugely successful career in boxing PR—with no previous experience in the area. She went on to set up her own PR firm in London, among other accounts, managing the launch of Dyson vacuum cleaners.

I have observed this kind of serendipitous happening with many successful people: They go into a situation with one idea (in this case, interviewing a boxer for a publication), but they are also open to the unexpected. It is often in these kinds of situations that serendipity happens—and often, *others* connect the dots for us then.

But it is easier to connect the dots if we have a feeling for what we are striving for. Our research at the LSE, at NYU, and at Leaders on Purpose has shown that central to many successful people and organizations is a broad ambition, a drive, a belief system, or a "guiding theory." This may be referred to as our *North Star*—the point, principle, or philosophy that consciously or subconsciously guides us in our respective context. Without it we may drift or sit becalmed.[7]

A North Star is not a precise guide. It is often essential, but it must not define our path or dictate each step. Rather, it gives us a sense of direction. The exact route, the twists and turns, the shortcuts and the diversions (many of which are extremely valuable) are a vital part of our journey and they are the life stuff of serendipity.

Paul Polman, cofounder of Imagine and former CEO of Unilever, where he reoriented one of the world's largest companies toward creating societal impact, told me that because he has so many interests—in business as well as in issues of climate change, poverty, and sustainability—people might think he is distracted when taking on projects that unexpectedly come out of conversations. But he is actually very intentional about what he does. He takes on a variety of projects but always with a specific intention that helps him focus. Throughout his life, his passion has been to help people who cannot help themselves. Early in life he thought that this would be via his becoming a doctor or a priest. Serendipitously, he did it via business. He created his own opportunity and then got firmly behind it.

Layla Yarjani, cofounder of education organization Little Bridge, which teaches English worldwide, and cochair of UNICEF's NextGen Europe chapter, captured how this broader ambition is not about a particular life goal, but rather about *how* we approach life. People like her, who have been inspiring others, often get asked how they have it all figured out. How did she find what feels right for her, what she loves doing? Was it that she chose the "right" career background and had the "right" life experiences?

Not at all. For Layla and many others that I have encountered on this journey, it comes from following individual curiosity, and a sincere desire to help others. It does not come from the belief that she's figured it all out. To her, the notion of figuring out her purpose is just that, a notion. She considers it a waste of time to look for justifications for why others have the right resources, connections, etc., to do what they do and how you can't replicate that because of your own limitations. Layla is no more or less special than anyone else; she chooses what she wants to do and wakes up every day and does it, because it feels right.

Layla follows her curiosity, and then once she stumbles on something that feels right, she explores it as a side project alongside her other activities. She talks to people about it, she tries out ideas as they occur to her, and she is open to see where they go. Many of her projects started out of coffee shops from her own curiosity and many of them are now, she says, "safely filed away in a Google folder." Layla and the late Albert Einstein have this in common: She believes she has no special talent, but is only passionately curious.

Successful people often place a number of bets on new ideas and then go with the one that feels right to them. They frequently do this while they are still working at their full-time jobs, which gives them the stability to experiment during their downtime, which is often an important hedge against uncertainty.

I have done this myself, with varied success. Almost none of my own journey was preplanned, and (almost) each big step felt right when it happened. Over the course of my life I placed a number of bets, learning something from each one. Life could have turned out very differently for me, but a dear mentor told me whenever I had to make a choice: "People like you always think that there is this one right way, one path that leads you to where you want to be. But there are many paths. The important thing is that you just start moving."[8]

Indeed, I sometimes need this reminder of *equifinality*—that there are multiple paths leading us to Rome—especially when my fear of rejection keeps me from moving.

Sometimes We Have to Play It by Ear

One of the most fundamental yet still under-appreciated truths of human existence . . . is this: everyone is totally just winging it, all the time.

OLIVER BURKEMAN, JOURNALIST AND AUTHOR

When the veil of control slips for a public figure, it makes headlines. Politicians who can't remember the key statistics in their policies, chief executives who stumble over details at a press conference, government projects that fail because it's all been thrown together at the last minute all are examples that often people in power and responsibility are *just winging it*.[9]

Oliver Burkeman, journalist and author, points out that of course, it's no different in daily life. The man in the street who can't calculate a tip in his head, the doctor who googles Osgood-Schlatter disease, the barista who can't tell the time from an analog clock, the teenager who can't get somewhere without GPS, the new parent who has no idea how to properly change the diaper but does it anyway. These people function perfectly well by avoiding certain tasks and situations and get by using other techniques, but they are all winging it. And by "they" I mean "we." An honest appraisal of ourselves reveals that all of us have moments in which we feel we are making it up as we go along.

Almost everyone feels completely out of their depth at times in their lives. And while many of us can hide it most of the time, sometimes it's impossible to maintain the fiction.

For many people and institutions this is a very worrying realization, and Burkeman points out that institutions invest lots of time and money pretending that everything has been figured out and that in no way is the company or organization making it up as it goes along.

Legitimacy, authority, and even the survival of companies often depend on the notion that they have the answers. Followers of organizations and leaders gain much of their psychological security from believing that the people who are in charge actually know what they are doing.

But after a couple of glasses of wine, even the most powerful, successful, and seemingly in-control people usually admit that they often don't know what they're doing all the time.

So why is the world, your life, and your company not a total mess? After all, if at any one time a significant number of us are winging it, then surely the wheels should be coming off the whole bandwagon? The counterintuitive answer is that not having all the answers is not necessarily a problem. Winging it is fine; it often works and works well, just as long as the person doing the winging has the right state of mind—being able to adjust based on unexpected changes.

We Can't Always Predict the Future, but We Can Handle It

We often try to project proficiency while inside we are in panic. But Burkeman's insight reminds us that everyone else is doing the same thing. Everyone feels like an imposter at times—this nagging, persistent fear of being exposed as a "fraud." Your doctor surely knows exactly what she's doing, right? Your pilot is always in control, isn't he?

Scientific and anecdotal evidence points to the fact that even in defined spheres like aviation or medicine, where presumably people know exactly what they're doing, they still have to wing it at times. In fact, people—including experts—are most likely to be winging it at the most critical moments.

An unprecedented medical emergency during surgery, or the multiple engine failures on an airliner flying at low altitude may be precisely the moments when the doctor or pilot will have to—pardon the pun—wing it.

What is more, it is these moments that are usually regarded as the apogee of brilliance and quick thinking. The case of US Airways captain Chesley Sullenberger, the pilot who in 2009 successfully carried out a water landing in New York's Hudson River after a twin-engine failure just minutes after takeoff, is an example of this. The normal procedure for dealing with a twin-engine failure would be to glide the aircraft to the nearest airport, but that textbook solution assumed the aircraft would be at a much higher altitude than US Airways Flight 1549 was. While air traffic controllers proposed heading for the nearest runway, Sullenberger correctly and quickly realized that at his altitude and speed, that would not work. He wouldn't make it. So he landed in the Hudson River, saving the lives of every one of the 153 passengers and crew on the plane that day.

None of this is to suggest that knowledge and experience were not essential. Sullenberger himself attributed his success to his years of flying, which he described as making small deposits in the bank of experience, allowing him to make a hefty withdrawal when he needed it. His years of experience and a mature gut feeling allowed him to do something unconventional—and to become one of the heroes of the twenty-first century.

Most of us will never have to think on our feet in quite such dramatic circumstances and when so much is at stake. But in smaller ways, each of us does it all the time—even the most in-control people. What is truly dangerous are not the moments when people think on their feet, but when they stick to the model and act as if everything is set in stone.

Self-confidence and a huge ego can be good for ambition, and often enable careers. But too much ego and a lack of self- and situational awareness are dangerous; trusting wholly to our existing models or templates can mean failing to see risks or to be ready for the unexpected.

In an interview series with thirty-one of the world's most successful CEOs I carried out with colleagues at Harvard University, Leaders on Purpose, and The World Bank, we found that most of those leaders had a deep awareness that they cannot always fully control, let alone predict, the future.[10]

For example, Emmanuel Faber, CEO of the food company Danone, reflected that he trusts more in vision and the emerging execution that starts paving the road than in a big plan. Why? Because the world is changing so fast that he doesn't think it makes much sense to overplan—but that you need a vision because you need to make sure you know where to go.

These leaders often lead by developing a strong yet malleable North Star—a broad ambition and purpose—rather than meticulous plans, enabling their teams to make their own decisions within this guiding frame. And they often portray a vulnerable strength—with clear vision and energy but transparent to the apparent limitations—which often develops even more support as people tend to trust leaders with whom they resonate.[11]

From Socrates to Serendipity

Throughout this book, you will find many approaches and tools that can help you assess and (re-) frame situations based on a serendipity mindset. For now, let us look at the Socratic method—persistent questioning dialogue—which is one of the most effective and time-tested approaches for stimulating fresh thinking, cutting down preconceived ideas, and uncovering something from within, rather than projecting templates from the outside.

The Greek philosopher Socrates, credited as one of the founders of Western philosophy, did not teach a set of beliefs or facts. The Socratic dialogues that have come to us through Plato are not lectures. They are conversations in which Socrates asks questions.

The questions reduced his fellows to a state in which they realized that their preconceptions were illusions and they must start to think afresh—and in dialogue with Socrates they established new understandings. The six types of Socratic questions are questions for clarification, such as "Why do you say that?"; questions that probe assumptions ("What could we assume instead?"; "How can you verify that assumption?"); questions that probe evidence ("What would be an example?"); questions that question perspective ("What are the pros and cons?"); questions that probe implications ("What are the consequences of this action?"); and questions about the question itself ("Why do we ask this question in the first place?").

During the last few years, I have used variations of these questions when faced with important discussions—especially in more confrontational settings. Once we are forced to clarify our assumptions, we often realize that our position is just that—a position.

Wisdom is not about having all the answers, it is often about asking the right questions. Socrates—deemed the wisest person in the world by the Oracle of Delphi—famously declared that he had nothing to teach. He was only asking questions. *He was winging it.*

Serendipity: An Education

What starts in childhood can be developed throughout our lives. As children, we learn how to look at the world. As parents or friends, we can have a major impact on how our children or friends see the world. My father used to say that "whatever happens, with the right attitude we will always work it out." This always made me feel that things would be fine as long as I did something about them—and that I could do something about them. And even if everything did not work out the way I wanted it, life would go on. Painful learnings would turn out to be helpful, and issues were challenges to be solved rather than constraints.

In fact, Carol Dweck in her inspiring work on growth mindsets has shown that even small changes in conversation and language can alter our approach to life. She suggests replacing "I'm bad at that" or "I can't do that" with "I haven't mastered that yet."[12] In fact, related research on brain plasticity has shown that the brain is not fixed—nor is our attitude and approach.[13] Our brain, much like our body, is a muscle that can be exercised and trained.

Believing that we can learn and do anything once we put our mind to it is essential if we are going to be ready for that chance encounter, the unexpected event, the unforeseen connection—for serendipity.

It is essential because without a belief that it is OK to wing it, that we can, and should, be engaged in a constant two-way interaction with the world, we might miss the opportunity to turn instances of chance into true serendipity.

Giving someone the self-confidence that things will work out is probably one of the biggest gifts a parent can offer their child or that a teacher or leader can impart to their students or team.

Unfortunately, most universities, and particularly business schools, still focus on the idea that the future can be planned out, subtly incentivizing people to pretend they had everything planned all along. Teaching strategic planning, templates, and business plans is all well and good, but often life (and business) is more emergent than that. In reality, as scholars such as Saras Sarasvathy have shown, especially entrepreneurs in fast-changing environments often do not work out a concrete target destination, but they look at what they have in front of them—resources, skills, connections, the marketplace—and build something based on that, often iterating along the way. If we don't take this into account, we fail to teach students that we do not need to (try to) predict the future and then pretend we know everything as long as we can control and adjust the key parameters.[14]

Take the example of Sandbox, now a global community of around fifteen hundred young innovators from over sixty countries that we cofounded in 2008.[15] Sandbox identifies the most inspiring young people in different fields (e.g., design, arts, business, law, entrepreneurship, social business), and connects them with one another as well as with outside mentors and resources.

We strongly felt that there are many young amazing changemakers in the world who already do innovative things in their twenties—but who takes those agents of change seriously? And where can they meet like-minded peers in an intimate setting? What if the leaders of tomorrow already met at twenty-five instead of fifty-five? How would their friendships affect the impact they can have in the world across their lifetime?

In German, *Sandkastenfreunde* are the friends you meet while quite literally playing in a kindergarten sandbox, and who sometimes become lifelong friends. We wanted to create a playground for twenty-somethings in which they could shape and exchange ideas and develop meaningful relationships in an informal and unforced way. The close-knit community is organized in a decentralized way: In more than thirty cities around the world—called hubs—local representatives ("ambassadors") identify members and organize both informal dinners and events such as "demo nights" to help members solve their professional and personal challenges. Members support each other in a number of ways by offering emotional support, information, feedback, and opportunities.

Sandbox emerged out of a future that was impossible to predict. It was late 2008, the American financial services firm Lehman Brothers had just collapsed, and the global economy was in tatters. So were we. The initial plan—bringing together the leading changemakers in their twenties from around the globe at an inspiring conference—did not seem feasible anymore. We had spent a year talking with potential sponsors and scouting for locations. Corporate partners had shown interest, but at this point, budgets were being cut—especially for initiatives such as a global youth conference.

We felt that it just wasn't possible to organize a global conference without a budget. At the same time, we were excited about the idea of shaping this community. We had started to host a couple of informal dinners in Zurich and London, and people seemed to enjoy meeting one another and letting their guard down. We started arranging more of those smaller events, and realized that they were an effective way of attracting more members—step by step, rather than in one big go.

While at first we had imagined our venture as a conference, we realized that a locally embedded approach would be more financially sustainable and make it possible to develop a healthy membership structure over time. We did not abandon our broad ambition—our North Star—of developing a community of young changemakers; instead, we abandoned the plan, the big conference.

We ditched the top-down approach of launching a huge conference and instead focused on a hub-based model, driven by local members. It was a simple, inexpensive approach, with events that were intimate and often at members' homes. Over time, we extended this to regional retreats—usually between two and four days in a cozy rented house somewhere in the countryside. These get-togethers helped cross-pollinate across the different hubs. They were often interactive and cocreated by members, with a focus on deepening relationships.

Once the first global conference happened four years later in Lisbon, people already had connected both offline or online via our internal Facebook groups (the sentence "Nice to finally meet you in person!" became one of the most-uttered ones at the conference). Sandbox worked because people felt a deep emotional connection to the other members. They did not show up as their "best self" but rather as their *whole* self—there was no need to hide the parts that might appear "crazy" to some.

In hindsight, unexpectedly having to reverse the model turned out to be a blessing in disguise. The global financial crisis could have spelled Sandbox's doom—but while it certainly caused us quite a few sleepless nights, it turned out to be a great opportunity to reframe our ideas and approach, and helped to kick-start not a conference but a tightly knit global community based on local gatherings. Of course, there were many challenges along the journey—but the initial barrier was overcome. The situation was *reframed*.

The ramifications of reframing extend into the way we establish a mindset to help us and future generations grasp unexpected opportunities instead of floundering when our rigid templates are shattered. Achieving this will require reforming our education and apprenticeship systems away from mere hard skills to a serendipity mindset that allows us to recognize and leverage the unexpected. We need to imbue a generation with the idea that we can all influence our own luck.

Unraveling the Surprising

Have you ever had a conversation in which someone described a job opportunity that you felt was not relevant to you? You are happy with your current job, so why would you want another job—or one in a different field? But a few weeks later, life has changed, and you feel that you are ready for something new. You recall the conversation and now the job might be exactly what you are looking for.

What if you hadn't listened, ignored the "irrelevant" chatter from your dinner companion, and thought about the ingredients of your lasagna instead? The opportunity would have been missed.

Curiosity and, crucially, openness to unsought information and events dramatically increases our chances of experiencing serendipity.[16] This is often coupled with the willingness to find an anomaly or the surprise in a given situation. Curious, open, and questioning minds are at the core of making discoveries and creating serendipity.[17]

One of the books on my bedside table to this day is *The Little Prince* by Antoine de Saint-Exupéry. The story is of a little boy who explores his world and is in wonder about everything and everyone in it. It is a timeless reminder of the value of always asking questions, even (or especially) if they might seem childish. (One of my favorite parts is when the Little Prince asks a businessman, who is busy counting the stars that he thinks he owns: "What good does it do you to own the stars?" "It does me the good of making me rich." "And what good does it do you to be rich?" "It makes it possible for me to buy more stars, if any are discovered." "This man," the little prince says to himself, "reasons a little like my poor tippler.") We will come back to this later.

The writer Walter Isaacson, a former CEO of the Aspen Institute, has studied many of the world's great minds such as Albert Einstein (who was close with genius Marie Curie) and Leonardo da Vinci. The common denominator among them: their curiosity across disciplines. Isaacson summed this up in a conversation with professor Adam Grant, explaining how Benjamin Franklin went up and down the Atlantic seacoast looking at how swirls of air resembled the swirls of the northeastern storms—then discovering the Gulf Stream. Or take Leonardo da Vinci, who saw patterns across nature. Or Steve Jobs, who would always end his product presentations with the intersection of the arts and technology.[18] An intersection—between ideas, observations, perspectives, areas of application—is where creativity happens.

Remember the three princes of Serendip from the Old Persian fairy tale. They became the emblem of what we now call serendipity not because they had a fixed worldview but because they went through the world with open eyes. Their curiosity allowed them to recognize different cues, such as the camel's tracks, which with hindsight allowed them to connect the dots.

This points to the important fact that we do not necessarily need prior knowledge before serendipity can happen. The meanings or opportunities in an event or piece of information may not be apparent at first. It may be years before another piece falls into place—a new book we read or another conversation.

However, curiosity and openness can backfire if they distract you.[19] The fact is, there is a time and a place for serendipity. It is often important during the early stages of a project, when alertness for outside influences tends to be higher.[20] During later stages, it is often time to focus on getting stuff done.

This book is itself partly a product of serendipity as thoughts, studies, research, conversations, and stories came together and the dots were connected. But in the later stages I had to move into execution mode: sit down, put my headphones on, turn off my cell phone, say no to conferences—and write. I had to close myself down to more serendipity to get the book done.

Even in a multinational organization, there are times and places when serendipity is key, and others where it is less so. Research on Japanese optoelectronics firms has shown that serendipity often plays a more important role at the beginning of exploration efforts, when alertness and mindfulness are higher, than in later stages.[21] In general, creative endeavors tend to be important in the early stages of science or product life cycles—it may even be the reason an idea exists at all. But later in the process serendipity might take a back seat and the process becomes more standardized and industrialized. At that stage, consistency and credibility of data might trump other concerns. So the core question then is—where is the creative process taking place, and when does it really add value to be creative?

But even in down periods it is vital that we never shut down our openness to serendipity. There are countless examples of entrepreneurs who launch several ventures during their career, each one the result of some serendipitous encounter or insight. There are also plenty of people who after a long and stable career have a moment of serendipity, give up the day job, and take a new direction.

But we often need to feel ready. Charlie Dalloway (name changed), a staff member at a restaurant in London, shared his story with me. For a long time, he felt he did not know himself well enough to decide which path he wanted to follow. He did not act on opportunities that came from unexpected encounters and conversations, for example from customers that took a liking to and shared opportunities with him. Yet the more he got to know himself, the more he began to trust that he was ready for serendipity. Now he's working to help his children feel safe enough to trust themselves and their judgment—to feel ready for when an unexpected opportunity arises. "Serendipity before I was twenty-five? Zero. Serendipity now? All the time."

The Conversation Is Never Boring
If You Know What to Look For

Let's go back to the dinner conversation where your friend suggests a job opportunity that you're not interested in. In this scenario, you realize weeks later that it was just the job opportunity you needed. Maybe you could have accelerated that realization by asking the right questions at the time. Questions like: "Why does the person think the job would suit me?"; "Has she perhaps already seen a problem or frustration with my current job that I haven't recognized?"

The most seemingly boring or irrelevant conversation can be transformed by asking the right questions. Too often many of us will complain that we got trapped at an event talking to a bore. We might say the person had "nothing to say" or that the two of you had nothing in common. But perhaps instead of dismissing this person, we should think instead about asking questions that could make the conversation more interesting.

Over the last fifteen years I have hosted hundreds of dinners around the world for global networks and local communities. I have experimented with the introductory questions, hoping to get people to open up, because the most interesting conversations usually occur when people feel that they can be their true selves—both who they truly are and, equally important, who they aspire to be in a context they feel safe in.

One successful conversation gambit is to ask people to introduce themselves not with their job title but with their current state of mind, or what makes them come alive, or what their current challenges are. As people answer—"I am currently trying to transform myself toward . . ." —it often turns out that quite a few people in the room have gone through similar challenges or are trying to achieve similar goals. And so the various experiences emerge, interact, and throw up fresh ideas, fresh solutions, and sometimes fresh challenges.

Once we talk about our real challenges of life, we realize how much we have in common, even if we come from very different industries or cultures. Then, often you will hear something like, "What, such a coincidence, I've been dealing with something similar, too!" Lost a loved one and not sure how to cope with it? Chances are the other person had a similarly painful experience in their life and might share some of their experiences, which could give you some further insights about how to deal with loss. They might just have found the spiritual practice that will change your life, or a great counselor to talk with. What a coincidence!

We always assume our challenges are unique, but we have much in common even with people whom we think are nothing at all like us. If we set up our conversations to make possible bisociations—opening up our potential for connecting the dots—that is when serendipity can strike. Often, the moments where serendipity can truly change a person's life are when the connections concern something they care about deeply.

The questions we ask are crucial. If when we first meet someone we ask, "What do you do?" then we are asking them to define themselves in a very narrow way. We may be putting them into a box in which they feel trapped. No wonder they're boring to talk to.

Even in the most inspiring of communities, if we ask someone "What do you do?" it will often lead to more monotonous and uninspired answers than if you asked a more open question that would allow someone to define themselves by what they find meaningful.

From Boring to Bonding: How to Have Better Conversations

Stuck for questions? Try asking:

"What's on your mind?"
"What are you inspired by right now? Why?"
"Which book are you reading at the moment? Why?"
"What inspired you most about this presentation?"

Once you advance in the conversation,
try something along the lines of:

"If you were to write a book, what would it be about? Why?"
"What's the last thing you've become obsessed with?"
"What would constitute a 'perfect' day for you?"
"Which person has the greatest influence over your life? Why?"
"What was an experience that contributed to shaping you into who you are today?"
"What ideas or thoughts scare you the most? Why?"
"What does 'success' mean to you?"

The more we shift our questions away from superficial facts to underlying reasons, motivations, and challenges, the greater the likelihood that we will discover an interesting theme or unexpected association. And if you get asked the dreaded "What do you do?" question yourself, why not answer with something unexpected, such as "Do you want the practical or the philosophical answer?" (Needless to say, having a follow-up in mind for both will come in handy.)

Bringing a conversation to life is an essential and obtainable skill if you are to open up the opportunity space for serendipity to occur.

Making the Magic Happen

Just as we don't want to restrict people's answers and conversations, we also don't want to over-define a problem or a need, as we can restrict the range of possible solutions.

Innovation researchers Eric von Hippel and Georg von Krogh have explored this question in detail. They discuss the typical setting in an organization: If you ask your product manager "How can we cut costs?" she will try to come up with measures such as reducing headcount or buying cheaper raw materials. But this may not be the most valuable contribution she can offer. If instead we were to say, "Our profit margin on this product is a bit low. Any thoughts?" then the product manager might come up with a wider range of answers. It might still include buying cheaper raw materials, but she may also suggest quite the opposite—use more expensive and higher-quality raw materials and raise the selling price so the margins are higher. Or she might come up with ideas for substituting the process or product with a more efficient option.

Adding more information to think about the problem and pushing deeper into what the underlying issue really is, rather than settling for the most superficial question, are surprisingly easy ways to generate a wider range of possible solutions. It also opens up the opportunity space for truly serendipitous events.

"Why?" is one of the most open-ended questions we can ask. It has driven scientific discovery for thousands of years, and is the question that children ask most, and that adults often find hard to answer. If we do not ask why, we often end up fixing symptoms and not the underlying problems. Understanding the "why" from different perspectives often leads to new ideas—and serendipitous associations.

Sakichi Toyoda, the founder of Toyoda Automatic Loom Works (his son Kiichiro established the automobile department, which as "Toyota Motors" took off to become one of the world's largest carmakers) and a pivotal figure in Japanese industry in the twentieth century, developed a concept known as the 5 *Whys* approach. The world has developed vastly since Toyoda's insight, and in some aspects it is outdated, but its core principle is still valuable.

When faced with any difficulty, Toyoda specified that one needs to ask "Why?" five times in order to get to the root cause of any issue. Every question probes deeper into the problem, but the root cause, and therefore the solution to the problem, is often revealed only at a late stage.

This can be valuable in all parts of life, from the challenges we face at work to those in our romantic relationships. A troubled couple may be able to trace their difficulties to an obvious event such as infidelity—but when asking why it happened might subsequently trace it to a deeper (root) problem, such as a feeling of loneliness.[22]

Thus, the way we ask questions is crucial to truly understand an underlying issue or problem (and, as we will see later, to create a force field in which serendipity can happen).

What Do You Want?

Traditionally, when we think about tackling problems, we tend to think in a linear way.[23] What we typically do—whether it's a problem at home, at work, in school, or elsewhere—is to define some objectives, along the lines of:

1. Identify and formulate the problem/need.
2. Try to solve this problem by either
   a) focusing on solving that specific problem, or
   b) progressively re-specifying or reformulating the problem as we get more information.[24]

Imagine you repeatedly get headaches. There is the immediate solution (painkillers), but your doctor will also want to examine whether there is a deeper root cause that needs to be addressed. In fields such as medicine, we have a clear, routine process of how to look at potential underlying causes. The real problem is not necessarily the headache itself, but perhaps an infection that underlies it.[25]

Therefore, the doctor might use a similar approach to the 5 Whys outlined by Toyoda—digging deeper into potential root causes. Then, once the true cause is identified and addressed, usually the symptoms, in this case the headaches, tend to be resolved.

A doctor's "search strategy" would be to first cast a wide net of possible issues, perhaps asking about accompanying symptoms, whether you have recently banged your head, or perhaps whether and how much you drink every night. The diagnosis then goes deeper and deeper depending on where the answers lead, stopping at the most likely—albeit not always correct—solution.[26] This is a typical funnel approach, trying to narrow down possibilities to zoom in on a solution. It is the most common way individuals and businesses approach their problems.

A marketing department might identify a gap in the market—a consumer need that is not currently satisfied by an existing product. This creates what's known as a *problem statement*: "What will satisfy this need?" This problem is then transferred to developers, who come up with a product for the company that (presumably) will meet this need. Formulating a clear problem statement can be useful as it allows us to define a clear objective and focus, as well as related measurements and incentives. It also allows tasks to be transferred to other entities, for example, a separate group of problem solvers. And it allows us to enjoy the feeling that a problem has been solved.

Not all issues are quite this simple to resolve, though. American polymath Herbert Simon defined two essential types of problem: "well-structured" and "ill-structured."[27] Well-structured problems—problems that can be clearly demarcated—can be solved by approaches such as algorithms or the procedures discussed above in the medical example.[28] While that's a perfectly effective method for approaching such problems, it is not usually the most effective for tackling ill-structured problems, which often cannot be clearly defined, at least at the beginning. And it can limit serendipity. Recent research has shown that if you narrowly define the problem, you are immediately restricting the field of possible answers and you may not find solutions that are both creative and valuable.[29]

There is another reason that narrowing the question can hinder finding the most effective solution(s). An individual or organization with a problem can rarely provide all the potentially relevant information about the actual underlying need. New information often emerges along the way as a problem is explored.[30] This becomes a particular challenge when the person articulating the problem and the person solving the problem are separated, for instance, by organizational barriers. This can cut problem solvers off from seeing other possible needs or problems, thus hampering the search for better solutions. How often have you seen a company's IT department solve a problem but in doing so placing an annoying restraint on how you can work, or even creating a new and different problem? This is not a matter of poor IT skills; it is about the problem solver being given a narrow problem to solve, and not having access to the bigger picture.

You might give the IT team the following brief: "We need team A to be able to read files of type X." The IT department will surely solve that problem. But perhaps team A needed to edit the files too, and the new solution does not let them. Or, conversely, it was important that team A should not be able to edit the files, and now they can. And so on.

Such confusion could have been avoided by bringing the IT department into the problem-solving process (e.g., by discussing the root cause) rather than giving them a narrow problem to solve. Only then will the IT department be able to devise a truly effective solution.

The same applies to any individual or organization: over-defining a problem will restrict the possible solutions and make a serendipitous outcome less likely. Defining a problem too narrowly usually results from putting a lot of initial effort into trying to work out exactly what the problem is. This can work if the problem is well structured, but in a situation that is fast-changing and uncertain, such as a start-up company, few of the important problems or challenges are this simple.

There is often a lack of full information available, and the situation can be changing rapidly. These kinds of environment rarely throw up well-structured problems whose potential solutions can be easily identified and measured. In fact, a good rule of thumb might be: If the problem isn't immediately and obviously easy to define, then don't force it to be. Forget the rigid approach and think about alternative problem-solving techniques.

One such approach is known as "iterative problem formulation," where a problem is approached repeatedly in different ways in rapid succession. Each approach is then assessed quickly for its efficacy.

Approaches such as this are increasingly coming to the fore, driven by organizations such as the design group IDEO. The method of idea development known as *rapid prototyping* sees the problem solver respond to an initial challenge by quickly developing and delivering an easy-to-modify, inexpensive working model. Users then work with the prototype and gather their own data on how well it works. They then modify their specifications, the new model goes back to the designer/problem solver, and a refined prototype is quickly produced.[31] Then the cycle begins again, as fast as possible.

Refine, try, repeat.

This iterative problem/solution reformulation and trial-and-error learning by both the problem solver and the user are repeated until a successful solution is found. Some may say this does not sound very different from the traditional approach of different departments doing specific jobs: department A asks department B for a solution; department B comes up with something that doesn't work; department A says "Wrong! Do it again!"

But the pace and, crucially, the attitude of those involved creates a different dynamic. In a rapid prototyping mindset, each iteration of the prototype is seen not as a "failure," but as a necessary step in the process. Carrying out this process relatively rapidly creates regular, constant contact between the user and the problem solver. You have a dialogue—or a dialectic, if you prefer—in which users and problem solvers (designers) develop the product together.[32]

But can we perhaps do something more radical, something that frees us from the illusion that everything is under control, that there is a system and a set of rules for solving problems?

In order to answer this question, we need to dive deeper into research on needs, goals, and problem solving in the areas of psychology, neuroscience, library sciences, innovation, and strategic management.

Beyond Problem Solving

If we could know not only all that affects the attainment of our present wishes but also our future wants and desires, there would be little case for liberty. . . . Liberty is essential to leave room for the unforeseeable and unpredictable; we want it because we have learned to expect from it the opportunity of realizing many of our aims.

FRIEDRICH HAYEK, ECONOMIST AND PHILOSOPHER

Recent research has shown that overly structured goals limit serendipity, while aspirational goals make serendipity more likely. In one experiment, participants interacted with a reading device. Some were given a specific task to find out some particular information. Others were given no task at all. The results were clear: While the first group often did find out the specific information they were seeking, the second group were much more exploratory in their interaction and tended to come away with all kinds of interesting information that was not previously sought.[33]

Other experiments have shown that groups with over-specified problems tend to be less open to unexpected moments than those with a broader purview—and that unexpected positive outcomes would happen much more often if we allowed them to, rather than forcing people or issues into particular boxes.[34] A focus on "food shortage" or "food scarcity" can lead development efforts to overfocus on one-sided designs on food, while the focus should actually be more broadly on nutrition.

This applies to other areas as well. In my teaching and thesis supervision I have encountered many wonderful students. Often I can tell after a few minutes of conversation which students are likely to achieve the best grades (but of course not letting myself be prejudiced by this first impression!).

Many students will come and say to me, "I know exactly what I want to do. I have this approach. Can you sign off on this?" But potential high achievers more often say, "I have read up on this subject widely and become inspired, but I'm not really sure yet which specific (theoretical) perspective I should pick. Can we talk about it?"

An "average" student often has a very clear road map and a fixed goal; they know their approach, and they will usually accomplish a very solid piece of work. But the exceptional student tends to allow for a broader search field. They read around their subject, trying to find potential touch points that might trigger their thinking in new (and often unexpected), dialectic ways. Many of the students I've worked with feel that such ambiguity is a weakness, but it is often the wellspring for real imagination and originality.

This ambiguity does not always feel nice, and can be downright uncomfortable, but it also tends to lead to the potential spark that leads to a truly valuable contribution. In fact, research has shown that insight often comes not only from curiosity and connection, but also from contradiction and "creative desperation"—sparked by the discovery of new patterns.[35]

I have also observed this phenomenon in the classroom. In one course, we asked students to work on ideas for businesses. Many times, the brightest students would admit that they had no clear idea yet of where exactly they wanted to go, but felt they wanted to do something to move the needle. That's a great starting point: an open and curious mind, paired with the motivation to find and do something meaningful. Intellectual curiosity and uncertainty can be powerful ways to avoid overconfidence, to question preconceived ideas, and to develop a healthy skepticism. If this is paired with hard work and motivation, often wonderful things emerge, as they did in this course.

It might be time to adjust our approach to how we approach problems and goals—and develop what I call our "opportunity space."

Eureka, Here We Come

Serendipitous encounters—making an unexpected discovery and associating it with something relevant—have the potential to save lives, and they have led to some of the most useful inventions and innovations. They often come out of nothing more than a pertinent observation.

When filmmaker Geneva Peschka moved to New York City from Toronto, she was open to creating a new life. Two years earlier, she had separated from her husband and realized that her life was merely a routine. She decided that she should start to change things by acting out her biggest and scariest dream—moving to New York.

A couple of months before making the move, she asked friends in New

York whether they knew of any available job so that she could start working when she arrived. A friend was going on an extended honeymoon and asked if she wanted to take over the work she was doing, providing after-school support to the autistic eight-year-old daughter of a family friend. Geneva leaped at the opportunity to explore the city, and spent a great deal of her summer getting to know Emma and her family.

Over the years, Geneva grew closer to the family, and saw the communication breakthrough that the girl, Emma, had at age ten. Emma's speech pattern was that of a younger child, and she started to work with the rapid prompting method, which involves pointing to letters to form words on a stencil board.

When Emma voiced that people needed to know what it is like to be autistic, it was an eye-opening moment for Geneva—and something clicked. She connected the dots between Emma's desire to be heard and her own background in filmmaking. Why not make a film that would give Emma a voice and in which she would own her narrative? As a woman of color, Geneva knew too well what it was like to have others tell her story, so she asked Emma if she wanted to codirect the film.

The resulting film—*Unspoken*—was Geneva's first film with and about someone she cared deeply for. Actress Vera Farmiga and her husband, producer Renn Hawkey, joined in as executive producers of the film that pushes the dialogue of inclusion, self-advocacy, and human rights. It has by now been screened at festivals and conferences such as SXSW and the UN's Girl Up Leadership Summit.

Today, five years after their first meeting, Geneva looks back at how everything has fallen together since then. Giving Emma a platform through *Unspoken* to tell her story allowed Geneva to find her own voice as well. "I would have never dreamt that I would find my voice by collaborating with the eight-year-old girl I met in Central Park the day after I moved to New York City," Geneva reflected.

To this day, *Unspoken* is the achievement of which Geneva is most proud in her life. It has created a shift in the dialogue surrounding the importance of self-advocacy and human rights, and has helped to open the hearts and minds of audiences around the world.

Such eureka moments as Geneva experienced usually arise from a feeling of making sense, creating an *Aha!* effect.[36] In cognitive psychology, it has been shown that this eureka moment occurs through a sudden gain in what's called "processing fluency." In other words, the insights of eureka moments are evidence of people filling in gaps in their own thinking, gaps that they were not consciously aware even existed.[37]

Take the rolling suitcase as another example of this.[38] When Bernard D. Sadow came back from a family vacation in the 1970s, he had to drag two heavy suitcases through an airport. While waiting in line at customs, he saw a worker effortlessly roll a heavy machine on a wheeled skid. He connected this observation to the fact that he had to lift, carry, and transport his heavy suitcases. When he went back to work at the luggage company where he was employed, he mounted furniture casters on a heavy travel suitcase. Putting a strap on the front and pulling it, he remarked, "It worked!" The rolling suitcase was born.

Bisociations such as these, linking two previously unconnected or even unknown facts or pieces of knowledge, lay the ground for serendipity to emerge.

Rather than happening because we have formulated a problem and are looking for a solution, serendipity often occurs when we see the problem and the solution at the same time. Once we realize it, we compare this new option to the existing arrangements in our life or in our business. If it is clearly superior, serendipity has turned into opportunity.

Often, we only realize we have a problem once we see a solution to it.[39]

Innovation experts Eric von Hippel and Georg von Krogh suggest to imagine problems or needs as existing on a landscape, like physical locations. They then imagine another landscape that has the possible solutions to each need or problem. We can in a sense lay one on top of the other, or connect a place on the need landscape to a potential equivalent on the solution landscape. A doctor's problem landscape, for example, represents all the symptoms and ailments that a patient might present. The doctor's solution landscape, meanwhile, includes the doctor's personal and professional experiences and information, as well as their respective working environment, available literature, research facilities—everything that could potentially be useful in finding a solution. Problem solving (in the doctor's case helping the patient) is about making the links between a specific point on the problem landscape and a specific point on the solution landscape.

As serendipity often emerges from the observation of a link between two things previously regarded as unconnected, often in hindsight we see a solution to a problem. We might not even have been aware of the problem, though later we might well rationalize our experience by saying that was the problem we were trying to solve all along.

Think again about Bernard D. Sadow and his rolling suitcase. In theory, a solution already existed to the problem of carrying heavy luggage through airports: using a luggage trolley provided by the airport. Because a supposed solution was in place, no one was seeing this as a problem, or at least not one worth putting any effort into solving.

But once you have a rolling suitcase, you realize the old luggage trolley *was* posing a problem—in fact, a whole series of infuriating problems. Are there enough trolleys available? (Rarely.) Are they in the right place at the right time for passengers to use them? (Not always.) Can you maneuver them through a check-in line? (Not easily.) Can you take them on an escalator? (Absolutely not.)

Only once we have a new solution does hindsight allow us to see the old state of affairs was actually a problem.[40]

Many of us perform this process intuitively and subconsciously—but once we try to make sense of it, we often tell the story in a way that makes it sound more linear than it actually was. After the event, we fool ourselves into thinking that we identified a problem and then worked out a solution when this was not at all how it happened.

I suspect that many readers will instinctively dispute this view. How can you come up with a solution unless you know the problem? The simultaneous identification of a problem and its solution is just not how problem solving feels to most of us.

But here it is worth recalling that we typically post-rationalize the way we solve problems. We tend to think that we identified a problem, and then looked for a solution. This is related to the phenomenon that leads many business leaders to recall their success as a series of carefully executed plans rather than a series of coincidental events. It is worth repeating that while this natural tendency is at face value harmless, it can have a corrosive effect, because if we start to believe this is really how problems are solved, then we start to expect ourselves and others to work and solve problems in this narrow manner.

Should the Exception Become the Rule?

We have already seen some of the techniques that work, for instance, reformulating questions and issues in a more open-ended way that gives a direction without superficially narrowing the solution space.*

There is, however, an exciting range of approaches that we can leverage,

---

* In the company context, the challenge a chief executive or a company might typically set for themself is, "To reach our financial goals, we need to produce our product better or more cheaply." But this could easily be reformulated as, "We are willing to produce anything we can sell at a profit with our existing distribution channels. So . . . ?" Then, the company could seek inspiration from looking at what similarly situated firms are producing at a profit (for more on this topic, see von Hippel and von Krogh, 2016). This is actually something I have observed with more and more companies that do not consider themselves "product companies" anymore, but rather now try to assess which of several different problems they might solve—understanding that their competitors of the future are the Amazons and Googles of the world (who have access to the data necessary to understand changing needs), rather than those that they are competing with now. Amazon's move into health care and insurance, among other offerings, exemplifies this shifting landscape. The Philips example in chapter 8 is an illustration of this shift.

all based on an open-ended style of questioning. They can help us break out of the rigid mental models that often define our lives and businesses and limit serendipity.

One example is what is known as the *positive deviance* approach.[41] This approach looks at a population (of people, companies, organizations) and identifies individual cases that deviate from the typical—in a good way.

If an organization's broad aspiration—its North Star—is to help a community in sub-Saharan Africa to improve the health of its families, then the strategy would be to focus on searching for families in the community that stand out as positive deviants—in other words, they're particularly healthy. The underlying assumption is that those individuals will have somehow found a successful way to maintain their good health, and their approach might fit others in the community.

Then you could try to understand what it is that these positive deviants are doing that might be linked to better health. If these life choices—certain food, say, or vigilance about clean water—look viable for others, we have found a best practice model. (In a similar way, researchers using qualitative methods often look for "extreme cases" to spot interesting, unexpected ideas).

The same approach can work very well in a business context. Which employee or teams are the most productive? What are they doing differently from everyone else? Could everyone else in the organization do that, too? The positive deviance approach is a way of identifying first what worked, and then seeing if these positive traits can be used for a problem that often you did not even know you had.

Sandbox ended up focusing on positive deviators—though we did not realize it at the time—when we asked people to apply to our community by telling us what they felt made them stick out.

An applicant would be asked to present a creative submission in whichever way or form they wanted—developing what we call a *wow factor*. Sandbox in effect identified creative misfits whose approach was unique and unexpected. With hindsight we can now see that this was a kind of search for positive deviance. It allowed us to identify creative approaches that could inspire others in this exciting journey that is life.

We had initially asked a headhunting agency to suggest a framework that could help identify the most inspiring people, but we realized that the criteria it suggested—educational pedigrees, corporate experience, etc.— did not match the people we considered to be most inspiring.

Take Fraser Doherty. He started a jam company in his grand-mother's kitchen when he was fourteen. His jam was being stocked in the supermarket chain Tesco's when he was sixteen. This young boy back then had little formal education and no corporate experience. But he made us go "wow."

The wow factor allowed the screening team to get a grasp of what made a person interesting instead of just a top-notch education and good experience. We still screened for some of these traits but the wow factor became the most important element of the process. For example, William Mc-Quillan, now a successful early stage investor, created a pop-up book about his work experience, his world travels, and his time in the jungle, relating it to how these experiences would make him a good Sandboxer.

Today Sandbox is a hotbed of serendipitous ideas and encounters, an environment in which serendipity is fueled by a combination of trust—anchored in common values and the members' commitment to the community—and the diversity of thought and perspectives that comes from bringing together people from different walks of life.[42]

These people are often also *lead users*—people who use new methods or products early. (Hackers are a kind of lead user, too: They often identify a problem before a company even knows it has it, which is why they can become valuable employees, especially of security agencies.)[43]

Sensing Toward Serendipity

Thus, the way we formulate questions, problems, goals, or application processes has a major impact on the creativity, novelty, and effectiveness of our solutions and our capacity to experience serendipity. Especially under conditions where needs and problems are complex and where the facts are evolving or uncertain, it may be best not to start by trying to over-define the problem.

Let us consider one simple day-to-day example on how we can broaden our opportunity space. Waqas Baggia, whom we met earlier, told me about an example from his life. He had a company that was in a tough financial situation. At that time, someone sent him a random request on LinkedIn, asking if he had a job for him. Waqas told him they didn't have the resources to employ someone, but that if that person brought in funding, Waqas might be able to create an opportunity to collaborate. The person asked, "Which type of project are you looking for?" Waqas answered, "Construction." Turns out the person's family's multimillion-dollar business was in construction, and he was able to pull it in for a new project.

Waqas has a problem: He has a company in financial difficulty. The LinkedIn contact has his own problem: He needs a job. At first glance neither has a solution for the other. Taking all this at face value, most people in Waqas's situation might have simply replied, "You need a job. I don't have a job for you, come back another day." However, he did what serendipitors do: He reframed the situation and opened up a possible opportunity space. By creating this opportunity space, he made it possible to create a new, unexpected option. Not taking things at face value, looking for overlaps in what might look like unrelated issues, is what can create a serendipitous outcome. Not taking questions or problems as given but rather as socially constructed opens up this space.

Reframing a problem can be the key to seeing more of the landscape and allowing the unexpected links to appear. This is what it means to maximize what I call our "serendipity field"—the opportunity space that holds all the potential bisociations/(connections of) dots that could happen. The magic of serendipity is when those links are unexpected or previously unimagined—which happens all the time—and come together to create opportunity.

This does not mean there is no place for specifying clear and narrow problems in advance. It has a valuable role, particularly in stable, established organizations and processes. The rigor of such an approach in identifying the problem—typified by Toyoda's 5 Whys—can be very effective. But genuine innovation, step changes in thinking, in designs, in products, and in problem solving often come from more organic, "semi-structured" problem solving.

Thus . . .

In this chapter, we have looked at the thinking processes and problem-solving techniques that can foster serendipity and that can expand our opportunity space. By *reframing* how we look at the world, we start seeing bridges where others see gaps. Not taking problem formulations or questions as given allows us to explore underlying interests rather than positions, and methods such as identifying positive deviants can help us understand and leverage what is possible.

However, the process of serendipity is often a prolonged journey rather than an isolated moment, and we need to have sufficient motivation and inspiration to stay focused to make it happen. In the next chapter, I explore the question of how we can set ourselves up for creating and acting on this opportunity space.

SERENDIPITY WORKOUT: SETTING
YOUR MIND UP FOR SERENDIPITY

1. When meeting a new person at a conference or other event, don't ask, "What do you do?" Ask, "What is your state of mind?" or "Which book are you reading at the moment, and why?" or "What did you find most interesting about . . . ?" These questions get us out of our usual autopilot response and help to open up conversations that might lead to intriguing—and often serendipitous—outcomes.

2. Once you know someone better, ask, "What makes you feel alive?" or "What is one word that encapsulates your aspiration for the coming year, and why?" or "What's something you believe (or believe in) that no one else believes (in)?" Dive deeper into whatever catches your interest from the answers.

3. Instead of asking for data and details, ask about experiences unique to the person you're talking to. Instead of asking something like "Where are you from?" or "When did you visit that country?" ask "What was that like?" or "What made you want to do that?"[44] If we already know someone, we can break out of small talk as a way to build rapport, and ask questions slightly differently. Instead of "What did you do this weekend?" try "What made you laugh this weekend?"

4. If in any situation questions feel too forced, make a statement that could pique the other person's interest, such as, "That was intriguing." It gives them the opportunity to ask you more.

5. When hosting a dinner or convening an event, don't just ask people to introduce themselves by what they do. Depending on the occasion and type of participant, use variations of "What is on your mind?" or "What are you currently most

excited about?" or "What are you currently exploring?" At more intimate dinners, ask questions such as "What was an experience that contributed to shaping you into who you are today?"

6. When someone tells you about something, listen closely and try to read between the lines. When they articulate a problem, don't take it as a given. Go deeper with a couple of "whys" or "how comes" to establish the actual underlying need or root cause.

7. Write down three things you would do if you had no constraints and if you couldn't fail. Write down the reasons why you think you cannot reframe the situation. And then three reasons why/how you can. Then act on them.

8. Find your story to tell. Write down on one page your area of interest and an interesting hook, relating it to your own story. If you are unsure what that could be, ask your friends questions such as, "When you think of me, which traits or themes do you associate most with me?" or "What do you think is the most memorable part of me or my life?" or "If I were to write a book, what should I write about?" Once you think you have an idea of what your story and hook might be, try them out at a couple of random events and reiterate depending on what seems to feel best. When people ask, "What do you do?" talk about it (the short version!).

CHAPTER 4

THE STIMULATED MIND

Acting On It

—

*If you want to build a ship, don't drum up people to collect wood
and don't assign them tasks and work, but rather teach them to
long for the endless immensity of the sea.*

ATTRIBUTED TO ANTOINE DE SAINT-EXUPÉRY

Imagine a jigsaw puzzle with some missing pieces. Initially, you might not have a clear idea of the final picture, so you don't know what the missing pieces look like. A bit of someone's face? A patch of cloud? The corner of a house? But as you assemble the puzzle piece by piece, you get a sense of the complete picture, and a better idea of what's missing. You start to see how the missing pieces fit into the overall image.

Similarly, in your personal life or career, the different pieces you have assembled—your skills, knowledge, and experience—might not fit together intuitively at first, but over time they start to form a bigger picture. Once you have that (perhaps based on a particular passion that connects very different experiences), you can search for the missing elements.

Perhaps you realize that you are missing a skill that could transform your life. Even if you cannot be specific, you may have a broad sense of what is lacking—"I have too little technical experience" or "I need to be a better communicator." Then you can search for the missing pieces with a clearer focus.

In these situations, hindsight and foresight complement each other. We often can make sense of things only in *hindsight*, but our *foresight* allows us to complete the puzzle.[1]

Everyone has their particular approach, perspective, and aspirations that lead them to spot unexpected opportunities. In fact, research suggests that having a certain broader motivation or "sense of direction" can help us to experience serendipity more often and with better outcomes.[2] Motivation of some kind is essential—we have to want to see the trigger, we have to want to connect the dots.

Naturally, everyone is motivated differently. For some, a search for meaning is paramount. For others, principles rule. For still others, caring is key. And it would be foolish to rule out other motivations such as abstract curiosity, a need to belong, a strong sex drive, envy, or greed.[3]

But in contrast to blind luck, serendipity is an active pursuit. An open mind is nothing without the emotional and aspirational setup, the willingness and motivation to steer ourselves in a desirable direction even if the exact destination is unknown. As we recognized in the previous chapter, we must actively want serendipity to happen to us, rather than just thinking idly that one day it might.

But how can we develop an outlook that helps us to truly experience serendipity and become the person we are truly capable of becoming?*

Our Search for Direction

When Evelina Dzimanaviciute arrived in London in the summer of 2004 for an extended holiday, little did she imagine that she would end up staying in the United Kingdom for good. Born in a small village in Lithuania,

---

* Serendipity is not only effective with regard to particular positive outcomes, but it can also be a powerful way to explore different potential versions of "who we could be"—and iterate toward a "better" or "more suitable" version of ourselves that we might not even have been able to imagine.

she was looking forward to exploring London with her then-boyfriend. They had been invited to the UK to stay with a friend and had planned to return home to Vilnius after the holiday, where Evelina had already secured a fully funded place in the city's university.

In a stroke of bad luck, by the time Evelina arrived in the UK, her friend was unemployed and she had to start charging rent, which meant Evelina had to earn money to fund her accommodation. The dream of exploring the country unexpectedly turned into a desperate job hunt, and Evelina eventually found employment as a cleaner in a small hotel. She worked long hours, often humiliated by the other staff for being a foreigner who only spoke very little English. Then, the unimaginable happened:

"I was cleaning the room when I suddenly heard the opening of the door behind me. There was this guy I worked with—a sleazy, overweight man with greasy hair, rotten teeth, and a permanent smell of whisky and tobacco. He placed a 'Do Not Disturb' sign on the door, locked it, and walked toward me, with a wide grin on his face, undoing his belt. I was shocked and frightened, and backed off as he tried to force himself on me. Fortunately, there was another unlocked door to an adjacent room, and I was lucky to make a narrow escape."

Evelina ran out into London's busy Oxford Street with her cleaning gloves on, still wearing her blue maid's dress and a white apron. She ran mindlessly to nowhere, among crowds of people, all dressed and suited, purposefully making their way to wherever they were heading. Suddenly, a voice began to play in her head like a scratched record: "I'm better than this, I'm better than this, I'm better than this."

She decided that there must be more to life. With purposeful optimism and drive, she wandered the streets of London the next day looking for a new job, and she was delighted to see the French sign of a Pret A Manger sandwich shop. Convinced that the fluent French that she had learned at school would be helpful, she found the manager, and started speaking to him confidently in that language. The tall Italian looked down at her with a smile and curiosity on his face, and after listening to her for a while muttered that he did not speak French, that Pret was not a French company, and that they did not need any new employees. He nevertheless found a job for her, although Evelina still can't understand why. After helping her open a bank account and acquire the necessary work permit, he sent her to another Pret shop that he knew was hiring. There, Evelina quickly climbed the career ladder, her hard work and positive attitude making up for her language deficit. Most of the staff spoke Polish, which she had learned as a child watching TV and used for fun to entertain Polish visitors to the famous churches of her hometown. Her holiday forgotten, Evelina remained at Pret and within a few years at the company, progressed to senior management roles, ultimately leading business development projects to expand Pret's operations to new locations, opening new stores, and training new managers and leaders.

More than a decade has passed since then. Evelina lives with her daughter outside of London, and has her own consulting, training, and coaching business, Elite Mind. She feels that she is living a happy and fulfilled life. Today, she uses her confidence and her energy to inspire others and to help remove limiting beliefs that might keep people stuck in ruts.

Evelina's experience in the hotel is truly terrible, so it is inspiring that, like many of the people I interviewed, she used this traumatic event as a starting point to reorient her life, redefining her direction on her own terms, rather than letting herself be defined—and crushed—by an event.

People like Evelina derive a strong sense of direction, drive, and meaning out of crisis. Others have an intuitive sense of where they are going, or strive toward a higher purpose. Those who practice a religion might seek such orientation in scripture. Others might rely on philosophy, or other guiding principles. A company's executives might articulate a "vision" that describes why they do what they do.[4]

But in more ways than one, I have been able to observe firsthand the fact that often we don't know where exactly we want to go. What I have observed with myself as well as with many other people is that we think less about a particular goal or venture, and more about an "opportunity space" that allows us to explore what excites us—and then usually we stumble over opportunities that feel right. Once we think about companies, communities, and universities as *platforms* that can help us determine and enable our own journey of experimentation, we can develop skill sets while at the same time exploring which setting is most meaningful to us. It allows us to place bets.

When I started my PhD, the deal I made with my then supervisor was simple: I would focus on my research and he would let me help to develop an innovation center. That way, I had the opportunity to research but at the same time was able to take on a role—as inaugural deputy director—that was relevant to the outside world and helped me find the area in which I felt most at home.

The LSE, and particularly the Innovation and Co-Creation Lab I helped to develop, turned out to be a wonderful opportunity platform and experimentation space for me. It helped me facilitate projects such as a Corporate Social Responsibility (CSR) society, the Sandbox Network, and Leaders on Purpose, based on the people I met and the opportunities that emerged serendipitously from these encounters. They naturally happened over the years, and I somehow felt certain that something positive would happen, even though I did not know what exactly it would be. How could I be so sure?

Insights from the natural sciences can help us answer this question. In particular, the famous theory in biology of "adjacent possibilities," which refers to the idea that every interaction in an ecosystem increases the potentiality of what can happen next. Jonathan Kalan, cofounder of Unsettled, a platform that gives people the opportunity to spend time with others in different locations around the world, lives life according to this notion. It helps him understand that even if something is not possible at this point, it will be as soon as some other intermediate possibilities happen. Like a piece of coal turning into a diamond over time, with every interaction a new infinite universe of possibilities opens up, ready to be discovered. And we can choose to be open to those new opportunities—turning the fear of the unknown into the joy of seeing what's possible.

This can make us feel vulnerable, and depends on how much uncertainty we are comfortable with, but it makes clear that it is impossible to map out everything in advance. If you run into the Dalai Lama tomorrow and he asks you to become his senior adviser, that might not have been on your radar, but it would open up a wealth of new possibilities. Every new interaction with a person or an idea broadens our opportunity space into areas we might not have been able to imagine.

In the social sciences, the notion of "unexpected utility" captures a similar idea with regard to the people we know already. Adam Grant articulated succinctly that you cannot know when you meet someone today where that person will land tomorrow. So if you make every decision by asking "What will I get in return?" you will miss out on this potentiality (and thus future serendipity).[5]

Focus is important—but so is being able to "place bets," to allow opportunities to emerge based on new interactions, insights, and revelations. This allowed me to sense the direction I would take in my life, and to develop the types of networks that could help me guess what could come next. (I did not have that sense of direction when I was younger—and without this I was channeling my energy into questionable pursuits.)

In some cases, this structured experimentation might mean joining a larger company that allows one to grow. The point here is to look at any job and related organization as a "platform" rather than as a particular career. You're working at Goldman Sachs to acquire skills and networks? Well, perhaps you have a cause, such as getting more women into entrepreneurship, that could be related to the company's longer-term goals? If we can creatively frame it, and once we find the first allies in the company (more on this in later chapters), we can move mountains at whichever stage of the hierarchy we are. This is how junior employees helped introduce the triple bottom line (integrating environmental and social impact) at a major accounting firm, and a fair-trade marketplace at a major e-commerce company.

Looking at organizations as platforms and placing bets allows us to instinctively navigate our way toward a potential North Star.

This parallels the approach that successful companies use in a world in which it is impossible to predict where life will take us. In an interview, Harald Krüger, repeatedly voted Germany's most popular CEO (then of car manufacturer BMW), told me that for something like sustainability he needs a strong vision to keep on going, but he then works with scenarios. To him, there is no perfect approach, but you have to take small steps forward and test out flexible areas for the future. "It's about curiosity, data, and benchmarking with others. There is not one point—one particular strategic point—but you have to trust to enter new areas," he said.[6]

But how we place bets depends on how comfortable we are with taking risks, and the "garbage can" model often still holds true: Most of what happens in organizations is by chance, and depends on how and when the relatively independent streams of problems, solutions, participants, and choice opportunities collide. Chance often determines which solutions get attached to which problems.[7]

But there's a shift happening. Traditionally, as Johan Torgeby, CEO of one of Sweden's largest banks, SEB, explained to me, people like him were thinking mostly in financial measures such as internal rate of return. But he increasingly shifts toward a "tech investor" mindset of placing bets in a world that is based less on Excel sheets and more on belief.[8] In a world where we often cannot predict what will happen, we need to "let a hundred flowers bloom and then spot the right one," as Anand Mahindra (CEO of Mahindra & Mahindra) puts it.

We, as individuals, can place our own bets. This can start as trivially as doing a couple of hours' work per week for someone we admire—often, that is where the unexpected opportunities arise.

An adaptation of a famous quote by Mark Twain can be helpful to keep in mind when determining your North Star: "When you look back twenty years from now, what would you regret *not* having done?" And if you don't have a feeling for that yet (which is understandable), what has the biggest pull on you? And then, which "platform" would allow you to develop toward that, or develop broader skills?

Answers to these questions can help shape the aspirations that intrinsically motivate us, aligning potential serendipity triggers with what we care about, and with who we are (or want to be). Then, connecting the dots becomes easy—because we have something to connect them to.

The Whole Self

Our aspiration is often born out of deeper beliefs and values. If we grew up in a collectivistic environment, "family" might be more important than "personal" ambition. If we grew up in a career-focused, individualistic environment, we might be more inclined to focus on individual rather than group aspirations.[9] And often it can be driven by deep emotions such as fear, despair, or revenge. Or, crucially, a search for meaning.

Some people have scripture on their bedside table—I have Viktor Frankl's book *Man's Search for Meaning*. Frankl, a lauded psychotherapist, placed the emphasis of his theory and practice on the human need for meaning.

Where others have seen humanity as driven by a will to power or a sexual urge, Frankl saw a will to meaning. He described this in his own life, reflecting on his experience as a Holocaust survivor. He thought that what kept him psychologically alive during that horror was that he tried to find "meaning" wherever possible. He tried to find it in the everyday by, say, talking with a fellow prisoner to give him hope, which in turn gave Frankl meaning. But in addition, he had a bigger aspiration as well: to write a book once he was out of the concentration camp.

Finding meaning in the small things while also having a bigger long-term aspiration helped him to survive (current research substantiates the important role of meaning in regard to health and other benefits).[10]

I have observed this interplay in people across all walks of life and in all life experiences: We thrive when we have both a North Star that gives a broader meaning as well as meaningful day-to-day interactions. We often need both the macro and the micro to thrive.

But there is a problem. We have often looked at life as a progression of stages, and many of us were taught about Maslow's "hierarchy of needs" in school or university—one of the most used (some might say abused) paradigms in history. It subtly informed much of how we go about life and work.

According to this idea, humans first fulfill physiological needs such as shelter, air, food, and water; then safety and security needs; then social needs like friends and family; then esteem needs such as achievement; then, and only then—if we still have time—do we focus on solving the problems we really care about, on fulfillment, on self-actualization, on deeper meaning.

People like Andrew Carnegie, Bill Gates, or John D. Rockefeller first fulfilled the lower material needs and climbed up the ladder, later on in life devoting themselves to philanthropic organizations and giving much of their fortune away.*

Some of our best students first work for a decade in a job they grudg-

---

* Intriguingly, recent research shows that for decades Maslow has been misinterpreted by "pop-psychologists"—he never visualized it as a hierarchy but it was interpreted that way (Bridgman et al., 2019).

ingly accept, to make enough money and contacts and to get the "right skills," to only afterward do what they really care about. This idea is based on the premise, "First do well, then do good."

A very linear approach to life that shows itself in the way many organizations have been set up. But increasingly, the goal is to combine money and meaning. Harald Krüger (of BMW) put it in a nutshell: "Today, only if people feel meaningful, do they remain loyal."

But it is not only employees and customers who feel that way. Expectations are changing, including those of a next generation of wealth holders who aim to invest in organizations that can deliver on both profit and purpose. This will force banks, pension funds, and others who rely on the money of these high-net-worth individuals to adjust their approach and their investments.

And despite what has been in the news in recent years, this deeper longing is not limited to millennials: It now applies across age groups, in an increasingly uncertain world where questions of legacy, contribution, and impact play an ever more important role. As they approach retirement, many senior executives that I work with begin to question what they want their legacy to be—and those who are close to death or have suffered a breakup have the "big questions of life" emerge.

Our choices are frequently shaped by, and in turn shape, our idea of who we are or want to be remembered as. Once we have the license to do so, there is no stopping us. Technological developments such as social media that showcase the lives of others let us see the different potential lives we could live and the different paths we could take; the desire to combine money and meaning is increasingly commonplace and is considered feasible rather than unrealistic.

In some communities our self-worth is attached to material value, and we accept money as a key measure of success—perhaps because it is so easy to measure and to compare. Not only Saint-Exupéry's Little Prince finds this difficult to understand.[11]

What is fascinating is that once people transition into a life that they consider meaningful and less driven by peer pressure, they often bring more authenticity to it. This can lead to more serendipity and even synchronicity—we now attract based on what we really desire rather than what we pretend to want. Danae Ringelmann, cofounder of the leading crowdfunding platform Indiegogo, described her observations of her sister, Mercy, whom she describes as a "serendipity queen."

Mercy brings her whole self to her different endeavors. She is an herbalist, a technology sales leader, a small business owner, and a mother of three. "In the midst of closing a multi-million-dollar deal, she'll be the first to whip out relaxation and immune-system-boosting essential oils to keep her team healthy and calm. She's also bringing her kids to her organic kale chip company while working alongside her kitchen staff packing kale chips," says Danae. She does not hide the parts of herself that might seem inappropriate in different circumstances. Danae reflected that since her sister has increased her conscious efforts to remove those artificial walls, serendipity has only increased. It also keeps her energy intact—hiding parts of yourself is hard and exhausting! To Danae, this lower friction of interpersonal relations when one is authentic is a key to success.

I have observed many of these experiences across private and professional contexts—people increasingly aim to combine what they truly care about with making money. Coaching platforms such as inSynch Global have started to integrate this into their practices, and organizations such as Serenflipity, a platform set up by entrepreneur Cara Thomas, use playful cards to get people to open up their "authentic selves." Sharing the "real us," pulling off the mask, allows for deeper connection, authenticity, and trust. Pretending to be who we are not can make us literally sick, and people who feel that they work on something meaningful (*even if tasks are monotonous*) have been shown to be healthier and more productive.[12]

Given the choice, why on earth would we spend the majority of our life in a way that makes us unhappy and sick? Why have we focused on "taking," while most research will tell us that giving makes us happier?[13]

A fundamental change is happening, and what used to be a pyramid might be more of a *circle of needs*, where we aim to fulfill the needs at the same time rather than one after another.*

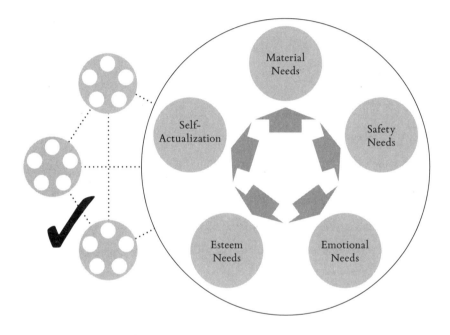

Then, a happy and wealthy life can be about "being a Buddha and driving a Benz with your loved ones" (as husband-and-wife team Krishnaji and Preetha Krishna, founders of the O&O Academy, a meditation school in India, put it)[14]—with a deeper consciousness of ourselves and the world around us that allows for a more meaningful connection with the people we love.

But is this not a sign of privilege, to be able to strive for meaning and a

---

* And our circle of needs increasingly depends on how well we can cater to others' needs—an *enlightened self-interest* becomes key in a networked world that relies on knowledge and information sharing. I am indebted to my excellent former colleague Brad Fitchew for helping develop this line of thinking and the related visuals.

higher purpose? Surely, this does not apply for people in poverty, where life is often about the basics of food and nutrition, education, and housing?

For decades, this belief has driven failed development efforts in the West and around the world. It disempowers local communities, because it assumes that people will be all right as long as they fulfill their "lower needs." It underestimates the strong desire for meaning, for the presumably "higher needs" that are often essential in giving people the hope they need to survive the toughest of circumstances. (Many discussions about guaranteed incomes similarly miss the mark—money is only one among several factors.)

Our work has shown that *especially* in resource-constrained contexts the importance of being an agent of one's own luck, of being able to solve one's own relevant problems, the problems one cares about, becomes paramount. It permits a more dignified and joyful life, but is also a way to moderate mental health issues. Remember RLabs' story: Only once their members reframed their role from passive victim of circumstance and receiver of basic help to active creator of their own did their lives improve considerably and serendipity happened en masse. It was not about receiving handouts, but about creating hope and tangible "meaning-making."[15] (Naturally, a lack of financial and other resources can let other things shift into the background, and research has shown that these pressures can lead to bad decisions as they can sap attention.)[16]

This is true in a variety of settings. Ajay Banga, CEO of MasterCard, told our Leaders on Purpose research team how the anchoring of purpose at MasterCard helped the company move mountains. He put out the goal of helping five hundred million consumers and forty million small merchants get into the financial system. He had no precise idea of how he'd get to five hundred million people—but it showed him what is possible once you put a target out there and you let creative people have at it. To date, they have reached more than four hundred million individuals. "It's not to get more cards into the market, but to move to a world beyond cash, and that's now embedded in everything we say and do." The underlying notion is that today's leaders need to navigate an ever-changing environment and inspire their teams to take responsible action driven by both mind and heart. Ajay and his team now cultivate serendipity because people know what they are working toward and are motivated by it.

That applies more broadly as well: In a study of thirty-one of the world's best-performing CEOs, my colleagues and I found that the best-performing individuals and their companies often try to operate on a duality of purpose, which often leads to serendipity.[17] In such a scenario, a North Star is combined with the day-to-day practices that instill meaning. In the workplace, instead of pursuing a passion project after work, employees are likely to transfer their energy into the everyday.

The truth is, often there are trade-offs. Following a deeper purpose (such as helping to solve a global challenge such as malnutrition) might feel like an unwelcome distraction from a company's goal of being profitable. But companies such as Natura show that holding dual objectives can in itself be a route to innovation and serendipity. Bringing together previously separate factors encourages new serendipitous connections—and motivates people to come up with more effective solutions. As a Natura senior executive shared with me, Natura's founder was a philosopher at heart who wanted to willfully create tension between potentially opposing forces. That's what often leads to real creativity and innovation—and it is how much of human progress has emerged.

Formulating and implementing a sense of direction remains important. But often, the notion of purpose can be misleading. Take Layla Yarjani, whom we met earlier. Layla, cofounder at Little Bridge, a children's learning and media company, is led by a deep sense of curiosity and of contribution, out of which passion can emerge. To her, it would be a waste of time to try to define the purpose of her life. Instead, she focuses on constantly questioning her assumptions about where she feels she is and where she wants to be headed, which helps her develop a sense of how potential dots could be connected.

This often requires rational optimism. Viktor Frankl's experience of taking flying lessons deeply resonated with me: The flight instructor told him that he will always need to aim slightly higher than he would actually want to fly, because the wind will usually pull him down. In Frankl's understanding of the lesson, this translates to the idea that if you start as a realist, you end up depressed. But if you start as an optimist, you end up as an actual realist.

And, as we saw in chapter 2, studies have shown that optimistic people tend to have more luck than others—it is almost a self-fulfilling prophecy that manifests itself.[18]

Doing the Right Thing

In 2017, when Hurricane Maria destroyed large parts of Puerto Rico where Best Buy—the world's leading provider of consumer technology products—has three stores, the management team there had to make some quick decisions. They organized private planes, food, water, and offered to evacuate employees and their families who wanted to leave. They continued to pay their workers, even though the stores were closed. The only provision was that the employees had to contribute to the recovery of the island once Maria had passed.

Best Buy's executive chairman and former CEO, Hubert Joly, told me that the company did "what we felt was the right thing to do." They shared their thinking with their investors, and that it had cost the company some money but "on those occasions, the way you deal with the unexpected defines the values and the culture of the company." The way the company took care of its employees sent a strong signal to them: We take care of you. We are in this together.

What happened as a result? Joly observed that Best Buy's performance on Puerto Rico is now around 20 percent higher, that "the employees are supercharged," and that their customers know what happened and credit Best Buy for its human and humane approach. Best Buy didn't take care of its employees to increase revenues, but by doing so this is what happened. It is an example of where doing good and doing well go hand in hand.

Similarly, Kaan Terzioğlu, CEO of Turkish telecom company Turkcell from 2015 to 2019, told me how company executives prepare for the unexpected based on a clear understanding of their capabilities and their role in society. In an emerging market setting, the unexpected happens all the time. Then, based on what Kaan believes in, he directly connects the dots. For instance, when there was serious violence in 2016 following an attempted coup d'état in Turkey, Kaan and his team made the internet free for a month, so that people were able to communicate with those whom they cared about, without worrying about bills. They reacted similarly to other unexpected events, sending drones to enable phone networks to work following an earthquake, for example. Kaan told me that they did this because it was the right thing to do based on their values, and that it also had the positive outcome of employees being proud to work for Turkcell—and of its customers being grateful.

Dealing with the unexpected and seizing those crisis moments becomes a powerful moment of truth that can positively define organizations and individuals.

As random as these choices sometimes feel, they are frequently shaped by, and in turn they shape, our idea of who we are, or who we want others to think we are. Unexpected encounters rarely give us much time to reflect, so we must decide based on what "feels right."* This is where real values, beliefs, and intuitive behaviors come into play. Getting to know ourselves better and understanding our principles can open us up to serendipity, as it gives us a guiding frame for reacting to the unexpected, and for seeing it

---

* Though we might then post-rationalize our decisions to convince ourselves otherwise. I have witnessed on a flabbergasting number of occasions how senior executives or politicians make decisions based on a hunch and then ask their assistants to find a justification for what they just decided.

as an opportunity rather than as a threat. (This does not discount the value of more "analytical" decision metrics or preexisting decision rules that could guide a decision—it is not always about either analytical thinking or intuitive action, rather an interplay between the two. The more instable, unknowable, fast-changing, and complex a situation is, and the more experience a person has, the more intuition tends to come to the fore.)[19]

We do not know what awaits us in life, so it is hard to plan for all eventualities—especially those that involve trade-offs. What we can do is shape the values and behaviors that we hold most dear. I still vividly remember an unexpected trade-off that I faced in one of the organizations I cofounded. Torn between different ideas of the future, different loyalties, and different assumptions of risk, I made a decision mostly from my head—and against my gut.

When reflecting on it later, I realized it was partly driven by fear: fear of failure, fear of loss, fear of conflict, and the advice of mentors to rationalize the situation. But what really happened was that we had neglected to take the emotional temperature of the team, and tried to avoid conflict at every corner. Instead of calming the conflict it just aggravated it, as everyone at some point felt they were not being heard.

I was not happy about some of my decisions at that time, but it did help shape my consciousness of what I value most—and made me resolve to decide differently next time. During important decisions nowadays I listen to my gut, and try to make decisions based on hope or vision rather than avoiding fear—and also to avoid a top deathbed regret: "I wish I had been true to myself when I had the choice."[20]

We can practice self-awareness early on. If you are a parent, the approach that Adam Grant takes with his kids might be interesting. Rather than just making rules like, "Be in bed by 9 p.m.," he tells them about the values that they represent. For example, "We value being well-rested." The kids then see that the rules are not arbitrary. Next, he gives them responsibilities, such as by telling the nine-year-old that lights should be out at

8:30 p.m., but that it's her responsibility to turn them off. He gives her two options: "Do you want to be responsible for it, or make me do it? If you don't do it, you lose the privilege."[21] Thus, he gives her a choice.

It is often easy to pay lip service to our principles or values, but do we really live them? Do they really guide our behavior? An increasing number of companies are attempting to make this transfer happen. At L'Oréal, a chief ethics officer (another kind of CEO!)—Emmanuel Lulin—helps integrate values such as integrity, respect, courage, and transparency by traveling to every corporate location around the world. People who join the organization are being trained in both those values and the ethical code, and they are increasingly manifested across the organization via face-to-face and web-based conversations.

At Omnicom's Ketchum company, CEO Barri Rafferty role-models values into behavior. What she calls "work-life integration" was a core principle of hers, but being aware that offering parental leave policies is not enough to actually have them picked up by employees, she changed the language to "family bonding policy." And she started what she called "leaving loudly" to show that it's OK to value your personal life. When her daughter has a volleyball game, she makes it known in the office that she's going to it. And when she started as CEO, she publicly announced in her welcome email that one of her leading principles is to not ditch family—and that she had a planned vacation coming up that she was intending to take. This gave license to others in the company to articulate when they needed to be home—in turn making them more present when they're at work.[22]

When facing tough choices, it pays to know when to say no—which applies particularly in moments of serendipity, as every unexpected opportunity can also lead us in the wrong direction. Take the serendipitous discovery of financial information that could tempt us into insider trading (where Warren Buffett is right when he says that it takes twenty years to build your reputation, and only five minutes to destroy it).

Our values and principles tend to emerge over time. We can take inspiration from Eastern philosophy—in particular, the realization that there is not "one authentic self" as we like to believe in the West, but rather, we are habitually in flow and adapt to different contexts. Learning to trust our gut feeling can help us navigate difficult decisions—as long as we have enough information so that we have an *informed gut feeling*. (I learned firsthand that our subconscious mind often has more information than our conscious one, and that it's actually quite rational to listen to it if it combines intuition with information. The more a conversation advances and the more information I collect, the more I realize how I feel about something. Rather than always having a rigid position at the beginning, I often try to sense my way to the right decision.)

This introspective approach also works with companies. Heiligenfeld, which runs a number of mental health hospitals in Germany, used largegroup reflections. Once a week, around three hundred people came together for an hour to reflect on a topic or value. It started with a brief "framing," then a presentation, then people broke into small groups for discussions, then the groups reported back to the larger plenum. This helped to manifest values across the organization and engaged employees, in the process reminding them why what they are doing is important, why it matters. This can also manifest in the very buildings we operate in. Michigan engineering group Cascade Engineering defined itself as a company "solving problems without creating new ones," and demonstrated this in one way by putting their offices in buildings that met the LEED standards (Leadership in Energy and Environmental Design), thereby showing that they care about their employees and the environment.[23]

Given that serendipity happens when we are open, the more our activities resonate with who we (think we) are or could be and what we care about, the more we can foster serendipitous moments. But while caring is a powerful motivation, serendipity can happen without us caring about related issues or even without any meaning or purpose at all. That is where kindness, generosity, and an enlightened self-interest come into play.

Love Thy Neighbor—A Serendipitous Maxim

Serendipity requires us to see and connect the dots. People such as my Sandbox cofounder Fabian Pfortmüller, who is also founder of the Together Institute, or Nachson Mimran, founder of To.org, a platform connecting creatives with potential investors and worthy causes, do this intuitively: When speaking with someone about a problem or a challenge, they try to think how they can help, whether through introductions or via ideas. They don't expect anything in return, but similarly to Viktor Frankl, they know that in the long run it makes them feel happy, and is often reciprocated at some point.

Indeed, the more we help, the more others have a tendency to help us, even if we don't expect them to.[24] (As an additional perk, research has shown that kindness and gratitude can also improve our sleep quality, happiness, and alertness.)

Adam Grant writes that "givers"—people who think about "what can I do for you" and who are intrinsically motivated to add value to others— are often more successful than "takers." This is especially true in fields where services are the ultimate product.[25] However, to be a giver while also succeeding requires good time management, clearly defining the boundaries of generosity, and thinking proactively about where they can add the most value to others and themselves by giving.

Without these limits and qualities, givers can become passive victims of their generosity, burning out by always responding to requests. Being an intuitive giver myself, I have experienced the importance of learning to draw boundaries—otherwise burnout is right outside the front door.

This also shows in the way we negotiate. When it came to equity negotiations in one of my companies, I sometimes was more interested in making everyone happy than in securing a big piece of the pie—sometimes losing myself in the process. I learned the hard way that in the long run this does not make anyone happy (least of all myself), as resentment or a feeling of injustice might creep in. Getting it out of the way early would probably have avoided it.

Of course, there are the values of self-care and fostering our own well-being as preconditions for mental health. We can be more helpful to others when we ourselves are in a good place. In this regard, inspired by Adam Grant and others, I have found it helpful to stop thinking about how I can keep everyone happy and rather think about how I can contribute to someone's happiness right now. This makes it much less stressful!

"Takers" might at times get the job and they might pretend to be more giving than they are—for example, via "cheap signaling," where they take on a highly visible role without having to do much work, just to be seen as charitable. But, in Grant's words, they tend to be "losers in life."

A third form are "matchers." They are relationship accountants, constantly making sure that they are even in every relationship they're in. The logic partly parallels game theory: When you are among takers, you do not want to be too much of a giver, else you might lose out. They want to be neither too selfish, nor too giving, and thus are matching. This works in the short term, but people often see through it.

Fascinating studies have shown that when people are told to focus more on being happy, in many countries they do get happier. But in some countries, the opposite happens. Why? Because in many societies, happiness is associated with doing something *for others*, which indeed makes us happier. In others, happiness is associated with "spending money on ourselves." That might give us short-term satisfaction or relaxation, but it does not really make us happy. In the mid-term, an *other-focus*, rather than a *self-focus*, makes us happier (but naturally self-care is paramount and we need good emotional health in order to be able to cater to others).[26] It also helps nurture serendipity: People have more incentive to help us connect the dots if there is goodwill.

How can we foster this kindness for ourselves and with others? One way is to focus on gratefulness, especially in difficult situations. When Cara Thomas's flight was delayed on New Year's Eve, she was annoyed. To offset her irritation she tried to find a number of "thank yous," including that she had had an interesting conversation with an Uber driver, and that she arrived at her destination just in time for dinner. This helped her get out of all the negative thoughts that clouded the bigger picture. The moment of gratitude helped her shift back to being in a state in which serendipity is possible, and where the Uber driver introduced her to a videographer that she needed.

But how does this play out in organizations? French engineering group FAVI starts meetings with a brief story of someone they wanted to thank or congratulate. It put people into a mindset of gratitude and enhanced willingness to collaborate.[27] (In chapter 8, I will talk about how to go about this in more competitive organizations.)

However, beware the blenders: Many people pretend to be altruistic to conceal self-interest, and some do-gooders have a hidden agenda. Take the story of a most-wanted man who escapes from Australia to build a new life in India. He helps construct a school, but he does it with money from the mafia, and perhaps mostly to impress the woman he loves. Does the positive outcome justify the means and the intent?

Sometimes it makes for a better story to say you have sacrificed yourself and that you want to make the world a better place. But you might have acted only out of guilt or obligation, or simply to seem relevant. This is common, particularly in the social sector: Some people claim they want to "help a million people," but really, they want to be *seen* as "the one who helped a million people." It is ego rather than altruism. Being true to our intentions—and being aware of enlightened self-interest where it does exist—can go a long way in building trust if communicated the right way.

In short, it is in our enlightened self-interest to not be too self-interested. This is both to feel better about ourselves, and to make others more willing to help us connect the dots and find serendipity.

But none of this will help much unless we are receptive to serendipity.

Are You Ready for Serendipity?

Fascinating research has shown that the willingness and motivation to engage in activities that nurture serendipity can be driven by adaptable (and trainable) traits such as proactivity, humor, openness to experience, and willingness to pursue untested ideas.[28]

In particular, proactive behaviors such as taking initiative and practicing forethought can help put us into situations where serendipity can happen, and overcome barriers. They can be linked to getting better jobs and incomes, to growth and success for budding entrepreneurs, and to escaping poverty.[29]

Creativity is particularly important in this regard, because it resembles many of the characteristics behind the emergence of serendipity: It is often dependent on our ability to attend to the unexpected, as well as to make unusual associations between ideas. People who are creative and original are often risk-averse—they are scared of failure. But they often overcome this through an even greater fear—the fear of not having tried.[30] Picture the writer or composer agonizing over their latest work and tormented that it is not good enough, but they can't stop trying.

There is a similar ambiguity when it comes to personality traits. Our dispositions are deeply rooted in brain science and evolution. When mammals emerged, they developed a neocortex. The neocortex allows us humans to think before we act, and to predict behavior. However, to work properly, it needs to be at an appropriate "level of arousal"—the brain engine needs to be revving adequately before it can be put in gear.[31]

While more extroverted[32] people reach their "optimum level of arousal" by interacting with others, more introverted people often have a high base level of mental arousal. For them, social activity drains mental energy and they need quiet or solitude to recharge. Susan Cain, in her brilliant book *Quiet*, tells the story of a Canadian professor who lectured at Harvard and was thought by his students to be highly extroverted. However, after lectures he would hide in the bathroom so he didn't have to talk to anyone.[33] When I once met this professor at an event (he serendipitously unveiled that he was the one!), I realized that this passionate introvert had many of the traits that I had observed in myself.

I have built communities for most of my life, so people assume I am very extroverted. However, many other community builders and I are often what I think of as "closet introverts." We have peaks of extraversion, particularly at events that we host, when we super-connect, and bring people together in settings that we can control. We have lots of serendipity happen to us and we cultivate it for others. And yet we often sneak out as soon as we can. For us, receptivity to new ideas can be very different depending on when you catch us.

If you meet me on my "introvert Sunday," I'm emotionally closed down; I have no motivation to connect any dots. Connecting the dots, while fun, can also take a lot of energy. I will need to sneak out of an event at some point to recharge. I sometimes have these moments when I'm in a more extrovert mode. What I do then is to hide somewhere—be it the bathroom, the patio outside, anywhere quiet and empty—to regain my strength, which allows me to stay longer than I would usually feel comfortable to.

University of Cambridge professor Brian Little calls the space in which we recharge our level of energy a "restorative niche." Often we do not give people enough space to restore themselves, process ideas and connections, and recover their optimum level of cerebral arousal. But without that, people become drained and serendipity is constrained.

Naturally, some extrovert traits are particularly valuable for serendipity—but both introverts and extroverts can train in those. Lots of community builders around me are passionate introverts—but we have learned how to survive in a world of extroverts.

Studies have shown that extroversion can increase lucky chance encounters in three ways: by meeting large numbers of people, by attracting people, and by keeping in touch with people.[34] This starts with simple steps such as chatting with someone in a supermarket or in the coffee shop queue. This can lead to intriguing conversations (and never to the excruciating "I should have talked to that person when I had the chance" feeling). So long as it is not intrusive, such behavior increases the probability of encountering someone (or something) that could have a positive effect.

Meet Christa Gyori. I still remember lining up for coffee at the TED Global conference in Edinburgh a few years ago, when Christa, then an executive at Unilever, started talking to me. We got along very well. Two years later I received an email in which she told me about her move to London and asked if we might meet for coffee to discuss the London scene. One thing led to another, and our conversation in a coffee shop at Holborn led to me joining Christa on her journey to set up Leaders on Purpose, now a global organization. Christa embodies the trait of sowing seeds of serendipity wherever she goes—and she takes people with her on the journey.

On a busy Monday in May, Tatjana Kazakova got a call from an unknown number. Working in strategy consulting, where days are long and time is scarce and high-priced, she would not usually take calls during the day except from family or a client. But something told her she should pick up. The caller said he had a team and "a super-exciting project," which he thought she would want to join as a side project. It struck her in the moment that "everything that I had done and pursued based on my gut feeling and interests made sense now, and I just needed to grab this opportunity." Without hesitation, she said yes.

When I put down the phone, I was excited. Tatjana joined our team, initially just to produce a report and related event on purpose-driven leadership, but within months, Christa's magnetism—and hard work and dedication—had pulled Tatjana in to join full time. She went all in—quit her job and sold her car—to become cofounder and chief of strategy of Leaders on Purpose Ltd.

Tatjana later reflected that she "couldn't grasp yet the sheer complexity of consequences this call and me saying 'yes' would entail." Tatjana and Christa turned what was a project into a full-fledged organization. And the company she had previously worked for, Horváth & Partners, became one of Leaders on Purpose's strongest partners.

Recent research by Richard Wiseman shows that lucky extroverted people like Christa tend to attract others and their ideas for a number of reasons, but it often comes down to the basics: These are people who make eye contact, smile often, and use gestures that are open and inviting.[35] Wiseman found that lucky people smiled twice as often as unlucky ones, used open body language, and fully faced the other person, which made others trust them and feel more "attracted" to them.*

Finally, and crucially, extroverted people are often easier to get to know and they tend to keep in touch with larger numbers of people. The idea here is simple: If we keep in touch with an adequate number of people, they themselves will keep in touch with other people. So if you are in touch with one hundred people and they are in touch with another hundred people, you are essentially in second-degree touch with ten thousand people (this assumes the hundred people don't know each other; if some of them do know each other it's a bit less than that, but the principle stays the same). This is one introduction or dinner party away from at least ten thousand possible chance encounters. And often one chance encounter is more than enough to change your life.

Having said all this, there is a major role in serendipity for introverted behavior, and there are good reasons to think that serendipity thrives from a combination of extroversion and introversion—within a group or even within the same person. As well as the spark of the unexpected that may

---

* Interestingly, this also applies to how we remember things. Psychologist James Douglas Laird and colleagues tested sixty students' mood responses to manipulated expressions. They were asked to read two passages of the same emotional content, either humorous or anger-provoking selections. One group was asked to put a pen between their lips (so to force a smile), others to frown. The ones that frowned remembered more about the sad content, and the ones that smiled remembered more about the happy content.

be derived from outgoing behavior, serendipity often requires inward focus, self-awareness, and time. Not all of our thoughts and ideas are necessarily sitting on the surface of our minds. Indeed, the most unexpectedly valuable bisociations may come from areas that are not obvious. Ideas may need time to percolate and turn over in a person's mind for their potential to be recognized. Or they might be hidden in calm spaces such as books, movies, or somewhere else. People who are more extroverted often benefit from being complemented by more introverted people, who help them reflect and connect their thoughts and experiences. In extrovert Nachson Mimran's case his thoughtful brother Arieh forms a "reflective base," reflecting on potential opportunities with him.

While all traits are malleable, don't worry if you're not too much of an extrovert; we can pick up the traits that are most aligned with our personality. But what is important to consider here is that our propensity for serendipity often depends on where we are emotionally. Positive emotions help with opportunity recognition, because they increase alertness to outside stimuli and give us the energy to explore them. They also boost responsiveness to events by broadening our scope of attention and action repertoire.[36] In fact, our emotional state is crucial, given that our decisions (such as acting on a coincidence) are often driven by our and other people's gut instincts. And have you ever noticed what a difference it makes to sit next to someone with "good energy" when you need to get work done or be inspired—or how much harder that becomes when you're sitting next to someone who yawns all the time? Energy travels.

Good Energy and Social Alchemy

People like Christa are "serendipity alchemists"—they create good energy wherever they go, a force field for themselves and for others to exchange positive energy and ideas. That's where physics and spirituality meet.

We know from quantum physics that energy comes in waves.[37] Once we see electrons as waves rather than particles located at one particular place, their impact is spread over a much broader space. This is true as well for how we look at the world: If we see ourselves as particles, we focus on particular elements such as life experiences, memories, bodies. But we can also become waves.[38] Radiating good energy then is more than just a positive feeling—it becomes a way to expand ours and others' serendipity fields.

In the end, energy is at the core of our existence. Take the second law of thermodynamics, which is all about entropy—the tendency for things to become obsolete or fall apart over time. Unless we keep a forward focus on progress, organizations, individuals, and even whole systems can fall into decline.[39] An example would be a business that seemed to be thriving but over time manifested a status quo with routines that quelled creativity and eventually went bust.

All this becomes even more interesting at the intersection of science and metaphysics. We have to take this with a grain of salt, but quantum physics might be able to give us a possible explanation of why focusing our energy on particular outcomes can accelerate serendipity: The interaction of an individual with a system might change the behavior of an electron. Experiments have shown that particles respond differently when the observer focuses on a particular path that they can take. Only a very small quantity of energetic occurrences are useful, and energy often moves in disorganized states—so if there is a certain sense of direction, this forward edge can help organize what could be.[40]

This sounds like magic. But perhaps you can think of examples in your life in which your focus on a desired possibility might have drawn it to you? Or perhaps you had a situation where the whole universe seemed to go your way? It's often self-reinforcing energy. People respond to positive energy. Like activation energy in physics that is needed to get a reaction started, we sometimes need igniting energy—or igniters such as Christa Gyori or Nachson Mimran—to help us spark something. This relates to the more abstract—and often debated—"law of attraction" that states that we are made from energy, and attracting like-energy might help us improve wealth, relationships, health, and joy.[41]

Things such as synchronicity—these meaningful coincidences in time—tend to happen when we put energy into the universe.* Fascinating studies have shown that people often tend to have similar emotional experiences as the people close to them. It's not only the menstrual cycles of roommates that might align—twins often have the feeling that they can communicate without language. In this case, we might share a consciousness with those we deeply care about, a real quantum entanglement.[42] French life sciences consultant and artist Sophie Peltre feels the same connection to her sister. Whenever Sophie is deeply sad, she feels that something is troubling her sister. And when she calls her, she learns that indeed her sister was feeling unhappy.

We do need to be careful not to justify implausible events using quantum mysticism. But many of the world's spiritual approaches, including most major religions, are anchored in the belief that everything is connected, that good things cause good things. Science and spirituality are increasingly saying the same thing.

Krishnaji and Preetha Krishna are founders of the O&O Academy in India, which has inspired millions of people. They see the power of consciousness at the core of their success.[43] To them, there is doing (achieving success, making important contacts, etc.) and being (how we experience life). Meaningful coincidences, they argue, happen once we are in a "beautiful state" and the universe starts arranging itself into patterns to fulfill our intentions, and solutions arise out of nothing.

Based on some estimates, we have between twelve thousand and sixty thousand thoughts per day, most of them repetitive and up to 80 percent of them negative.[44] Krishnaji and Preetha (also known as Preethaji) have

---

* Serendipity in its focus on an active process is different from synchronicity (see Jung, 2010) as a singular meaningful encounter.

experimented with steps that help us move from this "suffering state" into the "beautiful state." At the core of their system is to live with a spiritual vision—which is essentially about setting an intention. This focuses on discovering our inner truth—a nonjudgmental observation of what is happening inside ourselves.[45] We might sense a suffering state—perhaps some unresolved anger, anxiety, or sorrow—or a beautiful state of joy. Suffering states tend to perpetuate themselves into self-obsession.

Simply recognizing this state without trying to change the emotions can help to awaken us to what they call "universal intelligence"—they argue that it is not only our brain that leads us, but also our heart, our gut, and even our spine, and that all these elements possess intelligence. (According to some, old memories are often stored at different points in our bodies, such as in the spinal cord. We can access them, and can even change those that are stored in our cells.)

Practices such as yoga, meditation, and visualization can open our awareness and help us learn to let go. We then start solving problems not by trying to control the flow of life when we are in the moment (for example, in a negative emotional state), but by pausing and slowing down, and making decisions once we feel better. Instead of focusing on lofty ideals, we learn to take the unique circumstances of a situation into account, being present rather than self-righteous or entitled.

Krishnaji explains how he set himself the vision to create an ecosystem that would support the transformation of each individual who walked into their academy, helping them experience what he experienced. He recalls that less than a month after forming that intention, resources and people "began to flow" and "magical coincidences started to pop up." Despite major barriers and obstacles—including a lack of planning permissions—he found the land he needed and an architect who understood his vision, and the pieces fell into place. Today, around sixteen years later, thousands walk into the center every day. (It no doubt helps that Sri Bhagavan, a spiritual teacher with over fourteen million followers, is part of the family and founder of a related organization, but the application of serendipity in the center's journey remains no less relevant.)

Spiritual visions are different from goals: Goals such as strategic plans are future-oriented. A spiritual vision is not about a concrete destination, it is about the state you choose to live in as you go about reaching your goals. In a way, it is the mother of all visions. Holding a focused spiritual vision and manifesting it every day can also help us to loosen the grip of the past, of the wounded child that many of us have inside.

As an example, Krishnaji uses a YouTube clip of a small boy who tells his mother he loves her but he does not always like her—he only likes her when she gives him his cookies. We probably all have been this child. In this state, it is not about what we think society believes is right or wrong—we do not judge ourselves based on these feelings, we are simply joyful.[46] Feelings then are not right or wrong—they just are. This is a much more relaxed state to be in.

In his book *The Seven Spiritual Laws of Success*, Deepak Chopra, a man both loved by his followers and loathed by many scientists who see in him an embodiment of pseudoscience, points to the importance of karma—actions generate forces of energy that tend to return to us in kind.[47]

The scientific foundations of these ideas are scarce, and there has been a fierce discussion about how far scientific concepts might have been misunderstood or misused given that there are only anecdotal and self-selected reports.[48] But we can take inspiration from those that seem to align with patterns that we can observe in other areas as well, such as the positive role of energy flows and affirmation.

Importantly, however, like structural constraints that might keep us from navigating serendipity, we must never blame the opposite outcome—say, a debilitating illness—as having been "attracted" by the individual on its receiving end. Life is too complex, and we are all fragile.

Throughout my life I have been constantly reminded that, while I create and attract a lot of serendipity, things can quickly turn dark. Like me, my brother was almost killed in a car accident. My mother nearly died of an enterocele when I was a child. And my dad could have died of a heart attack if it wasn't for the fantastic ambulance services that rushed him to the hospital. This fragility of life is what makes us grateful for every day that we have together.

Sure, we were lucky in these situations, but our luck did run out when my young cousin drowned in the sea (even though he was a fantastic swimmer), or when a former classmate killed himself due to mental illness.

We all have periods of sadness, of despair. But serendipity can lift our life to a level that is more joyful, fulfilling, and successful. Even in bad situations, a "glass half full" attitude can indeed help us get better, faster. At RLabs, members have a "hype person" with them, someone who in a tough meeting echoes what they said, reinforcing their message without parroting it. Those who search for the positive are creating better energy even in dire situations where the odds are often stacked against them.

The Power of Imperfection

In this journey, embracing humility and vulnerability can be key.[49] Often, we need to overcome our quest for perfection, for total control, in order for serendipity to happen.

Hubert Joly, chairman of Best Buy and its former CEO, told me that in his experience, if you believe in having total control, you won't ask for help in situations in which you are not able to do something. And if someone else does something wrong, they're part of the problem. That is an inhumane way to live your life. In contrast, if you accept imperfection and you love your vulnerabilities and those of others, then if something unexpected happens, you will be OK with it. Then it is not an imperfection, it is simply something human; it is not about something wrong, but about seizing the moment. Hubert reflected that "it is in those moments of crisis where you can really make a big difference."

This also applies to others directing their search for perfection toward us, such as in the case of Danielle Cohen Henriquez. Danielle, a former-policy-analyst-turned-entrepreneur and impact investor, shared with me her experience regarding a job early on in her career. She had a terrible boss who had mighty temper tantrums. He was the kind of person who claimed the team's successes for himself and blamed the team for any failures.

In this toxic work environment, a third of his staff had quit or was on sick leave when Danielle joined. She was an eager trainee, and was soon overworked. One Friday evening around 7:30 p.m., she was on her way out of the office when her boss discovered a typo in an internal report that had been issued to the organization that day. Danielle recalls, "His eyes widened, he slammed on his keyboard, threw a bunch of paper clips against the wall and screamed at the top of his lungs: 'Is NO ONE capable of ANYTHING here?' My heart sank down to my toes. I had done everything to try to prove myself. I knew that this particular error wasn't on me, but his response could only mean that I just hadn't been good enough."

When she finally left the office, Danielle rushed to her train home but missed it by twenty seconds. "I collapsed in a dusty corner on the platform, feeling abhorrent and worthless." She knew then that something had to change, but what could she do? Talk to him on Monday about it? It didn't seem that was going to help much. Quit and be jobless? Not an option.

Then, an acquaintance of hers came onto the platform. He worked for one of the most powerful organizations in town, a competitor of her own organization in some ways. "Everyone wanted a job there; I hadn't even bothered to apply," she recalled. "When I asked how he was doing, he said that an exciting project had just landed on his team's desk, and that they would need a new staff member very urgently. 'Do you know someone?' he asked."

By the next Tuesday Danielle had an interview, and by Friday she was offered the job. What's more, it was one of the most rewarding positions she'd ever had. Her new boss was a remarkable leader: lighthearted, motivating, and knowledgeable. He opened countless career avenues to Danielle since, and is a mentor to this day.

In the moment, she was at rock bottom. But in hindsight, it was serendipity at work.

Danielle and Hubert both realized that serendipity often comes out of what some might see as crisis—but by embracing the imperfection of the moment they allowed positive outcomes to happen.

Relax!

Humans are not static; we change depending on our respective environments, circumstances, and priorities. Everyone is different, and we are each receptive and unreceptive at different times.

Take stress, for one. There is some truth in a Navy Seal's adaptation of Greek poet Archilochus's adage that in the thick of battle, you will not rise to the level of your expectations but fall to the level of your training. Almost all mental biases become worse in the face of stress, as our body goes into a fight-or-flight response, relying purely on instinct without the emergency brake of Daniel Kahneman's System 2 type of reasoning (our slow and controlled way of thinking).[50] Stress often results in hasty decisions, immediacy, and falling back into habit. I have made my worst decisions in periods in which I felt cornered and in fight-or-flight mode.

Lucky people tend to be more relaxed, and anxiety can keep us from grasping opportunities. In an experiment, Richard Wiseman gave people a newspaper to read, and asked how many photographs were in it. Most participants took around two minutes and counted through quickly. Some double-checked. None of them noticed the headline on the second page, "There are 42 pictures in this newspaper" in large bold letters. Nobody noticed it, because they were so focused on the photographs. They also missed out on the opportunity to win a hundred pounds—another large ad in the newspaper read, "Stop counting and tell the experimenter you see this and win £100." Again, the participants were too busy looking for the photographs. When Wiseman asked instead if they saw anything unusual in the paper, they looked at it differently and saw the messages immediately. By busily (over-) focusing on a particular task they missed out on the real value.

As long as we have in organizations a culture of hyper-stress, with people focusing on not losing their job or trying to get to their meetings on time, it is more likely that we will miss serendipity. (In settings of poverty, the feeling of stress and anxiety is arguably even greater, which can also have a negative impact on decision making.)

But while a healthy state of mind can be important, discomfort and pressure often can be sources of achievement—as usual, it's the balance that counts.

Furthermore, work on brain-body interactions has shown that changes in our digestive and cardiac systems are related to facial expressions. Essentially, physiological states can dictate humans' psychological and behavioral experiences. It's no surprise then that a soft voice or a kind face changes the way we feel, or that being ignored can shift us into states of fear or even mental collapse.[51] Equally, the day after your dog dies or you come out of surgery might not be a good day for serendipity.

Many of us benefit from calming our minds through meditation and/or yoga. The presence we develop from these approaches increases the chances of serendipity because serendipity thrives on alertness (and mono- rather than multitasking, for that matter!).[52] The idea of different states—different energy levels at different times—means that we are more receptive to (or good at conveying) ideas at certain times than at others. Finding people at the right moment—when they are in an open state and not in their shell—is crucial.

This is also true with regard to different phases in life: If you have just come out of school, reached the end of a life stage, or sold your company and are looking for your next idea, then you might be more open to unexpected turns. The same is true in business. There is a time for serendipity, and there is a time for focused execution.

Yet, it's not always up to us to choose, especially if and when we're fighting for survival (especially financially). Though even in those situations, serendipity can strike. And serendipity often strikes when we least expect it. Leaving expectations at the door—of a party, or an office—opens us to the most magical of moments.

Thus . . .

Serendipity is more likely if we care about spotting potential triggers and connecting the dots—and if we have an idea of what to connect a serendipitous moment to. It is all about seeing connections where others see holes, which is easier to do if we actually care about getting somewhere. We can derive our sense of direction in many ways, be it from a deeper sense of purpose, spiritual sensing, based on principles, or by experimenting. Developing an informed gut feeling can help us navigate.

That's why this chapter's serendipity exercise focuses on developing the underlying emotional foundation and motivation for serendipity.

SERENDIPITY WORKOUT: LAYING THE FOUNDATIONS

1. Write down what you value most in life. What are the themes that come to mind? Is there a dominant underlying pattern, perhaps a passion, a sense of direction that only unveils itself when you look back? Start experimenting with potential

North Stars—it will make it easier for you to connect the dots going forward.

2. Spend ten minutes a day meditating or repeating mantras. You can start simple: Sit in a comfortable chair or on a cushion, with your palms resting on your thighs. Take four deep breaths and slowly say to yourself, "May I find the answers that I seek; may I discover the solutions I need. May my life be beautiful. May the lives of the people I love be beautiful."[53] Apps such as Headspace also can give guidance.

3. Surround yourself with people who have positive energy. Identify two to three people who put you in a good mood and with whom you want to spend more time. Set up coffee dates with them.

4. Incorporate gratefulness into your life. You can use a gratefulness journal, or a mobile app such as Gratitude. Or you can integrate it into your daily routine, such as at the dinner table, where everyone can state three things they are grateful for.

5. Every week, send three thank-you notes to people who have had a positive impact on your life. Thank-you notes have been proven to have a surprisingly strong impact on both the sender and receiver.

6. Show the real you, starting with baby steps. Georgie Nightingall, founder of the human connection organization Trigger Conversations, uses the following approach: When someone asks you how you are, why not break out of the script and say something truthful and unexpected, like "a 6.5 out of 10," "caffeine-deprived," or "curious." People will be surprised but also intrigued at your unconventionality and may start a conversation.

7. Train your extroversion muscle. Talk to the person in the coffee shop line, connect with others by smiling with your eyes.

Talk to people you don't know at a party. Assume positive intention: Everyone has their own struggles, and in the spirit of Hanlon's razor—never attribute to malice what can be adequately explained by neglect—once we assume positive intention, we avoid negative spirals and self-fulfilling prophecies. If we assume that people actually want to speak with us— even if they might respond strangely, perhaps because they are surprised—conversations will start to flow.

8. Write down twenty of your aspirations and from that list pick the top five. We tend to overfocus on ambition and under-focus on aspiration, but success means focusing not only on what we want to do but also on who we want to be.[54] Ask yourself, "How will these choices shape my identity?"

9. Decide on two commitments (e.g., "I will have dinner every Monday with my loved one").[55] Pick an accountability partner—someone who will hold you accountable—to tell about them, and agree on when you will report back to them.

10. When organizing a staff or community retreat, reflect on five concrete behaviors that manifest the values your organization or community stands for. Can everyone tell specific stories of how this plays out in their daily life? If you are a parent, you can use the same approach with your children by asking them to share a story over dinner of someone who portrayed a core value such as kindness (perhaps they have a story of a child who was kind to them in school, or an example of how they were kind to someone else?).

CHAPTER 5

ENABLING AND SPOTTING SERENDIPITY TRIGGERS—AND CONNECTING THE DOTS

—

You miss one hundred percent of the shots you don't take.
WAYNE GRETZKY, FORMER PROFESSIONAL
ICE HOCKEY PLAYER AND COACH

Prompting the Unexpected

When Michele Cantos, an Ecuadorian educator based in New York City, sent out a life update email to friends and acquaintances, little did she know that it would lead to her becoming the director of a successful coding boot camp.

After four years of working in the philanthropy sector, where she had supported emerging student leaders from low-income backgrounds, Michele decided to take a few months off to travel back to her home country and think about her next steps. She sent an email update to around a hundred friends and acquaintances. It was an honest message about quitting her job and taking six months to travel.

It was a vulnerable moment. The email said something along the lines of "I will be back in six months, and am thinking about my next steps." She sent a couple of updates like this, related to her travels and her evolving thinking. It felt to her like an authentic way of sharing her journey. In the final email she sent after her return to New York, she specified that she was back and what her background and ideal next steps were. Just a short paragraph asking for ideas.

Several friends answered on a personal level, wishing Michele all the best in her future endeavors. But one acquaintance responded to her query differently. She had just gone through an interview marathon with a tech company and in the end decided to take another job. But she had made such a good impression that people there asked her if she knew anyone else who might suit the position. She thought Michele would be a perfect fit for the job and shared with her the research she had done into the role. The background information and endorsement in combination with Michele's enthusiasm went a long way, and Michele was offered the position.

For Michele, who had no previous experience in the tech industry, this job was entirely unexpected. Michele admits that she probably would have never applied for a job in the tech sector; it seemed so different from who she was. "That person saw it for me," she admits. "She changed my life." This job improved not only her salary, but also her quality of life. The four emails Michele sent as updates had a massive financial and life return.

Michele traces her key experiences and upward social mobility back to the power of serendipity, of which she now experiences "lots, everywhere."

But what is it exactly that Michele did here? She seeded a serendipity trigger. She put something, a prompt, out there that allowed serendipity to happen. She was proactive, open, and even slightly vulnerable. She set herself up for serendipity.

In this case, someone else connected the dots for her, pointing to the fact that serendipity is frequently cocreated and sometimes relies on the goodwill of others. Others can envision opportunities or talents in us that we don't—or, given their different areas of knowledge, they can connect dots that we don't have on our radar, opening the opportunity space even further. But if we don't let them know what we're interested in or what we're looking for, if we do not seed potential triggers, how can they know?

Seeding potential triggers is at the core of what people who experience serendipity en masse do. Connecting the dots helps turn it into a positive outcome. Both are key—sometimes they happen step by step, sometimes at the same time.

Seeding Serendipity Triggers

Let your hook be always cast; in the pool where you least expect it, there will be a fish.

OVID, ROMAN POET

When Oli Barrett, a London-based super-connector and founder of several start-up companies, meets new people, he casts several hooks that enable potential overlaps. If he gets asked, "What do you do?" he will answer something along the lines of, "I love connecting people, I set up a company in the education sector, I've recently started thinking about philosophy, but what I really enjoy is playing the piano."

This reply includes at least four potential serendipity triggers: a passion (connecting people), a job description (setting up an education company), an interest (philosophy), and a hobby (playing the piano). If he just responded with, "I founded an education business," the potential opportunity space for others to connect the dots would be quite small.

But by seeding four or even more potential serendipity triggers, he makes it more likely that someone might respond with something like, "Such a coincidence! I'm currently thinking about buying a piano, can you give me some tips?" It allows others to pick and choose the hook that relates to their life—and makes it more likely that serendipity happens, big or small.

Serendipity relies on serendipity triggers. How can we use this to our advantage?

Accelerating the (Positively) Unexpected

Our prompting of serendipity starts with an excursion into a subject that was part of placing me into the bottom 5 percent of my high school class: chemistry. While my appreciation for the subject then was shamefully low—to this day the only "table" I can remember is the timetable telling me when classes were over—it has increased considerably since. Especially once I realized how much chemical reactions have in common with social interactions.

In an exciting yet initially controversial study published in the leading science journal *Science*, David MacMillan, the James S. McDonnell Distinguished University Professor of Chemistry at Princeton University, and his colleagues showed that it is possible to accelerate serendipity.[1]

The usual approach in science is to take molecules that researchers believe will react, and then try to work out a way to achieve that reaction. In contrast, MacMillan's team took molecules where there was no obvious reaction and looked for what was called "accidental reactivity." By choosing chemicals that had never been shown to react with each other, the researchers prompted as-yet undiscovered reactions, thus enabling the development of valuable new drugs.

The researchers' core assumption was that serendipity is governed by probability and, thus, manageable by statistics. Therefore, increasing the number of possible chemical reactions in a laboratory setting had to increase the chances of a positive reaction—which is indeed what happened.[2]

This is roughly similar to increasing your chance of winning the lottery by buying more tickets or gaining a university admission by sending more applications in countries like Germany where that is possible. (I'm still pretty sure that the reason the university I attended accepted me was that there was something arbitrary in my application that resonated with someone on the recruitment team. I will never know what that was, but when you apply to more than forty universities, even with [very] below-average grades, the chances of someone, somewhere finding resonance in your application are greater.)

Perhaps the person who read my application had a son with a similarly tumultuous past—it would have been coincidence that they had, but the likelihood of such a coincidence was greater because of the number of applications I sent out. As in the chemistry example, and so many other areas in life, it is a numbers game. The more shots we take, the more likely we are to make a basket or hit a target, even if only by accident.

Unexpected connections often appear to come from unexpected sources. But think back to the birthday paradox example: The apparently unexpected is actually very probable because there are so many unexpected things (or connections) that could happen. If we add up all the potential possibilities, we realize that the unexpected happens all the time—we just have to open our eyes and pay closer attention to it to notice. And often we need only one of those encounters to change life for the better.

You might think, "I'm happy the way things are, why would I need to change?" Funnily enough, people who say that are often among the most joyful once serendipity starts to happen to them (including some of my colleagues). It's not necessarily about changing one's life, but about making life more joyful, meaningful, and successful.

For now, what is important is that we need to expose ourselves to unknowns. We are used to actively searching in fields where we are comfortable, but serendipity is more likely once we encounter random outside influences. This can take different forms and shapes: new information, resources, people, and ideas.

Information Is Not Only Power

Information is at the core of life's opportunities. In Michele Cantos's case, she was unexpectedly informed about the role that fit her best. Not by searching for that information—how can you search for something that you don't know?—but rather, by opening herself up to it. This can happen in the most trivial of ways.

The Slovenian philosopher Slavoj Žižek famously argued that what we think we want is not necessarily what we actually desire. Žižek uses the example of a man who has a wife and a lover. He secretly hopes that the wife will vanish so that he can be with his lover. The wife unexpectedly moves out of his life, and suddenly, the man does not desire the lover anymore. Why? The relationship worked well in one set of circumstances, but without those circumstances, the lover loses her appeal—she is no longer an "object of desire in the distance."[3]

Like so many things in life this is difficult to know beforehand, isn't it?

Indeed, as discussed in the last chapter, we often know what we actually desire only when we encounter it—often serendipitously—and discover that it just feels right or good.

Some of us can experience it through calm sources, say by skimming through the newspaper, scrolling through the internet, or reading a good book. Years ago, Keyun Ruan was shuffling through a magazine with a cup of tea in hand when she came across a piece about cloud computing. This piqued her curiosity as she was in search of a topic for her PhD research. Alert to potential serendipity triggers, she followed her interest and today, she is both a leading computer scientist and an expert in cloud forensics and security.[4]

Either way, exposing ourselves to new information is an important way to encounter serendipity.* This even includes movies.

When Bibi la Luz Gonzalez, an activist, political economist, and entrepreneur working as a journalist based in Guatemala, attended a conference in London in 2016, little did she expect that a movie would change her life.

While covering the Thomson Reuters Foundation Trust Conference on modern-day slavery, she attended the premiere of the movie *Sold*, about a girl who was trafficked from Nepal to India to work in a brothel. The movie had a lasting effect on Bibi, and after the screening ended, she told its director that she wanted to show the movie in Guatemala to raise awareness and perhaps feature it in the newspaper she worked for. The director agreed—but the movie needed Spanish subtitles, and it took two years to translate it. In 2018, Bibi received word that the subtitles were finally done.

By then she was no longer a journalist but among other things was now the curator of the Global Shapers Guatemala City Hub, part of a global community of young people interested in improving the state of the world. She used the movie as an opportunity to start a local project with other Global Shapers on human trafficking, a taboo topic in Guatemala, and planned to bring both the movie and the director to Guatemala to mentor local filmmakers, using it as a cross-cutting topic on women's and girls' rights.

Owing to a scheduling clash, the director wasn't able to get to Guatemala, but when Bibi had to go to Sacramento for an event, she contacted the director and asked if she could visit him in San Francisco on the

---

* Information is never just information; it is what we interpret into it, which depends on our context. In Germany, people tend to focus on the factual content of a text or conversation—sometimes missing the nuance that comes from the respective context. Whereas in cultures that have a high context sensitivity—for example most of Asia—messages tend to be more ambiguous and reading between the lines becomes paramount. In a low-context culture, someone might say "close the door," while in a high-context setting it might be something like, "it's getting cold in here," or "I don't want the cats to get out of the house" (Hall, 1976).

way back. He agreed, and Bibi went to see him with two other local Global Shapers—filmmakers Ramazan Nanayev and Meghan Stevenson-Krausz—to interview him at his home. She later screened the film and interview, and started promoting the project in Guatemala. She had cultivated this relationship for years, and it finally came to fruition. The project, Unshape Slavery, evolved into a global project within the Shapers community (comprising around eight thousand young leaders around the world), and she met a number of members on the way who became close friends. A movie and the meeting with its director were the serendipity triggers, but Bibi repeatedly connected the dots.

In 2019, she returned to the conference as a "Changemaker"—an award granted to those who have had an impact and gained expertise in the areas that Bibi encountered three years earlier at this very conference.

While serendipity triggers often happen via information that we get from books, newspapers, or movies, in the end, many serendipity triggers are seeded—and dots connected—by (often other) people.

It's All About the People

In the 1960s the Cold War meant that there was near isolation between the United States, China, and the Soviet Union. When U.S. Secretary of State Henry Kissinger bumped into an Eastern Bloc official at the Pugwash conference in the Polish resort of Sopot, he changed the course of history.

Kissinger, one of America's most effective (and controversial) secretaries of state, enabled the opening of diplomatic relations between the United States and Mao Zedong's China in 1972 based on a serendipitous encounter at the conference, which led to meetings that paved the way for a sitting U.S. president to visit China and change the geopolitical landscape. Kissinger, by virtue of his proactive networking behavior, made that possible.[5]

On a smaller scale, such random encounters can change, if not history, then at least our own lives.

More than fifty years later—in 2014—Amina Aitsi-Selmi faced a major crossroads in her career. Trained as a doctor, she was feeling lost and confused despite her glittering track record. People pointed her toward the safe career track, but to her, the safe road looked bleak and uninspiring. Her teenage dream of working in global health was receding into the distance, almost forgotten. One morning, she walked into an elevator in London and greeted the only other person there. They chatted about the weather and suddenly something clicked.

"Who are you?" the woman asked her. Amina explained what she was doing but said what she really wanted to do was meaningful work on health issues. The lady looked at her and said, "Come and see me, and find out more about what I'm doing."

It turned out the woman was the vice-chair of a technical group for a United Nations organization and was looking for someone with the scientific and technical skills (and a personality to match) to help her.

One thing led to another, and Amina found herself working on the UN's 2015 Sustainable Development Goal agenda, with a focus on health and disaster risk reduction. She ended up coauthoring a UN report and various other publications, which later helped her to achieve a senior clinical lecturer position and a consulting opportunity at Chatham House, a London-based international affairs think tank. UN and World Health Organization (WHO) panels started asking her for advice.

Her twenty-year-long dream had come true after a year of despair that Admina admitted had almost swallowed her up. A chance conversation in an elevator changed Amina's life.

Amina Aitsi-Selmi and Henry Kissinger were both able to leverage a serendipity trigger, and they were part of connecting the dots. But how can we recreate something similar for our own lives? Where does one start?

Setting Serendipity Bombs

A question I am often asked is, "How do I put myself in situations where I can find people that I can connect with? I just don't know that many yet."

Mattan Griffel, an entrepreneur and adjunct assistant professor at Columbia University, looks at it as "setting thousands of little serendipity bombs." This approach can include the practice of writing speculative emails to people we admire. Surprisingly often, they actually write back. And it is more probable that they will write back if you can refer to a project that they've been involved in.

Such was the case of Nicola Greco, who started to write a lot of code in the open source projects of Tim Berners-Lee, a computer scientist known as the inventor of the World Wide Web, in a way that Berners-Lee and his team would notice. He then sent an email saying, "Hey, I've done some work on xyz, it would be great to meet." They ended up meeting, and Berners-Lee became his PhD advisor, catapulting Nicola forward in his research and current activities.

Surprisingly often, there are unexpected interests or reasons to engage that we cannot know about beforehand, and that are known only to the other person. A researcher might have wanted to expand into exactly the area that a speculative email referred to. Even with all of the background information available to us with just a few keystrokes, we often cannot know this beforehand, and so sending an email that helps to map an opportunity space allows the person we admire to do trigger-spotting. And even if nothing comes of it immediately, at least we are on their radar now (assuming they read their emails, that is).

Why not write an email to the people you admire, telling them what you are excited about, and why you find them interesting? Even if they are not interested, they often know people who might be.

In many professional fields, academics are good starting points for making connections. Their email addresses tend to be on their university's home page, and they usually know people in industry who are relatively senior and are relatively open to making introductions. I have also witnessed people being successful by tweeting someone, sending messages to their assistant, Instagramming them, or using the InMail function on LinkedIn (where you can send an email to people you don't know).

That's what Alvin Owusu-Fordwuo, a young student from London's borough of Hackney, did when he left one of my workshops with the goal of setting serendipity bombs. A young man with a big heart and big dreams, Alvin dropped messages on LinkedIn to both the CEO and the copresident of a major company in which he was supposed to intern. Both agreed to meet him. His initial message was simple: "Hi [name of CEO], I'm an incoming spring intern at [name of company]. I'll be there for a week and I'd love the opportunity to speak to you or set up a lunch whilst I'm there to speak with you about your experiences and achieving success at [name of company]."

Alvin initially didn't get a reply to this message. But he reached out to someone more junior at the company who could support the social enterprise he was running on the side (serendipity bomb 2). It turned out that the president was mentoring her and she spoke to him about Alvin and made him take notice. After now a number of coffees, "the president has become massively supportive of my development and wants to use his platform to champion me after I finish university," Alvin said.

Sending random messages to strangers can be helpful, but following them up with someone who can nudge the person is even more effective. Perhaps there is someone who can introduce you who might be a mutual acquaintance on LinkedIn or Facebook? The point is that reaching out can be powerful—wherever or whoever we are.

Of course, it takes courage to put ourselves out there.

When Alby Shale, a London-based entrepreneur and philanthropist, lost his father, Christopher, to heart disease, he was beset by grief. The logical step was to talk to a therapist. Instead, he went to a party and found himself talking to a stranger about grief. Coincidentally, that stranger was going through a similarly tough period himself. The two came up with the idea of a mental health campaign that aimed to create a community of people committed to having difficult conversations about death and grief via means such as a podcast and symbols such as bracelets signaling that someone is grieving. Thinking through those ideas also turned out to be an effective remedy for them both.

Of course, all of this depends on how we communicate: People like Alby don't dive into self-pity or over-sharing. Instead, he shared his grief in short, succinct (and often learning-focused) ways so that others could relate to the core sentiment. In this manner, vulnerability becomes a way to trigger serendipity.[6]

Putting Ourselves Out There

How can we multiply the potential serendipity triggers and set up ourselves and others for connecting the related dots? Remember Michele's story: Newsletters, blogposts, and updates on topics we are interested in via email, Twitter, Instagram, and other means can be effective in prompting serendipity from the most unexpected of places so long as they are focused on relevant themes rather than self-indulgence.

Once we put ourselves out there, magic can happen. Ken Chua, a Singapore-based social entrepreneur, shared with me how the pivotal moment for starting his company—(these)abilities—was reading *Design Meets Disability* by Graham Pullin. Ken was looking for experts at the intersection of design, tech, and disability—of whom there are very few. He had long thought of sending Graham a speculative email but always procrastinated. One thing he did do was to continuously post content on (these) abilities' work and philosophy on social media.

One of these posts caught the attention of an interaction designer who was working at the Singapore office of the design firm IDEO and who had been a student of Graham's at the University of Dundee. Despite doing exciting design work for IDEO, the designer was missing the disability-focused practice he had under Graham. So when he came across Ken's activities on social media, he reached out.

Ken still didn't know that the designer was a student of Graham's when they met, but he dropped him a note when Graham was visiting Singapore to promote admissions for the University of Dundee. One thing led to another, and what was supposed to be a two-hour dinner with Graham turned into a multi-hour conversation in which they talked shop and life. They are friends now, exploring ways to collaborate.

How can we find our own authentic story to tell that sets the stage for potential serendipity prompts on a personal or professional level? I have found it useful to write a page about my area of interest and with an interesting hook related to my own life story.

We all have a story to tell, and we all feel like imposters at times, yet there are people out there waiting to find resonance in our narrative. We can also tell this "story of self" wherever we go. Its short version can become the new answer to "What do you do?"

It always feels like we need to be a true expert before we can put ourselves out there. Have you brought up a child? Have you worked in your job for many years? *You are an expert.* At most panel discussions, many of the panelists are just winging it, and many actually don't have a clue beyond their brief. Professors might be extremely well-trained in a niche but are considered experts for a whole field. They constantly need to wing it when they have to teach outside their direct area of research.

"Nice to Meet You . . ."

Of course, our serendipity score (which we will look to in more detail in the next few chapters) increases whenever there is a high concentration of interesting people. Public lectures at universities or institutions such as the Royal Society of Arts can be a hotbed of interesting people—and these events are almost always free and open to the public. Speakers are often surprisingly open to connecting with others, especially if there is a genuine interest in a current project.

Counterintuitively, often, the more senior the person, the more willing they are to connect if one sparks their interest. Mike Churney (name changed) shared with me how a senior executive he approached after a speech got in touch to donate hundreds of chairs to Mike's charity after the executive's company had sold some of its furnished buildings. Mike put himself on this CEO's map because he asked an interesting question and shared his story after a public speech that the CEO gave. When the executive had to decide what to do with the chairs, he remembered that they might be helpful to Mike's charity.

Mike had to overcome the same challenge as many of us: the feeling of not being able to contribute much to someone who appears to have everything. However, surprisingly often, these senior people can themselves be motivated by being part of a person's journey, rather than a particular material factor; this in turn is our contribution to them. After all, giving tends to make us happier than receiving, so letting people be part of our journey can be a powerful motivation for both sides if it is based on some kind of mutual interest or resonance.[7]

One trait I have observed in serendipitors is that they often introduce themselves to the host and/or their staff at the beginning of an event, whether it's a dinner, a conference, a business meeting, or something else. These people are rarely the stars of the event, but they know the key people, and if they like you, they can connect you or float your ideas with others. This is particularly true at community and coworking spaces, or events hosted locally. These events are often a good starting point to slide into other potentially interesting events.

Interest-based communities can be effective, too.[8] When I joined my Krav Maga martial arts class—where the main rule is that there are no rules—I overheard a financial markets specialist talking about his work on predictive models. Serendipity struck and we ended up discussing how their models are focusing on reducing error rather than developing resilience—which helped make this train of thought part of this book. Research on "weak ties"—people we do not know well—confirms that (unexpected) opportunities happen when we put ourselves into environments that are different from our usual setting.[9]

But even if we interact with more people, we might fail to stay in touch. I have found that one of the most effective approaches to keep in touch with someone is to offer to introduce them to someone who could be helpful to them. It's a nice excuse to ask for their card—and as a nice side effect, people often remember who introduced them to someone and they often return the favor.

How can we introduce people most effectively? Super-connectors such as Fabian Pfortmüller connect people via underlying interests ("This person is also excited about your chosen interest area") rather than merely their roles.[10] This focuses the conversation on common interests and passions and minimizes potential status differences. People connect differently when they connect with who or what they are truly interested in, rather than their professional self. Once we help to do that, serendipity can flourish.[11]

Designing for Serendipity Triggers

Countless studies have shown that the physical environment has a major influence on the likelihood of serendipity.[12] We can increase the amount and quality of serendipity triggers, not only for ourselves, but also for members of our organizations, communities, and even our families.

When Burning Man, one of the world's largest community gatherings, hosted in the western United States at Black Rock City in northern Nevada, placed art in some of its public spaces, serendipity was cultivated at scale.

Each year participants of Burning Man live in blocks of tents, and to get from A to B, they often need to cross public spaces, known as plazas. The festival organizers realized that people often need to connect with a diverse range of others to develop new ideas and innovation. By decreasing the size of these spaces and placing art in the middle of the plazas, the Burning Man team not only made people run into each other more frequently (given the lack of space), but also gave them an excuse to speak to strangers when stopping in front of the art and sharing their observations. It proved to spark serendipitous conversations. (Burning Man facilitates this with a culture of reciprocity and "gifting.")

Be it art that makes people run into each other, smart seating arrangements, or employing hosts to greet people and introduce strangers to each other, the ways we arrange physical settings have major influences on the amount and quality of triggers and can considerably increase individuals' and organizations' serendipity coefficient.

Serendipity-inducing space design can come in many different shapes and forms. In some collaborative coworking spaces, for example, the commonly used long tables do not follow the usual design logic. Instead, the tables "bend" after two or three seats—enough to sit next to someone, but at the same time giving you the opportunity to turn away if you need privacy or space. This combines the logic of openness with the logic of focus. Teams from different companies can sit at these tables, and often end up in seren-dipitous encounters. When I worked from one of these spaces in London, I often encountered new ideas from the most unexpected conversation part-ners, such as an orchestra singer who was about to start a company.

Pixar, one of the most successful film studios in history (with an aver-age gross revenue of more than $550 million per movie, including the *Toy Story* movies), took a similar approach. When Steve Jobs owned Pixar, he asked the architects to design its buildings "to maximize inadvertent en-counters."[13] At Pixar, artists and designers work hand in hand with com-puter scientists—connecting two potentially very different cultures.

Jobs, who has been credited with the turnaround of the company, took his liberal arts mindset into the design of the entire Pixar campus. When he purchased an abandoned factory in Emeryville, north of Oakland, Cal-ifornia, the original design was for three buildings, with separate offices for Pixar executives, animators, and computer scientists.

Jobs scrapped it. Instead, he wanted a single big space, with an atrium at the center. He believed that at the heart of the company should be the interaction of employees. How did he get people to actually go to the cen-tral space, especially given the two very different cultures?

He shifted the mailboxes to the atrium. He moved the meeting rooms to the building's center. He positioned the cafeteria there. And naturally, the gift shop and coffee bar went there, too. Jobs even wanted to locate the building's only set of bathrooms in the atrium. (This last idea did not go down so well, however, and he had to compromise, with several bathrooms across the campus.)

These elements led to people frequenting the atrium—and bumping into each other. Guess what the crest of Pixar University says? *Alienus Non Diutius*—a Latin phrase meaning "Alone no longer."[14]

In line with spaces, we can design simple processes for more and better serendipity triggers. Lunch Lottery helps large organizations have people meet across areas, and at NESTA, the British foundation for innovation, a "randomized coffee trial" (RCT) lets people meet new colleagues. In RCTs people are paired on a fixed frequency—say, monthly—to have a coffee with someone they have never met before. This can be a colleague from another unit, or from "the periphery"—someone they would not usually interact with. These meetings are open-ended and allocated randomly. If in-person meetings are not possible, video conferencing is, of course, a viable option.

These RCTs often lead to breaking down silos (groups not sharing information with other groups), developing higher levels of collaboration, and encouraging a higher frequency of serendipitous encounters. Organizations such as Britain's National Health Service, the United Nations Development Program, Google, and the Red Cross have subsequently applied it. At Google, you can even choose the days on which you want to be randomly paired up.

Or take Wok+Wine, a social dining experience purposefully designed to create the right conditions for serendipitous encounters, which its founder Peter Mandeno launched in New York and then expanded into eleven countries. Participants stand uncomfortably close to each other, eat with their hands, and literally break bread from a communal table. Events are held in unorthodox venues such as hair salons and abandoned buildings. The space is laid out to encourage movement, increasing the likelihood of bumping into someone new. For Peter, whose PhD at Imperial College London is on how to design for human connectivity, the experimentation across contexts allowed for what he calls "optimizing serendipity."

Technology as Game-Changer

Technology can be a powerful accelerator for serendipity. Web Summit, the world's biggest tech gathering, hosted annually in Lisbon, hired data scientists to engineer serendipity by programming which people to get to the conference, which people to focus on to connect at the summit, and who to help after it.[15]

Paddy Cosgrave, the founder of the conference that now attracts around fifty thousand participants, started Web Summit without a background in the conference industry, with few resources, and from what was at the time a relatively peripheral location: Dublin. How could he do that, in his early twenties? Paddy attributes much of its growth to this data-driven approach to serendipity.

Seemingly small items such as interesting typographic choices for name badges, specially arranged exhibition booths, signage, and queuing were meticulously designed. By using complex systems and network approaches such as eigenvector centrality (a measure of the influence of a person in a network), he brought science to the core of conference organizing, his team analyzing network data and personalizing its recommendations.

Web Summit does offline what many social media platforms do online, using graph theory to recommend people who might suit you. Cosgrave sees Web Summit as an "accelerated accelerator," facilitating creative collisions between over fifty thousand people.

You might think that the pub crawls during the event are just that. Not so. At Web Summit, they are machine-curated, and people are grouped based on their propensity to find commonalities. That is also mirrored in the seating arrangements: They are designed to cluster people who are expected to have interesting conversations.

The combination of offline and online happens even before delegates arrive: You can set meetings with attendees, and you'll be assigned a particular area that suits your interests and maximizes collisions. The organization also has GoPro cameras on the ceilings and uses computer vision to spot empty or congested areas, so that organizers can take action if someone seems isolated.

And if they want you to attend but you are not yet signed up, they might make sure that your Facebook newsfeed is full of people they know you respect, showing them to you as "confirmed members." They make you aware—sometimes painfully—of what you might be missing out on (but of course, the joy of missing out—JOMO—can sometimes be nicer than the fear of missing out—FOMO!).

On a more individual level, platforms such as Facebook, Instagram, and Twitter—particularly due to their tagging functions—have exponentially increased the number and quality of serendipitous encounters if we go beyond our small circle of friends.

Technology helps us expand the natural boundaries of social capital. Whereas only a few decades ago we were able to stay in touch with a limited number of people, today we can keep weak ties in larger numbers than ever before.[16] If used well, this can accelerate the number of our own and others' serendipity triggers.

This can unfold in a number of ways. Once you start sharing interesting articles related to your theme, and tag your favorite people—serendipity might happen more often. Others can tag others who might fit the bill.

On Twitter, authors like Adam Grant often like or retweet articles that mention them. They might even get back to you with comments or suggestions. Sharing what you learned at an event and using hashtags can also be effective—others who are at the same event might react and you could end up with a couple of exciting meetings.

This is multiplied in online communities of shared interests. In the Sandbox Facebook group ten minutes after someone posted, "I'm looking for ideas for an underwater-robot," several people chimed in with replies along the lines of, "my former professor worked on underwater robots, I can put you in touch!"; "a friend of mine works on a similar type of robot!"; and so on. This dynamic works much better in well-curated communities where people connect based on shared interests, develop a joint identity or vision, and have a basic level of trust than in looser-knit networks where people primarily connect one on one.

This is as true for high-income contexts as it is for settings of extreme poverty. Marlon Parker, founder of the South African Cape Flats' RLabs, told me that many of the people who come to the academy also like their Facebook page and follow RLabs on Twitter. People he hasn't spoken to in a while would come and follow this journey online, "and then immediately get that information and then 'okay, boom!' In some cases people can get involved immediately."

By constantly showcasing its activities online, RLabs has attracted random visitors from around the world. This quickly multiplied, and Marlon and his team developed products and platforms based on serendipitous ideas emerging from the most unexpected places. Once community members saw that young people were using their cell phones throughout the day, they became curious and discovered the value of social media. Out of this curiosity and the demand resulting from it, a "moms' program" evolved, which teaches older women how to use social media. Our related research has shown that often low- rather than high-level tech is key, seeing technology not as a solution, but a simple means to engage people.[17]

However, as *New York Times* columnist Thomas Friedman observed, the Arab Spring, Occupy Wall Street, and other protests showed one potential drawback of technology: It might allow us to *communicate* more, but not necessarily to collaborate more. Indeed, people often substitute activity on social media with real action.[18] Which comes back to the importance of a sense of direction that guides us.

Even more strikingly, if networks are not diverse enough, they make serendipity inaccessible. "Over-embeddedness" often discourages serendipity, as we get used to a shared thinking that doesn't lead to many anomalies or unexpected encounters. This is particularly the case in homogeneous, cohesive networks. *The Wall Street Journal* did a striking comparison between the Facebook feeds of Democrats and Republicans. The incredible self-referencing on either side reinforces belief systems and makes people on both sides feel confirmed and accepted—but often shuts us off from questioning our mental models and beliefs.[19]

Our research on tribes in Kenya offers similar insights regarding self-referencing. Only once tribal boundaries were bridged by creative means such as redefining shared identity (for example, based on shared interests such as sport) was it possible to connect across groups.[20] Lord Michael Hastings, chancellor of Regent's University London, calls it "understanding the other game," and moving from the 4 percent (in this case, the ethnic minority he refers to) to the 96 percent (the majority group) by learning about their modus operandi and interests.

This applies within organizations as well, especially when it comes to silos and information asymmetries. Take the example of Diamond Bank (now part of Access Bank), one of Nigeria's leading financial institutions, where former CEO Uzoma Dozie and his team integrated Yammer—a social tool that essentially tries to take the open-door policy into the digital world. Initially, it was set up to get feedback for some company policies.

In contrast to other organizations in which Yammer did not improve collaboration, in this case it did. Why did it work? Employees were allowed to use the chat function to communicate informally with each other about everything, from company policies to which movie they would watch that night. According to Uzoma, a 90 percent adoption rate happened not because people really wanted to give feedback—though that happened, too—but because they were creating their own informal groups around their hobbies, beliefs, and ideologies. Serious and less serious groups were being formed that were increasingly diverse in terms of rank, religion, and geography. The CEO in Lagos was now connected to a new employee in northeast Nigeria all because of a shared love of movies. This created strong bonds across the organization and allowed for unexpected collisions to occur at scale.

But all the serendipity triggers in the world are worth nothing without connecting the dots.

Connecting the Dots

Can you remember one of those moments when something fell into place? Often, the experience of serendipity is about that *aha* moment that gives us goose bumps. It can be magical when we see things that we thought were unconnected come together. And it can be magical if someone else unexpectedly sees something in us that we hadn't seen—and connects the dots for us.

Some of us connect the dots intuitively. When Aadarsh Gautam, an up-and-coming rapper going by the stage name Hyphen, uploaded a video on Instagram, the presenter of Soho Radio in London "liked" it. What would most people do with this trigger? They would probably be excited—and leave it at that. Serendipity missed.

But what did Aadarsh do? He direct messaged the radio presenter, indicating that he would be excited to meet sometime to discuss the song with him. The presenter wrote back, saying he would be happy to meet. Aadarsh asked if he might be able to perform—showing rather than telling! "Why don't you do it live on the radio then?" the presenter asked.

A date was fixed and Aadarsh eagerly waited for the day to come. Shortly before he was due to perform, he received an update: The presenter had moved over to the BBC and he was to stand in for a sick colleague at a major BBC radio show. Would Aadarsh be willing to perform there instead? Needless to say, Aadarsh was willing to do so—which led to a magnificent outlet for his work.

He saw a serendipity trigger and took advantage of it, but what made it happen was his connecting the dots and his persistence in doing so. This points to what makes a serendipity trigger relevant: bisociation. Noticing and then connecting unexpected bits of information is the key step in the serendipity process. This "What's going on?" step involves noticing an observation, and then thinking about what it might mean.[21]

Of Oil Spills and Growing Up in Houston

Alabama hairstylist Phil McCrory was sweeping his barber's shop at the end of a long day in 1989, watching the news about Exxon's oil spill in Alaska. The oil was clinging to otters' fur, and volunteers had difficulty cleaning the animals up.

Seeing how the fur trapped and held the spilled oil, Phil realized that the hair that he was sweeping could be used as an oil-capturing device. He collected the hair and put it in nylon tights to see how much oil it would absorb.[22] The idea of using human hair to mop up oil spills was born—resulting in products such as oil spill mats based on human hair. Phil connected the dots.

Some people do this intuitively, all the time. Frieder Strohauer, the owner of a legendary coffee shop in Heidelberg, Germany (and my first boss—I worked there during high school), told me that whenever he talks with someone, he thinks about what that person tells him and how it could fit into what he or others around him are doing. When a banker randomly tells him about an enterprise that's about to go bankrupt, he wonders who might be interested in buying it. When a neighbor tells him that he's looking for somewhere new to live, he tries to remember if he had a conversation recently where someone mentioned anything about houses being on the market. And of course, he tells people about what he enjoys doing. Often by what he thought was coincidence, someone always knows something; somehow it always comes together. Much of this is opportunity-seeking more generally, but it can lead to serendipitous connections.

That way, Frieder has developed a great network of people who enjoy talking with him—and on the side, he also developed a portfolio of projects that emerged from these conversations. He derives lots of joy from it, but also credits part of his success to constantly connecting the dots.

This ability plays out in different contexts. Take Pete Munger (name changed) from Houston. One day, Pete decided to try his luck. He grew up in a working-class family in Houston and was told that people like him were supposed to work in a factory. His dad used to tell him that "people like us don't go to college, we are just not made for that."

A couple of years ago, Pete had a random conversation with a lecturer whom he met at a local university at a dinner, who pointed him in the direction of some universities he should apply to. "Just to give it a shot," the lecturer said. Pete did give it a shot; he felt it was what he was supposed to do.

He got into college, but it was no easy route and it took a lot of effort. But he ended up being the first person in his family to gain a degree. Pete is sure that many factors contributed, but he feels that the most important one was that he took his luck in his own hands and acted on something that he would otherwise have missed. Pete recently was part of a global top-ten university's graduating class and is now an alumnus of one of the world's leading educational institutions.

How do we take control of a situation rather than being reactive? Once we shift our mindset, opportunities that we couldn't even dream of enter the realm of possibility.

What is common among people like Phil, Pete, or even Nathaniel (from chapter 1's TEDxVolcano story) is that they come into contact with the same serendipity triggers that others do. Phil wasn't the only one watching Exxon's oil spill on TV, and Nathaniel wasn't the only person who had his travels disrupted by a volcano. But they reacted differently: They connected the dots and made serendipity happen for themselves and for others.

Detecting the Universal in the Particular

What makes it easier to connect the dots is to have some knowledge that gives us potential points of reference. Often, we can only understand the significance of an unexpected event in context, and the unexpected *Eureka!*

happens after a preparation period of developing knowledge.[23] For example, Geneva, whom we encountered earlier, had a background in filmmaking, which made it possible to connect the dots to learning about Emma's desire to be heard. Detecting the universal in the particular often requires an informed observer.[24]

As experts in our own life experience, we all have some stock of knowledge—conscious or subconscious—that might come to mind when we encounter an unexpected event (*if* we are sufficiently excited and motivated).[25] We can't always know how we can use the knowledge until we see an application for it. Steve Jobs didn't know how and when his college-acquired calligraphy skills would be useful until he saw an opportunity to use them in designing multiple typefaces for the Apple Mac.

The same is true for the law. For viewers of law television series (such as *Suits*), have you ever noticed how many of the main characters' strategies, particularly in moments of crisis, emerge serendipitously from a random conversation or piece of reading? Only their ability to connect the new information with previous knowledge (e.g., of case law, or their opponent) makes it possible to connect the dots. Again, much of this knowledge was not acquired for a particular purpose but for the general ability to use it whenever needed.

Like humans, organizations tend to develop a collective memory. This is critical for serendipity, because we can retain knowledge from previous "experiments" and efforts. From that perspective, failure and waste are perceived differently: They are both important sources of establishing a stock of knowledge of what works and what doesn't.[26]

Understanding our own capabilities, combined with an open mind, can help us enormously to connect the dots when the unexpected happens. Keeping an open mind is particularly important. Marc Benioff, founder of Salesforce, a leading software company based in San Francisco, follows the beginner's mind idea of Zen master Suzuki: "In the beginner's mind there are many possibilities; in the expert's mind there are few." Benioff recalls that his "power" was that he didn't really want to do anything specific but was open to all possibilities.[27]

Steven D'Souza and Diana Renner in the book *Not Knowing* illustrate the importance of being comfortable with a beginner's mind—and that often real learning necessitates being out of our comfort zone. For Cara Thomas, whom we met earlier and who frequently encounters serendipity, the "not knowing" state is where serendipity usually finds her.[28]

In short, both previous knowledge and a beginner's mind can be effective if we use them in the right moments and if we do not let them hold us back.

Artistry and Serendipity

When King Solomon needed to resolve a dispute between two women regarding who was the true mother of a baby, he called for the child to be cut in half. Why?

In this famous story from the Bible, he wanted to observe the women's reactions, which would inform his judgment. In the days before DNA testing, he was limited in his options. As both women claimed that the baby was theirs, Solomon called for a sword and announced that he was going to slice the baby in two. One of the women pleaded with Solomon not to do it and to give the baby to the other woman—proving to Solomon that she was the baby's true mother, as she would sacrifice custody to keep her baby alive. He used a nonobvious, creative, and indirect approach that Edward de Bono would call *lateral thinking*,[29] i.e., lateral as opposed to vertical thinking, where we solve problems step by step.

Such an approach shows how we can broaden where we look for solutions and we can train ourselves in generating new ideas. Try picking an object at random, and associate it with your area of interest. De Bono used the example of randomly choosing the word "nose" in relation to a photocopier (the object in question), leading to the idea that the copier could create a lavender smell whenever it was out of paper.[30] From there, a creative session can get started.

There's much to be learned from the arts when it comes to facilitating serendipity triggers and connecting the dots. Artists tend to derive inspiration from happenstance, from the anomaly. Indeed, art thrives on the unexpected.[31]

Jackson Pollock, one of the greatest abstract painters of the twentieth century, famously said that he denied the accident. What did he mean? His point was that while some observers think of Pollock's technique as just randomly throwing paint at a canvas, Pollock believed he was following a method and intention behind each gesture.

Denying the accident doesn't mean mapping out a painting in advance. Pollock saw accidents as both intended and spontaneous at the same time.

Consider method acting, or improvised jazz, or stand-up comedy. In all these cases, the artists open themselves up to the unexpected, to the spontaneous. Sometimes it comes from inside themselves, perhaps from the audience, or from their fellow performers—frequently from all three. But when it's successful, the result is not meaningless uncontrolled chaos, but creative tension with often serendipitous outcomes.

Artists, notes Brad Gyori, an Emmy-nominated writer and university lecturer, are "serendipity hunters" who create strategies for serendipity "on demand." Indeed, artistic methods are often quite practical and much less mysterious than we might think. They are techniques for disrupting habits of mind to allow for adaptation and improvisation.

In the mid-1970s, the musician and producer Brian Eno collaborated with the artist and painter Peter Schmidt on a series of printed cards titled *Oblique Strategies*. Each one contained a phrase or remark intended to break an artistic deadlock, spark an idea, or set off a train of thought. Some of the phrases were quite practical, such as, "State the problem in words as clearly as possible" and others bordered on cryptic, for example, "Ask your body."

Brad Gyori calls such practices "disjunctive strategies." Disjunction involves breaking and reordering continuity, allowing audiences to make new and potentially interesting association via the intuitive recognition of patterns. Our innate predisposition to recognize patterns is often the wellspring of serendipity.[32] How does this work?

We achieve disjunction by changing space, time, perspective, and/or symbolic continuity.[33] Three effective strategies that we can adopt from the arts—and seemingly unrelated areas such as negotiation analysis—are 1) remixing, 2) rebooting, and 3) deconstructing. They challenge expectations and help us connect the dots.

Remixing

We tend to construct and defend positions and arguments.[34] We take a fixed position and try to argue our case. These positions are usually based on zero-sum game assumptions: The more you get, the less I get, and vice versa. An example is negotiating, where we often assume that our position and that of our negotiation partner are opposed.

At the start of term, students in the negotiation class I teach receive a briefing: They are supposed to negotiate a job offer. We break them into pairs so that they are in a one-on-one interview setting. One student is the applicant, the other one the recruiter. Both receive *general* information— which is the same for each—detailing a number of issues that they are supposed to agree on, such as salary, bonus, and location. Then, they each receive different *confidential* information that details their priorities, specified by the amount of points they get for different outcomes (e.g., "salary range between $40 and 60K" is worth x number of points; "location x" gets them x number of points). They do not know the other person's priorities or how many points the other person could get from these (or different) outcomes.

What tends to happen is that students assume that, for each item, their interests are opposed. The student who plays the role of the applicant assumes the recruiter does not want them to have a high salary and the recruiter assumes the applicant wants to earn as much as possible. When that is the case—and it usually is—it is indeed a distributive negotiation: the higher the salary, the more points for the applicant, and the fewer for the recruiter. Win-lose.

However, both also tend to assume that the other will prefer a different location outcome from the one that will score them maximum points. Surprisingly few people recognize the situation in which both have been offered a high points score for the same or similar locations. Such "integrative," win-win parts of the negotiation can be resolved only by exchanging information effectively.

There are many lessons to be learned from the exercise, but the main point is that we tend to see zero-sum games everywhere. However, often situations such as negotiations can be integrative: win-win. Then it is mostly about finding ways to make both people better off. This is possible if we focus on underlying interests rather than positions—trying to gain as much information as possible about the real underlying needs and priorities of the other party.

During the course, students tend to shift toward a more interest-based negotiation style, where they learn to increase the whole pie—by creating win-win constellations—rather than just increasing their piece of the (initially small) pie.

Interest-based negotiations depend on gathering information about the interests of the other party.[35] They are exploratory—they don't assume fixed positions, but rather regard positions as fluid and flexible, changing based on new information. Information is exchanged back and forth until there are possible—and often unexpected—solutions emerging.

This is most visible in another scenario used in the course, where there is no bargaining zone between the seller of a service station and a big company that aims to buy it. Students who focus on the initial positions will not find a solution: The price the company is willing to pay is far too low for the service station owner. In theory, there is no overlap if one looks at it from this perspective alone. We often see these kinds of (presumed) win-lose constellations in charged settings such as during the Cold War between the Soviet Union and the United States.

However, during the course of their negotiation, the students often discover unexpected solutions if they share information effectively. They recognize that they could still employ the service station owner even after the purchase, that they could sponsor his planned world trip with gasoline, and so on. This allows for buying the service station at a low price while keeping the owner happy.

Students realize that the price—their initial position—was merely a starting point, rather than an outcome set in stone. They learn to connect the dots when receiving new information—that the real interest of the service station owner is not the prices, but to live comfortably after the sale. In the end, it is about rethinking the positions they had at the beginning (here: focused on a one-dimensional price) and adapting them based on new information and the actual underlying needs.

This *fluidity* is also true more broadly, for example, regarding the development of people and their worldviews. There is a significant difference between the work of a young Karl Marx and an older Karl Marx, for instance.[36] In a similar way, many of us might have been drawn to political extremes at a young age only to become more centered and mainstream later in life.

What does all this have to do with the arts—and serendipity? Artists often eschew self-imposed ideological constraints. Shifting worldviews, embracing fluidity, denying a rigid, codified whole. By constantly combining and recombining ideas, they allow for new insights to emerge.

The Russian filmmaker Sergei Eisenstein proclaimed that when two independent strips of film are edited together, a "third meaning" is created—

tertium quid.[37] Or take the gestalt of art collage: It is all about combining disparate elements that suggest subliminal associations. The power of the remix, then, is not the individual elements but their relationship—and new, surprising associations.

Much can be learned from screenwriters, who note down scene summaries on index cards, then experiment with different narrative sequences.[38] The lesson is that a story can be told in many different ways.[39]

Disjunctive strategies such as the remix can offer opportunities to disrupt and rethink the status quo, and to look at unexpected insights and emerging relationships. By shuffling the different parts and considering different combinations, serendipitous associations can be made.[40] In qualitative research, this is often how interesting, counterintuitive contributions are identified. And it applies to business, too.

Take the Japanese motor company Honda. In the 1960s, their plan was to sell large motorbikes, given the usual preference of Americans for big-size items. However, when Honda employees in the United States used the smaller motorbikes common in Japan to drive to work, people frequently commented that such a version would actually be more interesting to them. Honda listened, and developed small motorbikes, taking on the U.S. market with its Super Cubs. They connected the dots based on emerging information. They saw something others did not, turning this observation into extraordinary success.[41] Management research has shown that strategic opportunities like in the Honda example often emerge serendipitously, often via different forms of remixing.

But it is not enough to just combine a wide range of perspectives. A basic level of trust and willingness to exchange are at the core of successful serendipitous encounters. Members of some well-curated, interest-based communities frequently exclaim "What a coincidence!" but the amount and quality of serendipity happening there is not entirely arbitrary—it is often accelerated by selection processes based on shared values and diverse ideas, as well as shared experiences and rituals.

Rebooting

Rebooting is about radical reinvention.[42] New ideas and projects and literature often build on previous work and change in radical iterations or "pivots."

Take comic books. Brad Gyori describes how story sequences usually have short shelf lives. After some time, when a narrative pattern seems exhausted, a new one overrides it, interrupting the continuity and returning the audience to the origin of the original tale with a reimagined version of the previous story.

Sound familiar? Well, I've certainly seen this pattern when observing friends go through midlife crises on their way to becoming a new person—though often in the end there was more remixing than rebooting! And I've seen it with myself after my car crash.

Rebooting happens when a whole sequence is reimagined. A remake reinvents a single work—a reboot reinvents a whole body of work. The remix reconfigures original source material, but the reboot wipes the whole slate clean. It creates a new origin story with new foundational concepts that can be built upon. It is not about shuffling the deck, but about a new deck altogether, with similarities to the old model and a significantly altered text. This frequently happens after periods of stagnation, for example, an intellectual paralysis in need of fresh insights.[43]

Rebooting requires a good understanding of both the original material and the disruption of familiar patterns to expose new (and often unexpected) insights. Take the same example for rebooting your life, or your organization. Sometimes it is just time to completely reinvent ourselves.

People often try to reboot via intense experiences, such as ayahuasca (a plant medication) retreats or hiking Kilimanjaro. At the LSE and at NYU, students collaborate with organizations in at-risk areas, where the students live among and engage with locals over a long period. This frequently leads to them questioning the preexisting assumption that one first needs to work a decade in a job one does not enjoy and realizing that one can work directly on projects that matter.

Where travel is impractical or impossible, virtual reality headsets can help people visualize contexts that would be difficult to get to—and at least in part experience what they feel like.

Deconstruction

Deconstruction is about looking beyond the structure of something and being able to discover what it might conceal. Instead of aiming to reach a predictable result or a final goal, deconstruction takes the logic of empirical wandering and blind tactics to deconstruct a text—often with surprising and interesting results.[44]

Grattage is a surrealist technique in which the artist flips her brush and uses the handle to scrape paint off an already painted canvas. Or take Gregory Maguire's book *Wicked*, a deconstruction of *The Wizard of Oz* that reimagines the life of the Wicked Witch of the West, a marginalized and vilified character in the original text.[45] This is about challenging assumptions and biases, rejecting cultural commonplaces in favor of exploring underrepresented voices.

Ancient Rome had the Saturnalia, an eight-day-long festival in which norms were challenged. Servants and masters changed places, men dressed as women and vice versa. This annual ritual temporarily redrew social distinctions, potentially serving as a means for catharsis.[46] More broadly, counterculture has often acted by inverting cultural norms.

Serendipity flourishes in these contexts, as these innovations are often spontaneous and unpredictable.[47]

Charlie Munger, Warren Buffett's business partner, in a celebrated commencement speech at the University of Southern California's law school in 2007 discussed the importance of "inversion," learning to think through problems backward as well as forward. He argues that problems are usually easier to solve if you start in reverse. Say, if you "want to help Somalia," the question you should ask is not "How can I help Somalia?" but something like, "What's doing the worst damage in Somalia? And how do I avoid it?" While we might think that they are logically the same thing, they are not. As in algebra, inversion can help solve problems that can't be solved in other ways.

Or as Munger's old saying goes, "All I want to know is where I'm going to die so I'll never go there!"[48]

Avoid Numb Data Mining

Remixing, rebooting, and deconstructing are about avoiding becoming data miners: simply going through information to confirm our existing assumptions. Instead, we can become *practical philosophers*, people who question, who do not take assumptions for granted, and who are open to shifting perspective and reading between the lines.

In many areas, questioning assumptions is at the core of living a good life. Murray S. Davis in his wonderful piece "That's Interesting!," which has inspired generations of PhD students, shows that there are different ways to make a theoretical contribution. One of the most important ones is to take a common assumption of the audience and try to deny it, or to show the conditions under which it does not apply.[49]

We see this with academics and artists, but it's also true for many of the world's most successful leaders. For our Leaders on Purpose study, we interviewed thirty-one of the world's best-performing CEOs. Most of them constantly question the way the world works. They allow for questioning and reversing assumptions—opening up an opportunity space for serendipity to happen.

Instead of looking for absolutes, we are better served by looking for what is significant in the context we are in. Meaning is not contained in one place, but things make sense in relation to each other—when perspectives collide. Then, in those moments of collision, we can spark serendipity.[50]

Indeed, an effective way to spark serendipity is to embrace opposing thoughts. Smart people often think dialectically: They allow for a thesis and an antithesis, which then helps find a synthesis (very Hegelian!). This is because reality is not black-and-white; nuance is the essence of life.

Humor Me

There are many other ways to train ourselves to connect the dots. Creative people often use analogous thinking—they take information from one area to help solve something in another domain.[51] Some ways to train analogous thinking include, for example, priming someone with potential analogies that will help them map possible opportunity spaces, which then increase the probability of finding a solution to a given problem.[52] Once we try to see parallels, we can find a potential solution.

Another way is to use provocative ideas to generate new ideas. Exaggeration or wishful thinking can be effective strategies to come up with the most radical ideas—and to then focus on emerging patterns.[53] In particular, stimulating playfulness has been shown to be useful for prompting serendipity and innovation. Many activities we undertake for pleasure fuel discovery, because they are often about breaking the rules and experimenting. They can take us out of what we already know and show us things we haven't yet figured out. That's where the magic happens.

Some communities use retreats into nature to help participants reconnect with their younger selves. They encourage people to not take themselves too seriously. And by helping them let go, they remove barriers and status lines. Indeed, Albert Einstein considered play to be the essence of productive thought, calling it "combinatorial play." Like a child with Legos, Einstein constantly combined and recombined ideas, images, and thoughts into different combinations—often visual. Combinatorial play under-scores a distinct skill, namely, to deduce matching pairs or sets of events that appear to be meaningfully related.

It's a skill Steve Jobs mastered. He famously reflected that creativity is just connecting things—and that when you ask creative people how they did something, they feel a bit guilty because they didn't really do it, *they just saw something*. It just seemed obvious to them after a while.

This is deeply engrained in human history. The ancient Roman phi-losopher and statesman Seneca (c. 4 BC–65 AD), who inspired many Re-naissance thinkers and artists, suggested we engage in what Einstein would later call combinatorial play: gathering ideas, sifting them, and combining them into new creations. In his *Epistles,* he tells us about the example of bees: They flit about and cull nectar for the production of honey, then arrange and sort in their cells all they have gathered. Via fer-mentation, separate elements are unified into one substance—honey. He likens it to sifting different readings, then bringing together these differ-ent sources in one. We must digest them, or they will feed only our mem-ory and not our reasoning.[54]

When we play—either with a new game, a challenging puzzle, or a new spectacle—we often make new bisociations. And while we're being playful, why not try some humor, too: Serendipity-prone people often have a good sense of humor.[55]

It's true of Alexandre Terrien. When Alexandre visited Paris, little did he know that he would end up at the wedding dinner of a friend even though he was not invited to the wedding. Having had a packed day, he arrived late at the dinner, and the only unoccupied seat was next to the bride's sister, Riwa Harfoush. He had been introduced to her online years ago, but they'd never met in person. When Alexandre arrived, he joked to Riwa and her parents, "I've been waiting for this moment for ten years!"

Riwa still remembers and treasures this serendipitous meeting with the man who became her husband.*

Thus . . .

Serendipity is not a single event but a process that depends on creating and seeing triggers and connecting the dots—allowing us to turn chance into good fortune through our own efforts. We can seed triggers in many ways, including by casting hooks and setting serendipity bombs—and we can connect the dots by constantly linking what someone tells us to things we have learned in other domains, even if they seem disconnected at first. Then we can expand our serendipity field.

But none of this matters if we don't put it into practice, so let's indulge in another serendipity muscle exercise.

SERENDIPITY WORKOUT: PUT IT INTO PRACTICE

1. Come up with a number of hooks that you can use in your next conversation, especially if someone asks you "What do you do?" Try to integrate three to five hooks in your (short) answer, allowing the other person to choose the one they relate to the most. Enjoy the conversation!

2. Write down a one-pager on your area of interest, with an interesting hook, relating it to your own story. Did you grow up in an impoverished area and find a way to unexpected success?

---

* Riwa herself is no stranger to using humor as a way to build rapport. She uses it as a way to prompt what she calls "moments of cosmic perception," those moments that allow us to look at the world in similar ways, that help us build trust. Humor can plant seeds and serve as incentive to connect the dots—and it's never too late to train to be funny!

Tell that story. Did having to repeat a year in high school help you find yourself? Tell that story. Then, put yourself out there: Reach out to your old school or university, or the university or school nearby to see if you can speak at an alumni or student event. You can start with a simple theme around "How an alumnus found their way to x." Or write a blog post on a platform such as *HuffPost* on a similar topic.

3. Set serendipity bombs: Identify the people you admire the most and whose details you could discover, whether via In-Mail on LinkedIn, email, or in other ways. Send them an honest message on how they have already shaped your life and how you would want them to be part of your journey. This is a numbers game, so be precise but do send this to as many people as possible—no fewer than five.

4. If you speak to groups, prepare for the unexpected: Have a joke ready for when a phone goes off in the audience; have a joke ready for when the projector breaks down; have a joke ready for when a joke you make falls flat. These are the moments that can bring an audience onside by portraying a comfort with the unexpected.

5. If you live in a city with a university or other public center (such as your local library), go to one public event per month. Prepare a good question that you can ask the speaker, ideally at the Q&A after the talk. This will make it easier for you to connect with the speaker later, as they will already recognize you. Try to get their contact details, and follow up immediately.

6. When you meet someone new, think about how you can contribute to their life and to whom you could introduce them. Introduce one new person per month to someone else. Think about how the two might overlap and mention this in the introduction, but do not over-specify.

7. When you run an event that is about connecting people, ask people to share 1) what they are currently most excited about, 2) their biggest challenge, and 3) their favorite serendipity story. Be an active listener when the other person speaks: How could something that you heard recently relate to their passion or challenge?

CHAPTER 6

TURNING SERENDIPITOUS
ENCOUNTERS INTO
OPPORTUNITY

—

Keep on going and the chances are you will stumble on
something, perhaps when you are least expecting it. I have
never heard of anyone stumbling on something sitting down.

CHARLES KETTERING, FORMER RESEARCH LEAD,
GENERAL MOTORS

Charles Kettering, who led General Motors' research from 1920 to 1947, knew back then what recent research is now starting to confirm: Practice and you get luckier.[1] It is not enough to just have a serendipitous encounter. No, you need to have the sagacity and tenacity to turn it into positive outcomes. This can often be the difference between a humdrum life in the lab and a Nobel Prize.

When Aaron Kellner, a professor of pathology at Cornell University, recognized in his lab that the ears of rabbits "flopped" when they received injections of the enzyme papain, he was not the only one. At around the same time, Lewis Thomas, a professor at New York University, noticed it, too. Both of them thought it unusual, but neither continued to investigate, as they were focused on other activities. The floppy ears popped up again and again in their work, but still they did not follow up.

In 1955, Thomas finally decided to follow up on why the rabbits' ears flopped and discovered that papain had an extreme effect on the ear's cell structure. This led to a breakthrough in understanding diseases like rheumatoid arthritis and eventually won him the Nobel Prize. Kellner, on the other hand, never pursued the idea further.

This was serendipity missed in the case of Kellner, and serendipity found in the case of Thomas.[2] But what had really happened here?

Before we get to the answer, meet Daniel Spencer, a technician who, quite literally, saved this book from drowning. I ran into Daniel at a repair shop after I had spilled coffee over my laptop. We talked about photography, his new side business. It was an idea that had taken six years to mature.

Daniel worked for Apple as a technician while following his enthusiasm for songwriting. However, more and more he realized that he also had a real passion for photography. There were two photographers on his team who taught him a lot without knowing it. Daniel treasured the peace he got from photography, and the joy of creating it. He reduced his time at Apple and started his first photography studio out of a friend's garage. When the first money came in, he left Apple.

He started shooting portraits and headshots for actors and businesspeople and called his venture "Turn and Shoot Photography." He wasn't sure why, it "just felt good." At that time, 360-degree images were starting to become popular online, with fashion company ASOS and others publishing rotating items to get a better view of them. The more Daniel thought about it, the more he noticed things rotating everywhere. "It was ultra-focus, like time slowed. I would see mannequins rotating in shop windows, or I'd play a game on my iPhone and the characters were rotating . . . it was as if life was screaming and waving at me to notice."

Something clicked, and Daniel had the idea of producing rotating actor headshots. He had done some acting and remembered being asked to turn left and turn right at auditions, and it occurred to him that there must be a better way to shoot headshots. He ran the idea by a friend, who said it was a million-pound idea. Yet he set it aside for months, even though he was so excited by it. He credits his procrastination to his fear of failure.

Eventually, he started to look into what he would need to make it work. He searched online for a turntable that could support the weight of a human but they were too expensive for him. He came across a competition to win one on Facebook. He entered and won. "It gave me a rush of 'This is it!' Not in a psychic way . . . but I knew I was going to win. I had no doubt whatsoever."

Daniel tested the idea with some actor friends and, after some persuasion, a casting company in London agreed to feature him on its homepage. The company called it "Headshot 360." The name "Turn and Shoot" started to make more sense. "Did I pick the name and choose my path? Was I already on a path and just taking the right steps?" Daniel reflected. "Who knows."

What the stories of both Lewis and Daniel illustrate is that we often have thoughts that might later percolate into ideas, based on a serendipity trigger that brings them to mind again. We might hold them back for some reason—perhaps we feel unworthy or "too busy," or that they're not important enough—but our brain is continuously and actively processing information, even when we think it is at rest.

This high level of unconscious activity can be traced by equipment that measures electrical activity in the brain.[3] This network has a major impact on day-to-day problem solving, error detection, and conflict resolution. We tend to unconsciously integrate multiple pieces of information over time[4]—and at some point, the eureka moment occurs.

People use the term to describe what seems like a spontaneous idea, but in many cases people have forgotten previous and linked ideas until some kind of insight, and later potentially a positive outcome, materializes and perhaps connects the dots.

This happens everywhere, all the time. In a recent Leaders on Purpose study, we found that many of the world's most successful CEOs stumble around before alighting on significant developments that end up shaping their own or their company's life.[5]

Only with hindsight and reflection did these CEOs realize that they had created an environment where, at some point, a positive coincidence had to happen. But it was only because of their tenacity and sagacity that it was possible to turn potential positive coincidences into positive outcomes.

The Joys and Perils of Incubating Serendipity

This points to an exciting phenomenon: Often, there is an "incubation time" for serendipity that requires tenacity and wisdom. We tend to perceive serendipity merely as a one-off surprise, but there can be a lag between trigger and bisociation, and then again until the ultimate opportunity comes to pass.

Research has shown that the incubation period of an idea (or bisociation) often can take a long time. We might not initially make a link, or might not feel ready, or might not assign importance to an idea at the time. This is the period between setting something aside and the "sudden" insight.[6]

Mundane activities—such as browsing shop windows in Daniel's case—can alert us to something that we might not have considered cognitively and which then, randomly and unexpectedly, pops into mind. At that point, we might suddenly have a complete, rapid understanding of how we could reach a solution—a typical eureka moment.[7] That's what happens when we have those sparks of insight in the shower, or when we wake up at 3 a.m. with a brilliant idea.

Incubation times are typically between five minutes and eight hours.[8] But this can be much longer—sometimes years, as in the floppy ears example. Either way, the true origin of an insight or connection is often forgotten or cannot be traced back to the moment of its birth.[9]

People tend to trace their eureka moments to a more recent meeting, even though the seed may have been planted earlier,* which is why it's good to stay on someone's radar, for example, by sending thank-you emails.

What does this mean for us? The legendary American advertising guru James Young employed a simple practice to engineer ideas that seemingly come out of nowhere but in reality were orchestrated. Imagine you are looking for an idea for how to design your new living room. You google examples, ask friends for their opinions, and look at the challenge from different perspectives. What is your style? What's your partner's style? Do you feel excited about the project? Would your friends feel excited about it?

Eventually, you find living room designs you like. Then you sleep on it. And then, one day in the shower, the *Aha!* might occur. It comes all at once but not out of nowhere. Rather, it comes from all of the potential dots and potential connections that your mind considered in the meantime.

What did you do? You gave your mind as much information as possible, then left it to your subconscious to figure it out. In fact, many people read about a challenge in the evening, so their subconscious can work on it during the night. That might not be ideal for a good night's sleep, but it can lead to a eureka moment after some incubation time.

This applies across contexts. Many of the world's most visible and successful serendipitous discoveries, such as Post-it Notes and penicillin, took a long time to emerge. The value of the respective discovery had to be interpreted and others had to be convinced of its merits.

But how can we develop the ability to turn coincidental encounters into positive outcomes?

---

* This has been a major challenge particularly for global innovation communities—how can you measure your impact if people do not trace back their serendipitous outcomes to the actual source? The hero stories that often are told usually cut out important pieces of the overall story, or people do not give feedback about it.

Overcoming What's Holding Us
Back—and Embracing the Next Chapter

Daniel's story is a reminder that we often, intentionally or not, hold back from sharing our ideas and thoughts for specific reasons—from being stuck in a particular relationship or situation to a more general fear of failure or being exposed as an imposter.

This book actually came out of serendipity—and of trying to overcome what was holding me back. I had planned for a long time to write a book on integrating profit and purpose, but I never felt ready. The book proposal was done, but something was holding me back. Then, a few years ago, I went on vacation with my good friend Grace and her family. Over drinks one evening on a beach in Myanmar, I told them about the latest developments in the realm I was planning to write about. Their faces were clear indications that perhaps the book was indeed not as original as I had thought it was.

They gently asked, "Do you have other book ideas as well?" What somehow came to mind at that moment was that in both my personal life and in my research, serendipity was popping up everywhere. It seemed paradoxical to me that some people appeared to create it all the time while others never encountered it. There seemed to be evidence that we can tweak our minds and that there might even be a science-based approach to cultivating serendipity. I had aggregated a lot of material over the last fifteen years that I could use.

Their faces changed immediately. "Now, that's interesting!" they exclaimed. That night, I wrote down everything that came to mind about what this book might be. The idea was seeded—serendipitously.

But while I attempted to start the book several times, I let it drift to the end of my to-do list. My imposter syndrome told me that I needed to do more research, talk with more people. And I felt insecure about opening the next chapter in my life while other chapters were still ongoing.

It took me a while—and many conversations with smart, wonderful people—to discover the power of letting go. Letting go of my own and others' expectations for making the book perfect. Letting go of the idea that I needed to close all the other chapters in my life before opening this one. Letting go of focusing on a particular outcome—and instead focusing on the joy of having space to reflect and make sense out of the last fifteen years of my life. Accepting previous decisions I was not happy about, remembering the context, seeing them in that context, and letting go.[10]

As someone who aims to be prepared for all eventualities—and to be agreeable with as many people as possible—I had to learn that not everything will always be fixable. Once I understood that, I started to wholeheartedly write this book, turning the potential serendipity that was seeded in Myanmar into what I hope is a positive outcome.

Brené Brown's research on vulnerability has provided ample inspiration in this regard. To her, vulnerability and bravery are two sides of the same coin. Vulnerability is often about showing up when you don't know the outcome. Brown actually credits her becoming "the vulnerability person" to a coincidence—and to seeing it through.

Several years ago, she was asked to give a talk at TEDxHouston. The organizer gave her no guidance on content, but told her: Just make sure it's a great one. She decided to not give her usual academic spiel, but to talk about how she often has to endure what she herself talks about: feeling vulnerable. She told her own moving story, and actually *showed* her vulnerability. This catapulted her into another orbit in terms of visibility because her research became relatable. She started embodying it.

TED featured the talk on its site, and it became one of the most-watched in TED's history, with over forty million hits to date. When she received harsh online feedback from several people, she tried to escape, going on a binge-watching weekend with the TV show *Downton Abbey*. Once she had finished it, she tried to continue distracting herself by googling who the key politicians were during the *Downton Abbey* years, and ended up scrolling through the lists of U.S. presidents.

One of those turned out to be Theodore Roosevelt. That's when she came across a quote of his that now is the foundation of much of her work, her belief system—and indeed, the title of her book, *Daring Greatly*:

> It is not the critic who counts; not the man who points out how the strong man stumbles, or where the doer of deeds could have done them better. The credit belongs to the man who is actually in the arena, whose face is marred by dust and sweat and blood; who strives valiantly; who errs, who comes short again and again, because there is no effort without error and shortcoming; but who does actually strive to do the deeds; who knows great enthusiasms, the great devotions; who spends himself in a worthy cause; who at the best knows in the end the triumph of high achievement, and who at the worst, if he fails, at least fails while daring greatly, so that his place shall never be with those cold and timid souls who neither know victory nor defeat.[11]

I have saved this quote on my screen to remind myself to pull through whenever I feel my courage is fading. It is something I have observed in many different circumstances, such as those of Charlie Dalloway, the restaurant staffer in London, in chapter 3—serendipity happens once we learn to trust ourselves.

And once it starts flowing, it tends to keep flowing, and it transcends our often-intertwined personal and professional lives. Bibi la Luz Gonzalez, a political-economist-turned-health-educator from Guatemala, was in the process of detaching herself from an unstable ten-year-long relationship with her boyfriend when she learned this. Bibi was already part of the Global Shapers, a youth community of the World Economic Forum (WEF), in which during the time, she found the companionship she needed. To get through the roughest days, she went walking, inspired by the book she was reading, *Wild*, about a woman hiking the Pacific Crest Trail (PCT) in the southwestern United States. She immediately connected with the writing—especially the aspect of "from lost to found on the PCT."

Bibi applied to join a regional Forum of the WEF in Mexico and was selected. She promised herself that she would get out of the relationship as soon as her project—connecting local Guatemalan bracelet products with global markets—succeeded. She attended the event in Mexico and met another Global Shaper who told her about another event, One Young World, a youth summit.

The experience in Mexico made Bibi feel that she was ready for her next chapter. She rediscovered her dream to be a nutritionist and saw the opportunity to link it to developmental issues. She was admitted to Oxford to study for an MBA (having graduated from the University of Warwick years earlier), but couldn't go because she didn't secure a scholarship. She decided instead to set up her own food security organization, Eat Better Wa'ik, and that year attended the One Young World Summit in Thailand as a selected delegate speaker—her first opportunity to address a larger audience about her organization. She had to crowdfund her trip and sent hundreds of emails to potential sponsors. In a serendipitous twist, one of the emails later landed her a job as an independent journalist and partnership specialist.

When she arrived in Thailand, she lent her power adapter to someone in desperate need of one. It turned out to be one of the staff members. When she later picked up the adapter, she got to know more staff members, in particular a sustainable development goal leader who introduced her to another organization working toward those goals. With her new contact's support, Bibi uncovered several opportunities in that area, and positive outcomes began to spiral, including speaking at the United Nations Headquarters and receiving the Obama entrepreneurship fellowship. This fellowship—a Young Leaders of the Americas Initiative—coincidentally placed her on the northern border of Nevada and California—and

Bibi found herself exactly where it all started (in *Wild*), on the Pacific Crest Trail.

At the fellowship, she found again a community that she felt close to. A "room full of weirdos like me, so I felt comfortable," she said.

No Grit, No Oscar

It always amazes me when I hear stories of overnight successes, when most of the time, the success is the result of years of hard work and perseverance. At any point on this journey things could have spelled bad luck were it not for the person's grit and persistence.

Grit—defined as "a trait based on an individual's perseverance of effort combined with the passion for a goal or end state"—and tenacity—"working hard and well"—are at the core of (compound) serendipity.[12] They can be the difference between longer-term success and what often feels like failure.

LinkedIn founder Reid Hoffman uses as an example of what he calls "positioning for luck" to debunk the myth that some people are just in the right place at the right time. Sure, timing is important, but it is the passion and grit that are at the core of success. Take Evan Williams, cofounder of Twitter and Blogger, and CEO of Medium, who coined the term "blogger." With Blogger, it was good timing, but what turned it into a success was the grit he had when Blogger ran out of money (as many start-ups do).[13]

At Sandbox, we initially planned a huge conference for inspirational young people, but the 2008 financial crisis hit and sponsors dropped out. We had to shelve the conference idea and started local community events instead. That's how our hub structure became a defining hallmark of Sandbox and subsequent communities. The whole team needed a lot of tenacity and a capacity for sleepless nights to make sure Sandbox would not close down. It became an opportunity to change course, and to develop a tight-knit community from the bottom up. We now credit the community's close-knit relationships to the fact that people first connected in smaller groups on a deeper level, only later meeting at a larger conference.

It might seem obvious that tenacity is important. But while we tend to say that hard work is often more important than talent, deep down we tend to believe the opposite. When your idea fails or you don't get the promotion, you might think, "I'm just not talented enough." Chia-Jung Tsay conducted a fascinating experiment: She told two music experts they were about to hear two recordings of the same piece of music, one by a "hard-working, striving" musician and one by a "naturally talented" one.[14] Both experts had a clear preference for the rendition by the "naturally talented" musician. Why is that surprising?

Because the exact same recording was played in both cases.

Angela Duckworth, in her great work on grit, shows that we tend to tell ourselves that we believe hard work is important. When times get tough, however, we often assume it was lack of talent that got us into trouble. Duckworth analyzed successful people in a variety of areas and showed that grit is indeed exponentially more important than talent.[15] What we tell ourselves might be right, even if we feel differently. What does this mean and what can we do about it?

Duckworth suggests we can develop grit by combining lower-level, daily goals that bring small wins and show progress with a broader dream or vision that is meaningful to us and keeps us focused. If you combine the two, you make it more probable that something positive will emerge. That means that good leaders and good parents need to be demanding and supportive at the same time.

Lady Gaga said it beautifully in her acceptance speech in 2019 when she won the Oscar for Best Original Song: "If you are at home and you're sitting on your couch and you're watching this right now, all I have to say is: This is hard work. I have worked hard for a long time. And it's not about winning. What it's about is: not giving up. If you have a dream, fight for it. There's a discipline for passion: It's not about how many times you get rejected or you fall down and get beaten up, but how many times you stand up and are brave and you keep on going."

Keep On Going

To keep on going often requires resilience. Robyn Scott, author and co-founder of Apolitical, a global learning platform for government, documented the work of a group of maximum-security prisoners in South Africa. Many had never been trusted in their lives. Many never felt they mattered.

Eight inmates who wanted to do something that mattered to make up for their crimes decided to support people suffering from HIV both inside the prison and outside in impoverished local communities. The prisoners had heard that a particular social worker was trustworthy. They asked him to help them help others. At first, he thought something like this was impossible. Gangs ruled the prison, white and black factions were at odds, and even musical instruments were banned.

But eventually, he decided to trust the good intentions of the men. The group of prisoners, supported by this social worker, connected with an eleven-year-old orphan boy nearby who had AIDS. They started to help him by sewing him new clothes, and they won the right to plant a vegetable garden on prison grounds to grow him food. His biggest wish was to fly, and the prison social worker managed to find a pilot who offered to fly with him. Together with the social worker these inmates made the boy's biggest dream possible.

These men, who called themselves "The Group of Hope," went on to change the lives of scores of men in prison, as well as hundreds of other orphans in the local township. The prisoners helped out the kids by growing food for them, throwing them parties in the prison, sewing them clothes, and giving them love. For the orphans, visiting the prison was the highlight of their month.

The self-imposed code of conduct among the prisoners was so strong that there was no major incident in ten years. The human connection between the inmates was intense, and orphans who wished for a family found one in the group. The meaning and dignity that helping out the orphans makes the prisoners feel, in the context of bead crafts they made and sold to support the children, that "we are rolling not only beads, we roll children's futures."[16]

People who are given responsibility become more responsible and take more agency, which in turn makes them good candidates to be given more responsibility—it's a self-reinforcing circle. The high-security prisoner who never in his life had the opportunity to feel that someone relied on him now feels he matters. The prisoner project in South Africa shows how recovery is possible.

While this arguably is a situation that most of us will not have to endure, many a lucky streak is preceded and will be followed by many unlucky ones. People will not usually tell us much about those periods, but they certainly happen.

How can we rebound from bad luck, to turn it into good luck over time? Lord Michael Hastings, the chancellor of Regent's University London we met earlier, develops a peer group around his mentees, many of whom grew up in disadvantaged areas in the UK. He helps shape role models and shows his mentees that the "truth" rests with them, that everything is possible. Mentee Sam, who served two years in prison and was released in 2017, became one of Leadership College London's "Students of the Year 2019" by developing this resilience—and turning bad luck into positive outcomes. For Sam, a strong faith in God helped him stay on course.

Michael inspires in his mentees what research has shown to be important all along: the importance of having the belief *that we matter; that other people rely on us;* and *that our behavior has an impact on others.*[17] Are there people in your life who make you feel like this—or whom you can help feel like this?

Bad Luck Today Might Be Serendipity Tomorrow

Our assessment of luck can change over time. We might interpret the same event very differently depending on the context and information available.[18] But if we stop once things get tough, it will always end up as bad luck. We close the chapter without allowing for other potential endings.

When an organization I cofounded almost went bankrupt, I felt as if bad luck was everywhere. Both our organizational and personal identities felt threatened. In the long run, it turned out to be a blessing: Moving away from investors and toward a more community-embedded approach was positive for alignment and longevity. But only in hindsight and after many unwanted emotional rollercoasters did it turn out this way—and it could have ended very differently were it not for the tenacity of some key protagonists.

And I still remember the day I was expelled from high school. Not only was I asked to leave the school and find a new one, but I also had to repeat a full year. Being expelled didn't feel great, especially when I already had a fear of rejection and a tendency to feel like an outsider.

When I went to the new school, I had wonderful teachers, but it was still a miracle that I somehow got through the German Abitur (a qualification required for attending a university).

With my miserable high school certificate in hand—and lots of "additional learning efforts" like voluntary presentations in my last year to at least have *something* on my CV, I applied to more than forty universities, and Furtwangen, a small up-and-coming university of applied sciences, gave me a chance. I went on to earn a master's and PhD at the LSE, and ended up teaching at both New York University and at the LSE.

There are two ways now to tell the story: that I went from high school to Furtwangen to LSE to NYU, "working my way up and having that bit of luck." Or, what rings truer, that I was expelled, had trouble finding first a high school and then a university that would take me, and then finally woke up and applied to dozens and dozens of universities for my undergraduate studies, then did parallel studies at a distance university to develop additional skills, and then applied again to dozens of universities for my postgrads. Only then did LSE accept my application and help me kick-start my career.

How does telling my story matter? My life now is full of serendipity. I found a platform that gives me the opportunity to encounter serendipity every day (apart from my introvert Sundays).

That was not the case in my early life, and everything could have turned out very differently had I stopped at the first barrier. What changed? My approach, sensing that there was more to life, trying to keep going even when it got tough. I have rarely encountered anyone who was lucky over the long run without being tenacious. Often, a road of failures or missed shots precedes the one on target.

Take Ben Grabiner, a successful entrepreneur in London: He pitched venture ideas to a number of venture capital (VC) firms in London—and was rejected. Rather than seeing this as the end of the story he kept in touch with them. He stayed on their radar and tried again and again. In his words, he was "pestering them."

At one point, one of the VCs reached out to him, impressed by his tenacity. Would Ben be interested in cofounding one of their new ventures, Platoon? Today, Ben co-runs the venture that was just acquired by Apple.

He allowed it to happen by being tenacious—and once an opportunity came up, he was ready to see it through. He is tenacious serendipity in action.

The Price of Admission to a Meaningful Life

Rather than trying to predict everything that could come next, these examples illustrate that we can work on being ready to cope with whatever life throws at us.

Our immune system works in a similar way: eat a bit of dirt when you are young, and you develop antibodies that help you later in life. Avoid all kinds of bacteria, and your immune system will be less prepared to cope later in life.[19]

Suppressing rather than embracing the unexpected makes us more vulnerable, not less. Rather than try to constantly manage risks and reduce potential error, we can instead develop the resilience and tenacity to be ready and see things through. Then, the unexpected is not a threat but an opportunity.

If we try to overcontrol situations, we make ourselves more vulnerable to randomness—because now we are trying to avoid, rather than embrace—the unexpected.

In complex systems such as societies, families, or our bodies, there are many interdependencies and nonlinear responses. Drinking alcohol might make life more fun, up to a point, but then it makes life much worse. Screaming louder at your brother doesn't necessarily increase the effect of your message—sometimes quite the opposite. Doubling your medication intake doesn't have double the efficacy—again, potentially quite the opposite.

Intervening in complex systems often has unexpected consequences: Just look at the wars Western countries failed to "win"—from Vietnam to Iraq.[20] Interventions often lead to worse outcomes, because we are often not aware of—or do not understand—unintended consequences. We make people, communities, and whole systems less resilient if we try to intervene and control without an understanding of the effects. Picture the overprotective parent whose child becomes anxious around people later in life. Nassim Nicholas Taleb in his writings on anti-fragility makes a strong point: Systems regenerate continuously by leveraging, rather than suffering from, unpredictable shocks and events.[21]

This is particularly important when it comes to emotions. We often try to push away bad feelings and see emotion as a flaw in ourselves and others. But rather than avoid them, we can develop ways of dealing with negative emotions. We will never try something new if we are afraid of the negative emotions that might come with failure.

Research by Susan David, a psychologist at Harvard Medical School and author of *Emotional Agility*, suggests that we view tough emotions not as something unwanted that needs to be avoided but instead as part of a contract for life. "You don't get a meaningful career or raise a family or leave the world a better place without stress and discomfort. Discomfort is the price of admission to a meaningful life." Indeed, a dissatisfaction with the status quo comes from high expectations, and productive unhappiness can often be effective.[22]

Similar to embracing uncertainty and the unexpected, embracing pain and negative emotion can help us thrive rather than thwart us—as long as we frame it that way.

Developing Resilience

How can we develop resilience more broadly? In earlier chapters, we encountered the importance of general motivation, adaptability, and learning from mistakes—in Samuel Beckett's words: "Fail again, fail better."

But resilience needs more than that. Adam Grant has studied this topic in depth, and his work suggests two approaches that can help us to develop resilience.

First, we can develop the ability to get in touch with our past self. Facebook's chief operating officer Sheryl Sandberg, who has gone through challenging times, including widowhood, has practiced this in many situations. When you are in a difficult situation, imagine what your past self would have done. Often it makes you realize that you have new skills that help you cope better. And if that does not work, think of an adverse situation you have gone through, and how you overcame it.

We can make mental notes of situations we have dealt with successfully, then remind ourselves what we did when we face a new one. I have done this frequently when starting to write a new research paper: it is gruesome to sit in front of a blank page but knowing that I have done it before takes some of the despair away. It also helps to write everything down roughly at first, and only in a second iteration try to get it right.

Second, we can change perspective. Grant describes how he makes his kids think about a challenging situation through the eyes of others. Building on the lauded work of Daniel Kahneman on decision-making processes, Grant argues that, in tough situations, we are in Kahneman's "system 1" mode (our fast, automatic, intuitive brain) but we need to be in "system 2"—the slower, analytical mode in which reason dominates.[23]

So what does Grant do? When his kids tell him about a challenge, he turns it around and asks them for advice. He asks them questions such as "What can I do to help you?"—to help them think through the situation from a reasoning perspective.

Related research shows how effective this approach can be. A study led by Hamilton College psychology professor Rachel White showed that self-distancing ("taking an outsider's view of one's situation") has a positive effect on perseverance, our ability to stick with something. Perseverance is critical but challenging in an age of distraction.

The researchers asked 140 children aged between four and six to complete a repetitive and boring task for ten minutes. The children were given the option to take a break by playing an attractive video game on a nearby iPad. The researchers split them into three groups. One group was focused on the usual perspective: The children were asked to think about their own feelings and thoughts while going through the task and ask themselves, "Am I working hard?"

The second group were asked to think of themselves in the third person ("Is [child's name] working hard?"). Those in the third group were asked to think about someone who was particularly good at working hard—a fictional character such as Bob the Builder or Batman. They were given a costume of the respective character to wear, and then asked, "Is [character's name] working hard?"

The children were then told to start with the work, and every minute were reminded of their condition ("Is [name] working hard?"). Everyone was told, "This is a very important activity and it would be helpful if you worked hard on this for as long as you could." The measure for perseverance was time spent on the work tasks.

Unsurprisingly, the children spent most of their time (63 percent) on the iPad. Intriguingly though, those children who impersonated an exemplar other (a character such as Batman) spent the most time on the tasks, followed by those who thought of themselves in the third person. Those with a first-person perspective spent the least time working.[24] The focus and perseverance increased the more the children distanced themselves.

This builds on previous research related to the marshmallow effect, where kids were asked to work on a repetitive task in the face of tempting distractions, such as marshmallows.[25] Those who could delay gratification and practice self-control were shown to fare better later in life with regard to money, education, health, and happiness. Researchers have called this "executive function."

Those kids who did well were able to reframe the respective object of temptation into something more abstract. For example, some of the kids imagined marshmallows as pictures—essentially, cooling the hot aspects of a temptation. This means establishing an imaginary distance—by imagining a cloud, or focusing on unrelated experiences.[26]

A similar effect was observed in the persistence study mentioned above. Pretending to be another person allowed the kids to better resist temptation and identify with the traits of the respective superhero.

The difference is this: Building self-control is about developing an ability to delay gratification. Developing cognitive control is all about the ability to ignore distractions and stay focused—which is arguably even more important. I have increasingly tried to apply these insights to my own life, in different ways. When I'm anxious—for example, about whether a license I've applied for will be granted—I tend to think about worst-case scenarios. Might the officer have interpreted my attempt to help ("Is there anything else I can do?") as an attempted bribe? Or could there be the risk of a formal irregularity, perhaps because I have two addresses in two countries, and they might think I wanted to trick them?

Such thoughts are huge distractions, and make me less focused on activities that I usually prioritize. In these situations, I now try to ask myself, "What would I tell a friend if they had these same questions and would ask me for advice?" It often makes me realize that from that perspective, the questions seem almost ridiculous. Once I adopt this approach, I understand that the probabilities of these worst-case scenarios happening are slimmer than the sausages I tried to sell back in high school.*

Developing resilience and perseverance is of course important in all areas of life. Going on a first date, we cannot predict the outcome. But we can learn to live with rejection and try again and again—until we find "the one(s)."

It takes effort and perseverance to turn potential serendipity into opportunity. People who make great things happen and who are "lucky" are, paradoxically, often very focused. They are good at filtering (see below) and persisting with the most valuable opportunities. Developing the ability to see a project through is particularly important in workplaces where there often is resistance against new ideas.

---

* Another option is, of course, to directly discuss these questions with a grounded friend—in my case, often my great roommate Nico Watzenig, whom I ended up sharing with serendipitously when we were both searching for an apartment and ran into each other in an elevator.

Seeing It Through

Harvard's Leith Sharp mapped the flow of hundreds of ideas and people across different industries, and across different hierarchical levels. Her findings are clear: The journeys of (serendipitous) ideas and projects are never truly linear, but are often what she describes as a "squiggle." Developing an emerging idea through an organization can cost a lot of energy—and not everyone prevails.

However, as we saw earlier, these ups and downs, including the rejections and drawbacks along the way, are often casually omitted from our narratives. This is dangerous, both because we set goals and position ideas in the logic of linear progressions, but also because we do not really learn from linear stories of success, which are often very different from the real story. In our need for the illusion of control, we often use language that is more decisive than it actually was at the time. In the stories we tell, linear tends to beat squiggle—but in real life, squiggle beats linear.

Often it is not even about overcoming the resistance of others. It's about being tenacious enough to follow through. We get in our own way. If I had a penny for each time I've heard the sentence "I have serendipity all the time—but I don't follow up on it!" then I would have upgraded to a new Mac already. It is the practical steps of sagacity and tenacity that turn something into opportunity—we need to do something with it.

In organizations, one way to do so is by developing touchpoints for employees to integrate their ideas into the organization. At white goods company Haier, employees can directly pitch their emerging ideas to an investment committee as they come up. At Sandbox, we used a simple customer relationship management (CRM) system to tag each contact after a conversation, and directly included a next-steps note. This worked to keep the team updated about the respective encounter, to keep it on the radar—and to create accountability and a bias toward action. RLabs has experimented with similar approaches. The team uses training material that includes questions such as, "What do you do if you meet somebody for the very first time who's interested and wants to know what we're doing?" or "How can I see the potential for collaboration?" Then, CRM systems can be used more effectively to determine whom to invite and with whom to follow up. In the end, tenacity and persistence can be navigated and facilitated.

But how can we know which serendipitous encounter we should see through? How do we avoid getting distracted? Or more succinctly: How can we recognize the value of serendipity, and filter those incidences that deserve our attention?

Having the Sagacity to Realize the Value

Original people do not necessarily have better ideas than others—they just tend to have *more* ideas, which increases the probability of developing a great one. Shakespeare is said to have written both his best and worst work at the same time—indicating that even geniuses have reasonably bad ideas—at least in the eyes of this beholder.*

I will never forget the first academic conference I attended: With high hopes, I went to a session by a management guru whom I had admired as a student. I expected to learn all about the future of management, but I was completely disillusioned by the quality of the idea in the paper he presented.

The reason? It was the early stage of an idea, one that would take another five years to be formed. He would go on to present it at numerous workshops, conferences, and in one-on-one conversations to get feedback.

---

* This is also why it's dangerous to compare ourselves to others, especially if we don't know them. People usually portray only their best work and experiences—and we get completely unrealistic expectations of what our life should look like. We might come to believe that there is a need for consistent greatness—though *even the greatest people are mediocre much of the time*. Everyone from the most wonderful management gurus to the most incredible poets has produced extremely bad work. A main cause of misery is that we tend to compare other peoples' outsides (such as their curated Instagram or Facebook feed) to our insides.

This feedback helped him to develop the paper so that when it was finally published it was an idea worth reading about.

This points to the importance of feedback at every stage as a major way to select and improve our ideas. Almost no one starts out with the big idea—often we have an initial intuition, and then we incrementally improve it over years of hard work, throwing out the bad ideas along the way. The quality of feedback—and filtering out the ideas that do not have potential—then is a major indicator of later success.

How can we determine which ideas or encounters might be worth persisting with, and how can we inform that decision? In some organizations, such as at Turkcell, artificial intelligence helps to filter ideas.[27] But there are nontechnological ways to achieve the same goal. Decision making and serendipity have this in common: The more information or potential triggers there are, the more opportunity there is for serendipity or a good decision. But only up to a point. After which there is information overload (see figure).[28] Exciting triggers do not help much if we are not able to filter them for those that are relevant.

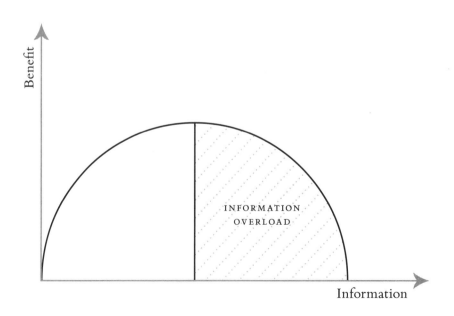

This means that we need to make information as relevant as it can possibly be—and avoid serendipity triggers becoming distractions. In a world in which distracting triggers are more commonplace than those that are actually valuable in the long run, we need filters.

Being Wise, Alone and Together

Filters can take a number of forms. A starting point is often some previous related knowledge, heuristics, or some sort of theory that helps make sense out of observations—and that makes them valuable to us.

We have touched on some of those, such as a sense of direction that we might develop at the start of our journey. But how do you go about this once the unexpected happens, and more important, how can it help us as a filter?

In 1982, when Howard Schultz was employed by a small Seattle-based coffee company, he visited Milan to attend a homeware trade show. Strolling through the city, he fell in love with Italian coffee bars. He recognized a potential solution and need at the same time.[29] He connected the dots and realized he wanted to recreate the Italian coffee bar culture in America.

When the founders of the company did not buy into his vision, he started his own company, and in 1987, he bought a Seattle coffee shop called Starbucks. He rapidly expanded it, and it became an iconic brand.

But Starbucks' key to success was not just about Schultz observing Italian coffee bars and how they could apply in the United States. Schultz composed a whole, implicit theory of value creation, which he iterated via feedback and experiments. This theory included questions and problem solving related to merchandising, store format, product sourcing, store ownership, customer education, and incentives.

His implicit theory of how to create value—making sense out of how everything fits together—guided these choices. Coincidence might have led him to the initial idea, but what Starbucks became was about solving a bundle of problems—and testing solutions related to delivery and customer experience. His sense of direction helped him filter. This was true for many of the iconic individuals and companies of our time, including Disney and Apple.[30]

While a theory can help us filter, we need more tangible approaches, too. Companies such as Pixar have developed structures such as "brain trusts" that allow them to screen and filter emerging ideas effectively by bringing in external people who evaluate upcoming ideas. I have found this works on the personal level as well: I have a small group of people who are part of my sounding board, or informal brain trust. When serendipitous insights emerge, I ask them for feedback. I usually ask two or three people at once—so that I don't over-rely on one opinion and not have an idea get shot down prematurely just because of a personal preference. Mentors, in contrast, have not always led me in the direction I felt most comfortable with. While asking a mentor for advice and using them as a filter can be effective, it can also shut down ideas or lead us in the wrong direction. We often receive advice based on "that's what worked for me"—which is idiosyncratic to the respective person's situation, and not necessarily useful for someone's living reality.

We—as mentors or as friends—often don't understand the complexity of the other person's situation. Some of the decisions I'm least happy about came from taking advice of mentors where perhaps I wasn't able to communicate the whole picture or articulate in full my priorities or values. The advice felt helpful in the moment, but in the long run I realized it might have been better to stick to a mature gut feeling—and a career coach or friend who has a better idea of the complexity of a situation and its context.

Functional fixedness might take over, and we might look at what we know to be true. Take the discovery of pleasure circuits by Peter Milner and James Olds, who are credited with the discovery in 1953. They showed that electrical brain stimulation made it possible to condition particular responses in rats. But Milner and Olds were not the first ones to discover this. Years before them, Robert Heath found "pleasurable brain stimulation" in schizophrenic patients. But Heath did not recognize the wider significance of his observation—in part because of his preconceived notions about the causes and effects of schizophrenia.

So, as mentor, it can be more useful to provide mentees with a framework for self-discovery, to allow for self-directed outcomes. Some psychotherapists, for example, use the (reverse) Socratic method, along the following steps: First, make your mentee imagine a desired state (e.g., reconciling with a friend). Then ask, "How/why/what needs to happen?" Then help them visualize the potential paths. Then help them believe in their dream/path, until they have a better idea of the potential puzzle pieces. Finally, ask, "What would it mean now to go 'all in'?"

This applies in companies as well, with the added bonus that it helps to develop buy-in. For example, a student in one of my executive education courses shared with me that once her company realized that management is often the bottleneck, they reframed the usual approach of people coming to management with questions, and management giving answers. (This outsources responsibility.) Instead, management now reframes questions back to their staff (of course, in some cultures this works better than in others; more on this later). So, when someone asks, "How shall I do x?" they ask, "How would *you* do it?" The employees know most of the answers better than management as they are closer to the action—and they take more ownership of the decision.

This is about letting people figure it out themselves—by giving them a simple toolkit, rather than strong advice based on potentially incomplete information. Helping people prioritize based on their own values and preferences, rather than ours.* This highlights the importance of prioritization.

Prioritization as (Inexpensive) Filter

You are on vacation and need to buy shampoo. The village shop stocks only two brands: one promising shiny hair, the other offering thicker hair. Depending on your preference, the choice should be an easy one. But suppose the only shop you can find is a supermarket with a selection of forty shampoos, all smiling at you with the same white teeth and the thickest, shiniest head of hair you have ever seen. Which one do you pick then?

If you are like me, you prefer the first shop: The choice is easy; you just pick the one that suits you better. If you can't decide then toss a coin. Interestingly, when there is a larger variety of items people tend to spend more time looking, but actually buy less than when they are faced with a smaller selection.[31]

When it comes to serendipity, we face a similar problem: How do we choose which serendipitous encounter to act or not act on, and avoid being overwhelmed by the various possibilities? How do we focus?

On a bus trip in Oslo, the former CEO of one of the world's leading cell phone companies revealed to me what has been most important in his life when it comes to serendipity: learning to allocate time. When to say no to things that we are not fully behind and focus on those we believe in. Of course, this differs as we age: Early in our careers, we often need to be

---

* However, we need to avoid routines that shut down creativity. The introduction of management system Six Sigma at 3M produced a culture of discipline with focus on execution that discouraged exploration and openness to the unexpected. Routines are usually designed to reduce outcome variation—we often want to be as sure as we can that we reach a result that we can predict (Austin et al., 2012). But these "predictive logics" limit our opportunity space, and we can design systems that allow for induced variation, for example by injecting some randomness. In the words of Ed Catmull, "Creativity thrives on the unpredictable!"

pragmatic with regard to the potentially limited choices we have. The older we get and the more wiggle room we have, the more we are able to choose based on what feels most right, being aware of opportunity costs and the like. This is reminiscent of the experience of PayPal's CEO Dan Schulman, who disclosed to our Leaders on Purpose team how he believes in experimentation—but what really matters is to have the systems in place to say when it's over and to learn from the outcomes.

Mike Flint, Warren Buffett's pilot, once asked his boss how he should prioritize his career ambitions. Buffett told him to write down his top twenty-five goals and once he had done that, to circle his top five. Flint said he would start working on them immediately, and Buffett asked him what he would do with the other twenty. Flint said they were still important, so he would give them some time when he wasn't working on the top five. Buffett responded that no, the other twenty are now on the "Avoid at All Costs" list; he should give them no attention until the top five are dealt with. (Fortunately, as my wise book agent observed, in the process of tackling the top five many of the other twenty might actually be achieved anyway.)

Once again, this underlines the importance of focus in turning serendipity into productive outcomes, particularly after the initial gathering of ideas. Often, the more senior we are, the more formal filters there are: We may have a personal assistant, or a chief of staff. But beware: These gatekeepers might keep potential serendipity from us. If your assistant says no to everything that does not provide immediate value to you, that is a problem.

Approaches such as opportunity engineering allow us to open the opportunity space a bit more while still limiting risk. They are about finding ways to select opportunities with a reasonable chance of a high upside or a very small downside. It's about breaking down a project into stages and dropping it cheaply if the early stages don't work out—or redirecting once it does not appear to work, as in the inexpensive, fast-prototyping methods discussed earlier. But that still often does not allow us to capture the unknown unknowns.[32]

In the workplace, training ourselves—and our support staff—to be alert to potentially serendipitous information and encounters that could be valuable in the long run—for example, by defining potential theories of value or opportunity spaces—becomes important.

At Nigeria's Diamond Bank, one approach was to include "low probability options"—options that were supposedly not core products but which might gain traction with some people (in other words, Diamond *placed bets*). The bank released a digital innovation to its 3.1 million mobile app subscribers. It aimed to digitize the traditional group savings scheme by allowing its mobile app users to connect with each other and save as a group. After a specified period, one member of the group receives the pool of savings on a rotation method. The solution was well received by the market, and adoption has steadily grown. But the surprise, according to the bank's CEO Uzoma Dozie, was that customers immediately adopted a feature that Diamond hadn't advertised: individual target savings. The adoption of individual savings was more than ten times that of the group one. It turned out to be an example of where digital can really work for organizations, as customers can pick it up and start using it for something unexpected. Diamond repositioned its advertising to promote the individual savings aspect—because it was something customers wanted to do, not just what the bank wanted them to do.

But how do we know when to focus on the unexpected? How can we filter the potentially relevant observations? Researchers Nancy Napier and Quan Hoang Vuong, whom we met in chapter 2, suggest that once we have noticed an anomaly or an unexpected encounter, and if we have the basic willingness and ability to evaluate it, we can do either a *flash evaluation* or a *systematic evaluation*. A flash evaluation is a quick assessment based on a gut feeling about the unusual information. Experienced eyes may spot ways to connect this to other information. Within companies, particularly numbers-driven companies, this will need to be packaged according to the respective dominant logic, standard, or language to be acceptable.* A systematic evaluation, in turn, is a more analytical assessment that can lead to a clearer indication of the information's possible value. This evaluation can include criteria such as level of uncertainty, timing, risk tolerance, and additional information that helps substantiate or invalidate the unexpected information.

The quality of the outcome will depend on this initial screening process, determining the nature of the potential opportunity. In the business world, the systemic evaluation of an investment committee can act as filter. Alternative filters could be peer evaluations, wherein people screen the ideas of their colleagues—assessing factors such as feasibility, desirability, and viability. Creating filters such as the above that help to increase the number and quality of meaningful encounters prepares the ground for serendipity at scale.

But frequently, in our own lives the question of filtering comes down to how many people to meet and how many ideas to explore. How can we evaluate that?

The Power of the Curated Encounter

Timothy Low, an entrepreneur and nonprofit executive from Singapore, describes how he developed his filter for what he calls "optimizing serendipity." His key challenges were to decide how many events are enough to optimize opportunity and how many is too many. He sees the scaling down of events and networking sessions like an hourglass: He started at

---

* Columbia University professor David Starck has researched into what he calls different "orders of worth." Every area (be it business, philosophy, or engineering) has its own logic of what is valued. A brilliant colleague of mine who is a psychologist by training accepted a job at a start-up company. She is an extremely deep, reflective person and has skills that would be valued in many contexts, but that were not valued in this fast-paced, fast-decision-making start-up. What this tells us is that we need to make sure that we align context with person, and vice versa. Or that we reframe the context. There will always be different orders of worth in every situation that will define the criteria we use to value ideas.

the top, where he crammed as many as he could into the limited time he had, and slowly filtered down to events that he personally felt inclined to go to.

His first phase was when he was new to the scene and immersed himself in as many networks as possible to understand fully the nature of the start-up world. He had to find out who its key players were, what the norms were, what the inside lingo was, where the cool clubs were, etc. He went to as many as ten events a month, and he felt that for a newcomer, this was extremely valuable. The learning was fast, and he made important links with people who would prove essential in his life. However, as time went by, the value began to diminish rapidly. He was no longer a newcomer and the learning had reached a plateau. The "value per event" was in danger of falling drastically.

This is when he entered phase two, where he began to scale back the number of events he attended, albeit without structure or much filtering. This allowed him to spend his time more efficiently, whether in terms of professional development (meeting the right people) or in emotional well-being (meeting friends and chilling out). This scaled down the number of events, and through a simple binary filter of professional versus emotional purpose he could maintain a high average value.

Phase three happened when he began to close himself off from new events. This meant that he only attended events where he could discuss various issues with people he was already comfortable with, and occasionally meet new people there who had already been "vetted" and curated by the event organizers. These were his "high-yield events" and networks. By eliminating his "low-yield events," in Timothy's words, "my average value per event skyrocketed. I was spending less time but getting more value."

Finally, phase four was based on the realization that the problem with phase three is that one siloes oneself into an echo chamber of sorts. This caused him to apply a more specific and well-thought-out filter to slightly increase the size of the funnel. His filters were:

- At the event or network I would be participating in, can I help?
- Is what they do related to what I would like to do or learn?
- Is there ground for constructive and intelligent conversation, or even discourse?

He reflected, "The average value per event remains similar to that of phase three, but because I'm able to expand my scope a bit through purposeful filtering, I chock up my cumulative value in a month to be double or even triple that."

Tim went through a process that is familiar to many: Start broad and then funnel down using evolving criteria based on a "theory of value" or current priorities to select which events to go to. But then, importantly, try to avoid the echo chamber many of us fall into.

What are some other potential filters? One is to use technology for relevance rather than similarity.[33] For example, to not only search by known items but also by items that might be meaningfully related. Technology nowadays offers to search by "known items" or by "serendipitous search." We can turn context filtering for recommendations on or off, change search parameters to reorder results dynamically or to control the level of range regarding suggestions.[34]

Just like in real life, narrow and rigid personalization can become a problem if it filters out proper serendipitous interaction, and we can find ourselves trapped inside a filter bubble.[35] New products and ideas usually are tracked from our search history and location—so might miss true serendipity by not integrating truly different (unexpected) results.[36] Personalization further narrows this down. However, research has shown that narrow search results do not necessarily lead to better outcomes, because narrow perspectives limit serendipitous encounters.[37]

Would the election of populists around the world or the vote for Brexit have happened, or been such a surprise, if we had come out of our bubbles? Our echo chambers have deep political ramifications. I will never forget riding with a Pakistani cab driver in London who was in favor of Brexit and said, "Now finally all foreigners are equal!" (referring to the fact that previously Europeans had more rights than other foreigners). Or a Syrian cab driver in Boston shortly before Trump was elected, who argued, "Trump needs to win. My family were legal immigrants and worked hard for it, so it's only fair that the illegals should stay out." I would not have expected these responses, and in my usual filter bubbles I would have grossly underestimated the existence of such perspectives.

But interests are dynamic and change based on different situations or over time. Like serendipity triggers in real life that can be either helpful or a nuisance, online providers have developed ways that allow for the incubation time of serendipity to unfold. Good platforms allow us to defer serendipitous ideas and bookmark items for when the time is right.[38]

We can also use an ideas journal to jot down our thoughts. Facebook strategic partner manager Victoria Stoyanova uses her iPhone's notepad to do this. That way, she is able to focus on the task she is doing—and to get back to those serendipitous ideas when the time is right.

Some companies I've been involved with used a parking lot system to store serendipitous ideas on their internal wiki when they came up in focused discussions. The planned agenda could thus continue uninterrupted and those ideas be revisited later rather than forgotten.

Filters are everywhere.[39] When paired with setting deadlines that challenge us without choking us, they can be very effective.[40] For instance, when writing this book, I made a deal with my publisher that I would deliver one chapter per month. The deadline kept me focused and accountable. I have practiced this in every project, especially in those where I am my own boss: Setting clear deadlines allows for motivation and accountability—and for getting things done.

But beware of those filters that are based on biases rather than effective screening devices. When J. Robin Warren and Barry J. Marshall handed in the report of their discovery that ulcers are caused by bacteria instead of bad diet or stress, as had previously been assumed, the report was not only rejected by the scientific community, but also they were described as "crazy guys saying crazy things."[41] In 2005, they received the Nobel Prize for Medicine for their work on understanding ulcers.

Even if we have effective filters, a core challenge is to give time and space to those ideas that deserve it. While serendipity may sometimes come in a flash, if often requires an incubation period. How can we make the necessary time for—and dedicate the necessary attention to—incubating serendipity?

Timing Is Everything

We need to give ourselves the time and space to let ideas emerge and shape up. Paul Graham, one of the world's most intriguing computer programmers and investors, in his excellent essay on "maker's versus manager's schedule" discussed how—depending on our type of work—we need to think differently about how we structure and manage our time.[42]

One of the best essays I have ever read, it has changed my life since I integrated it into my daily routine. It helped me to make more out of serendipitous encounters, and to be more productive.

At the core of Graham's argument is that a manager's day tends to be structured around short slots of time that are usually focused on particular issues. Lots of it is around managing people and systems. It is often reactive. The ability to make decisions quickly and smartly is essential in this context. For managers, meetings are a means through which work gets done.

A maker's day, in turn, is made up of long blocks of time that are about focusing on a particular task—for example, writing a book on serendipity, developing software, writing a strategic plan, or making a painting. Take Daniel Pink, the bestselling author. He goes into the office in the morning and sets himself a general objective, such as writing five hundred words. Until he has written those, he does nothing else, whether it's 7 a.m. or 2 p.m. No emails, no phone, nothing else. Pure focus. When you do that day after day, you end up with a book.

Admittedly, Daniel is among those people with the privilege of being able to control their time. If you cannot, there are also the many other ways to achieve focus discussed throughout the book. But even then, this approach can also apply to restricted time periods, such as a Saturday morning or a Wednesday evening. Even if we believe we are a slave to email and other people's demands, when we set boundaries people accept them surprisingly often. But if we don't set them, we will never get maker time.*

Blocking out emails and meetings is at the core of this approach. Meetings are costly for makers because they restrict the time they need for their work. A meeting cuts a block of time into two smaller pieces that now might be too short to get something substantial done. That's why makers often try to avoid meetings, reduce them by merging several into one, or put them into parts of the day where energy levels tend to be low, such as in the evening.

When I am working on a new idea, whether it's for an academic paper or a venture, I am creating or making something. I need a couple of hours in a row to get deeply into it and then shape a good text. In contrast, when I am in entrepreneurial funding mode, I run from meeting to meeting, one after the other. However, what I used to do until I came across Graham's essay was to mix my day: I would write a bit, then I would meet people, and then write a bit more, checking emails in between. It often left me frustrated but I couldn't point my finger on why.

Graham argues that when you are doing an analytical or creative task it takes time to get into it and you need to be immersed. If you then get a

---

* I have found a variant of the *paradox of weakness* especially helpful here: If we give ourselves an excuse—such as, "I'm sorry, but tonight is scheduled for strategic work" (and literally put it into the calendar)—it makes it easier to say no to people who "just want to grab a quick coffee/drink."

call, check an email, or have a colleague ask you out for a "quick coffee," the cost is not only the time that you spend on the coffee. You need lots more of it to reimmerse yourself into your work.

In contrast, when you are on a manager schedule, the coffee costs you exactly the time that you would usually spend in another meeting. The mistake I made for a long time was that I spent my maker time in a manager context and surrounded by manager people. At Sandbox I had the wonderful opportunity to connect with many amazing people, often for a quick Skype call. I did enjoy it, but I felt that I never really had the time to go deeper into ideas. The switching costs of moving between tasks and the attention residue were very high. I missed out on deepening the really important ideas. And I didn't feel productive. I now usually reserve my mornings for developing ideas, papers, and research, and use the afternoons for meetings. After half the day it feels like the making has happened already. As a nice side effect, it also takes the guilt out of sometimes being in meetings that don't feel productive.

I also intentionally slow down email communications: I usually check only at particular times of the day, and even then I tend to not respond immediately. People tend to get used to the rhythm, and many problems solve themselves. (Again, this is a technique that works better when one is not in a role that needs immediate sign-offs several times a day.) This allows me to be more present and motivated in *both* my maker time and my manager time—a key requisite for serendipity. This has had a major influence on my health as well: My stress levels have reduced considerably.

Companies have started to integrate similar approaches. For example, at some companies, Wednesday afternoons are reserved for analytical work, with no emails and interruptions permitted. Companies such as Google and 3M famously experimented with variations of a 20 percent rule, allowing staff to spend 20 percent of their time on whatever they are excited about.

This is even more important for introverts—who might need time to digest ideas or potential bisociations to make them truly fruitful. As Forward Institute founder Adam Grodecki reflects, many good ideas—and good leaders—"are growing in solitude, not in busy-ness." Indeed, we often mistake being busy for being productive. Almost everyone I know is busy and many people shut down to serendipity when they are too busy. But few people actually are really productive. Tesla CEO Elon Musk famously protects his maker times and reduces meeting times to short slots. Others have used office hours to cluster meetings and allow for sufficient maker time. Paul Graham, at Y Combinator, which provides seed money for start-ups, used office hours for founders, scheduling them at the end of the day so the day was not interrupted.

I have found variations of this clustering approach to be very effective: Whenever I have people contact me about having a coffee, I usually invite them to join an open dinner I'm organizing. It helps me focus my time, and it often leads them to meet other interesting people as well (in itself often prompting serendipity).

This logic can be used to structure both days and much longer periods of time. Adam Grant—one of the most productive people I have ever seen—makes sure that he puts hard and important intellectual work into long, uninterrupted stretches. He then clusters teaching and other manager-related tasks into particular periods, for example the fall semester. Other periods then are more focused on research, the maker work. These periods might include an out-of-office auto-responder on his email client so that he can focus several days on a particular research project without interruptions.

Experiments that compared the outcomes of programmers—some outperforming others by a factor of ten in terms of outcomes—showed surprising results. We might have expected characteristics such as experience and salary to be good predictors of outcomes. In these experiments, however, the most relevant factor turned out to be whether the programmers had sufficient space to immerse themselves. The most successful programmers worked for companies that gave their employees control over their physical environments, freedom from interruption, personal space, and privacy.[43]

This also explains why open-plan offices for makers such as researchers is often a terrible idea. (They can actually precipitate more sick leave and can have a negative effect on productivity, attention spans, and job satisfaction.[44])

The people calling the shots in organizations usually operate on a manager schedule and assume that their subordinates adopt a similar logic.

They often do not, leaving many makers frustrated and less productive than they could be. The way many makers take breaks are different, too: They might not be about interaction but rather about getting water or fresh air—the latter nurtures focus, the former takes it away. When I'm in maker mode, I try not to bump into people on my way to the bathroom! Multitasking and bumping into people might be effective for less immersive activities and for having opportunities emerge, but "mono-tasking" is often key when it comes to deeper analytical tasks. When my old university department introduced open-plan office spaces for researchers, I started doing most of my research in coffee shops and at home—and only came in for lectures and meetings.

Not everything that seems to bring people closer together actually does so—in many fields, we need to allow for a balance of making and managing, to allow for serendipity triggers, and for making something out of them. Otherwise, we not only limit serendipity—but also potentially harm health, well-being, and productivity.[45]

My Serendipity Might Be Your Bad Luck

Serendipity can change our lives. It can bring us success and joy. However, serendipity is in the eye of the beholder, and a positive coincidence for one person might be bad luck for another.

A police officer might randomly discover a small marijuana garden in a backyard because she tried to rescue a cat that was stuck on a tree. Good for the police officer, who might win the police officer of the month award. Bad for the retired pensioner whose last pleasure in life was having his homegrown weed for his own consumption without having to leave the house. Or take Theresa May's ascent to power in Britain, which was preceded by many unexpected events including the Brexit referendum result. This led to the resignation of her predecessor David Cameron as well as backstabbing among her main opponents, such as of the most probable winner when the leadership contest began, Boris Johnson.[46] Serendipity in this case is in the eye of the beholder, certainly not Boris Johnson's or a majority of the UK public's (even though, based on a similar chain of unexpected events, he became prime minister a year later).

And while we aim to enable and cultivate serendipity for "good use," like any tool or approach it can, of course, be used by the wrong people and/or for the "wrong" outcomes. Would you want to help Darth Vader turn what was for him a positive coincidence into a positive outcome? What might be positive for Vader might be bad for those we care about.

Thus . . .

Serendipity is not always about a single incident at a particular point in time, but requires tenacity, resilience, and the ability to see the value in, and to filter, a situation.

We must learn to let go when a connection proves fruitless or hold on and persevere when a spark is glimpsed to turn it into a practical reality—and have enough self-distance to make this careful balancing judgment.

At the end of the day, tenacity, sagacity, and filtering matter only if the potential outcome is meaningful—to us and to those that we care about.

SERENDIPITY WORKOUT: MAKING IT HAPPEN

1. Schedule times in your planner that are reserved for making. Treat that calendar item as if it were a real meeting. Build in an introvert evening or an introvert day. (But please note: If you are a maker and in a personal relationship with a manager, clarify it with them. It will reduce misunderstandings along the lines of "You don't treasure having me around.")

2. Start managing your energy based on when you feel most energetic—it's not just about showing up, it's about *how* you show up.

3. If you are an executive or event organizer, allocate physical space and time for makers within your company or community.

4. Start clustering your meetings—are there individual "going for a coffee" meetings that could be merged?

5. If you have children, ask them, "What would your favorite superhero do?" (Of course, ideally that character is someone who could actually help fix a problem—if not, go through different characters and see it as a fun game.)

6. Go through the most relevant business cards you collected at recent events. Send a follow-up, even if brief. It can refer back to what you enjoyed talking about or include a relevant link to

something that they might find interesting. Better late than never!

7. Once per week in a team meeting, have people reflect on three things that surprised them or that were unexpected. Ask if there could be value in them and if they can commit to a follow-up.

8. Set up your own informal sounding board that challenges your ideas. Reach out to them when you have new ideas. Ask people to question your assumptions, to help you rewire your mental models and connect the dots.

9. Reach out to top people in your field and ask for feedback on your ideas. Indicate that you were inspired by their work (the quality of your idea will depend heavily on the quality of the feedback that you receive).

10. If you are a student or researcher, send a short paper draft or pitch to the top five people in your field and ask for feedback. This is also a nice way of developing a relationship, as you create buy-in (naturally, it should be a reasonably good piece of work that you pitch!).

CHAPTER 7

AMPLIFYING SERENDIPITY

—

Never doubt that a small group of thoughtful, committed citizens can change the world. Indeed, it's the only thing that ever has.

ATTRIBUTED TO MARGARET MEAD, CULTURAL ANTHROPOLOGIST

An instance of serendipity is often seen as a transitory event, never to be repeated—but that is not the case. We each start life with a certain likelihood of being exposed to serendipitous events, what we might call our base serendipity potential, but this can be built upon, its process accelerated, and its results multiplied. That brings us a kind of *compound serendipity*—a process where each new instance of serendipity has greater potential because of the ones that have gone before.

The driving force behind this is the groups we are part of, such as our families and our communities, which includes our local network, professional circle, and interest groups. They can all help expand our serendipity field by creating a social opportunity space. But groups come with their own biases and preconceptions, so they can either accelerate or stifle serendipity. That means we must evaluate and map our networks with our eyes open to the risks and opportunities.

Remember Michele Cantos, the New York–based Ecuadorian educator who learned about the Sandbox community while working at a foundation that brought together children from less privileged backgrounds.

Her story does not end with a single incidence of serendipity: "When I entered [one particular community], serendipity started to happen all the time. That's great for me now. But coming from a background of poverty, it scares me to remember how little access I had to the opportunities I have now."

The biggest influence in her life was not access to money or education, but to specific information and opportunities—which are often guarded. When she started encountering those, her experience of serendipity fundamentally changed.

Or take Alvin Ross Carpio, who grew up in an area in East London where knife crimes were endemic. His father passed away when he was nine years old, and growing up without a father in East London was tough. He used to carry a knife with him when he was a teenager, but when he read that you are more likely to die when in possession of a knife than without one it got him thinking. When his little cousin asked him for a knife, he realized his actions had consequences. He convinced his cousin that he didn't need one—and in the process convinced himself, too.

Going to a good school changed Alvin's life. As the son of a waiter and a mother who came to England to work as a chambermaid, he was surrounded by people who had access his family didn't have, and he started to connect with intentional communities such as the UpRising Leadership Program and the World Economic Forum's Global Shaper community. He now runs a global movement to help tackle global problems, and is a familiar face on the Forbes 30 Under 30 list. In addition to a loving family, hard work, and the belief that everything is possible, he credits both his access to opportunities and his success to learning how to develop and access effective networks and communities. To him, embedding himself in these settings made the difference between ending up in prison (or dead), and running the global project he heads today.

Not everyone from disadvantaged and underrepresented backgrounds is as fortunate as Michele and Alvin in finding the networks and communities that can help them thrive. Some people get stuck in unfulfilling relationships or jobs. They might face severe systemic challenges based on race, gender, sexual orientation, or income. The ability to join the "right" communities has a huge social justice component. The groups we are born into have a strong effect on our base serendipity potential. We grow up in a particular family, a particular neighborhood, and so on. They determine the quality of our decisions and our initial levels of anxiety, fatigue, and stress, all of which are related to serendipity. Over time though, we can adjust and rearrange these groups—and expand our serendipity field (though if, and only if, we have the motivation to do so!).* Research on social networks can help us understand how.

Don't Be a Stranger

Social networks can help us develop productive benefits—our *social capital*—such as access to resources and opportunities.[1] They can help us improve our well-being. But those of us who don't have connections to relevant others—bridging or linking social capital—tend to have a lower base level of serendipity potential than those who do. A comprehensive study published in the journal *Science* looked at national census data on the socioeconomic well-being of communities in England.[2] The researchers had access to the largest-ever record of England's national communication network—the data from more than 90 percent of the nation's cell phones. They found that a more diverse range of relationships was strongly related to economic development: If you grow up in a disadvantaged UK region, your general access to diverse groups—and thus opportunities—is likely to be lower.

---

* I have spent much of my life in extremely resource-constrained environments, and have witnessed serendipity even in the most challenging of environments. However, there are major constraints such as disability or structural poverty that can make it nearly impossible. It is a reality for many people around the globe to start out with an extremely low base serendipity potential.

But that does not mean that you don't have social capital. It just means that it is hidden. We might well have more social capital than we think. Perhaps your teacher knows the local city council member? Or your spiritual leader knows the manager of a nearby drugstore? Maybe the corner shop owner's cousin is the mayor's personal assistant?

Jonathan Rowson and colleagues worked with communities in Bristol and New Cross Gate, in London, mapping and examining how social networks can improve well-being. They showed that "familiar strangers," such as postmen, are effective in spreading local news and information. In lower-income contexts in particular, they can provide interesting links to other parts of society.[3]

The problem with hidden connections is that we usually can't see them, and thus cannot factor them into our social opportunity space. Doors are often opened for us or could be opened for us, but we miss the opportunities behind them. Ever talked with the local priest about your dreams? With the local rabbi about what you're hoping to do next? With your imam about where life might lead you? These local super-connectors often relay information and opportunities even in the most resource-constrained of areas—but you have to know they are there. The yoga teacher, gymnastics coach, professor, schoolteacher, councillor, local police officer—they all meet and talk with lots of people. They are all potential social-capital "multipliers." It is up to us to develop and leverage this latent social capital.

Amplify It

Have you ever considered mapping your professional network to identify your latent social capital? That's what Brad Fitchew, a former community manager at Sandbox, did. The figure is the visual representation of his LinkedIn network.

Each dot—or "node"—represents a contact. The bigger the dot, the more connections that person has—and the more potential they have for connecting you to opportunities, spreading an idea, or getting an insight. They are the "multipliers."

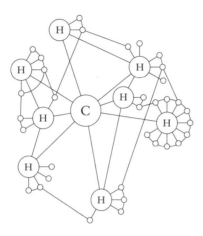

To get or spread an idea or opportunity across the LSE network (or any other network, for that matter), we do not need to contact everyone at the LSE. We target the key multipliers—the big dots that are well connected and much more credible to their peers than we could ever be. They can help access information, accelerate the flow of ideas, and put us in touch with others.

We can map any formal or informal network to identify the key multipliers. This is particularly important in organizations. We tend to be very aware of our formal network—our company's hierarchy, for example. Everyone knows who, in theory, is responsible for what, or at least they will be able to figure it out. But in reality, things tend to get done via informal networks. Then, our focus shifts from asking "Who is responsible for x?" to asking "Who do people go to first for advice about this?" or "Who do people call when they want to get this done?" Mapping these kind of networks—for example, via "name generators" that ask people about their respective network partners—can be extremely effective in enhancing your (or your organization's) serendipity score. And in getting stuff done.

But of course, this is a balancing act. Nobody appreciates being in your address book just because of what they can do for you. Rather, we should build our networks by cultivating meaningful relationships. There are many ways to do so, including developing an empathy for the challenges the other person faces—and perhaps trying to be of help.

It is far better to build those networks before we need them than when we need them. Remember Nathaniel, the creator of TEDxVolcano. He made something improbable happen because he contacted several multipliers. Rather than building networks from scratch, which takes time and energy, he leveraged his existing networks. Without knowing exactly what he would one day need, he had already developed relationships with key people, such as his contacts at TED. When serendipity struck, he was ready.

Nathaniel didn't build those relationships just in case an erupting volcano would see him stuck in London. He had built them based on being helpful and generous—not with a particular benefit or goal in mind—and so was well placed to benefit from the proxy trust given to him by the multipliers he connected with, in this case a TED organizer and a Sandbox member. Based on introductions from a few multipliers, Nathaniel could mobilize dozens of volunteers who acted as if they knew him already, because they trusted the multipliers who made the introduction and the communities they represented.[4]

What does this mean for us? We don't need to know everyone, and we don't need to build enormous networks. Rather, we can develop meaningful relationships with multipliers—and join or cultivate interest-based *communities* that give us proxy trust.

Compounding Your Serendipity Score

Communities are more than just networks. While networks can help us with particular relationships, communities—networks of interpersonal ties that provide a sense of belonging and social identity—can change our base level of serendipity.

As in the example of Michele, effective communities don't just accelerate serendipity a little (linearly); they do it a lot (exponentially). They follow a power law.

How do we lay the foundations for that? Understanding how effective communities function can help us navigate them. Well-curated communities can help us to qualitatively change, and improve, our experience of serendipity. We can develop our own interest-based communities or join existing ones.

Making Weak Ties Strong by Affiliation

Historically, communities were built on what sociologist Mark Granovetter calls "strong ties"—people we know well.[5] Think of tight-knit neighborhoods and church-based communities. These relationships tend to be local, trusted, and supportive. But they don't often reach far and they tend to not be very diverse. It takes lots of time and effort to maintain strong ties, and we are limited in how many we can develop—there's only so much time (and energy) in the day!

"Weak ties," in contrast, tend to be widespread, diverse, and potentially far-reaching, but often are not very actionable. Think of the person you met on Twitter, with whom you've interacted only a couple of times. Weak ties can be effective for general information exchange and access to opportunities, but you probably won't move mountains for that person—and vice versa. If you have only strong ties, you might receive great emotional support, but your reach and access to information and opportunities will be limited. If you only have weak ties, your support system might not be strong enough. However, well-curated interest-based communities, in the words of Fabian Pfortmüller, use "weak ties as if they were strong ties." These communities combine the power of strong ties with the power of weak ties. There is a proxy trust that makes weak ties strong by affiliation.

What does this mean? Remember Nathaniel. He was able to act on the unexpected: He had a great idea, a moment of opportunity, and some experience in organizing events, but that wasn't enough. He needed to find locations, volunteers, food, speakers, technology—everything necessary for a good conference. What did he do? He connected with multipliers and tapped into existing communities. He connected with TED, which gave him the brand and access to speakers; he contacted Sandbox, which helped him with volunteers, logistics, and exposure. People connected him with a TechCrunch.com editor, a multiplier in the technology and media space, who helped promote the event.

Essentially, people Nathaniel knew only slightly or not at all gave him their brand and helped him organize a full-fledged conference. He used weak ties as if they were strong ties—legitimized by the respective "multipliers" (TED) or being a member of the same community (Sandbox). Nathaniel did not know what he would need in advance, but given existing proxy trust and diversity in those communities and his interesting cause, he activated their members as if they were his friends.

Not every example is as extreme. When Sandbox members are traveling, for example, they will often be able to reach out to members in different cities even if they don't know them. Members will offer a couch to someone they have never met. In an increasingly networked world in which boundaries of tasks and organizations are fluid and permeable, we are more reliant on people outside our usual spheres of influence. We need weak ties—and effective interest-based communities can be a way to make them actionable as if they were strong ties.

Effective communities—be they of two, ten, or hundreds of people—provide an environment that fosters meaningful exchange and trust. How do you develop such an environment?

Building a Tight-Knit Community

To begin with, consider why the members of the community have come together. Is it their background, their interests, their passions, their shared values? The question of "common denominators" is at the core of community building of all kinds, from football to painting, to innovation, you name it. The larger the group, the more we need to implicitly or explicitly articulate this common denominator. Larger interest-based communities use language (e.g., "family"), rituals (e.g., hugs), or welcoming people in particular ways online or offline (e.g., by introducing them at the next dinner).

But communities that are too strongly knit can hold us back, especially if they are not diverse enough. Over-embeddedness in particular communities can lead to parochialism and echo chambers. Can you imagine the difference in the Facebook feeds of a Republican or Conservative voter and those of a Democrat or Labour voter? We are often born into those kinds of communities, and often out of convenience or necessity we stay close to our roots.

An extreme case arose in my research with Kenyan economist Robert Mudida, who runs the Centre for Competitiveness at Nairobi's Strathmore University, where we studied ethnic networks in sub-Saharan Africa. In this context, tribal affiliations are at least as powerful as political divides in the United States or the UK, and many people tend to stay in their homophilous ("similar to me") networks—with little opportunity to develop weak ties, which tend to be crucial for serendipity.

The successful, enterprising individuals in our study, in contrast, developed cross-ethnic networks. They redefined the in-group by framing it away from ethnicity and toward interest-based networks, for example, centered on sports or religion. A Kenyan entrepreneur in our study sat next to the other-tribe governor in church, reminding him—and any observers—that they have something in common. Studies in other contexts show similar results.[6]

How does this play out in your life? Are you operating in the close confines of your in-group, perhaps a close-knit friendship group or a siloed department? Are there common denominators with people in other groups to whom you could reach out?

Opening up to other groups can start with small actions. Groups that bring together people with diverse perspectives tend to nurture serendipity. But there needs to be a common denominator that helps people trust each other and have an incentive to share ideas. Diversity alone does not help if there is no glue to hold people together.[7]

Growing Without Losing Touch

Communities need to be inspired rather than controlled, and anchors that shape the conversation can help with this. This is why the multiplier approach is particularly effective for larger communities and organizations.

A major reason the Sandbox community expanded into over twenty countries in a few years was that we introduced an "ambassador" system. We identified people who were temporarily in the cities where we were based, perhaps because they were studying there, and nominated them to become ambassadors when they returned home.

How? The founders listed all inspirational people we knew on a shared wiki document, agreed on who would be a good fit, then contacted them.

At the beginning, they mostly got involved out of friendship, but later on, more and more out of excitement. As in many other communities, the incentives were nonmonetary but comprised, for example, increased status or visibility, which can potentially compound serendipity for the person because they are at the core of the action and so people tend to tell them first about new ideas, etc.[8] Ambassadors tended to be most active when the role integrated with their other activities, especially their professional life. Someone who organizes events for a living anyway is more inclined to perform a similar role in other groups than, say, someone working as a trader on Wall Street.

These ambassadors—usually in teams of two to four—put together local events and identified potential members in their respective cities. Using a snowballing approach, we asked them to refer other inspiring people. They contacted potential members, organized events for them, and developed local spaces for experimentation (such as challenge nights, which provided a space for members to present current challenges or projects). We, as the central team, supported them with best practice manuals and internal Facebook groups, and by linking it all together.*

By developing these super-nodes, Sandbox very quickly created a tight-knit, global community of over a thousand people. We initially limited local hub membership to between 80 and 130, based on the finding that we can only develop truly meaningful relationships with a relatively small number of people.† Then, people have a strong local base, and whenever they travel, they can just plug into other hubs, or connect directly with other members online.

---

* Later on, as the number of candidates increased, we took a more structured approach toward the application process. But often these multipliers emerged informally, and we identified them, for example, based on their higher level of engagement—and then "legitimized" them. More generally, showcasing examples of members being helpful to each other can be an effective approach to inspire others to do the same—behaviors are stronger than words!

† This resembles the logic of Dunbar's number: Robin Dunbar suggested that the maximum number of connections for a human being is somewhere in the 100–250 range (Hernando et al., 2009).

This approach of linking local multipliers with a global platform has enabled communities such as Sandbox, Nexus, Global Shapers, and TED/TEDx to develop a global presence with a very small core team and limited resources. Local multipliers bring in social capital and help adapt the global framework to local traditions.

At the core of these trusted environments are events that nurture meaningful interactions.

Nurturing Meaningful Interactions

During many years spent building communities, I've often come across people who say, "Great, let's do a networking event" or "Let's build in a networking break at the conference." The term "networking" gives me shivers—it misses the deeper significance behind meaningful relationships: trust. Have you ever met someone who genuinely enjoys going to a networking event? A focus on making connections tends to attract the wrong people—those with an agenda. It puts people on the spot, and it makes for artificial and superficial conversations. It's like attending a speed-dating event: You attract people who tend to be focused on a particular outcome.

Good relationship-building events, in contrast, focus on particular themes, interests, or passions, so that people can dive deeper into something together, or exchange ideas on subjects they care about. Based on meaningful conversations, more trusted relationships can be developed, and thus, seeding viable ground for the really interesting potential serendipity.

Well-curated events are a powerful way to embody what you or a community stand for. At Sandbox, we used informal dinners, where members would come together in a relaxed environment to share stories and develop relationships. The relaxed venue—particularly for people who are not used to spending time in such informal ways with near strangers—leads to a more open, and potentially more trusting, mindset. Games such as "rose, bud, thorn"—which ask questions such as "What was the highlight of your day/week/month/year?" (rose), "What went wrong during your day/week/month/year?" (thorn), and "What are you looking forward to tomorrow/next week/next month/next year?" (bud)—help people reflect on their real challenges—rather than bragging about how great they are (or think they are!).

Good relationships tend to form when people share interests or passions. They naturally happen at events that focus on developing meaningful relationships rather than on collecting business cards. Indeed, at almost every Sandbox meeting that I have attended—whether in London, Zurich, New York, Singapore, Mexico City, Nairobi, or Beijing—I have heard someone exclaim "That's such a coincidence!" (In fact, sometimes what seems unexpected to one might not be unexpected to another. Bertrand Russell's allegory, whereby a turkey that has been kept for weeks and fed daily is surprised to be killed before Christmas, does hold here as well.[9])

Over-engineered networking—or for that matter, serendipity—leads to the opposite effect. In a recent paper, LSE's Harry Barkema and I show how an incubator created an environment for serendipity. Having realized that standardized programs to support ideas and enterprises can go only so far—especially given that the ideas and needs of aspiring enterprises often change, and that overly structured events could kill rather than facilitate serendipity—the team realized that it needed to set up an environment to "engineer serendipity" instead.

This included seating a diverse range of people—for example, of different cultural or professional backgrounds—with shared values next to each other; setting up a coffee shop that would let people bump into one another; and creating an atmosphere in which serendipity is celebrated, supported, and invested in. Well-curated events allow people to come together in a more natural way than more "sterile" experiences.[10]

Keeping One Another Accountable

Even tight-knit groups can fall victim to the "tragedy of the commons." This is when a shared resource such as a trusted platform is depleted and ultimately fails because no one takes responsibility for it. Many communities die because of this neglect, and many others have freeloaders who enjoy the benefits of the group without putting any work into its upkeep. Perhaps you have joined one of the millions of online communities that have become inactive? Or perhaps you had a person on your team who didn't really contribute but still basks in the glory of what the rest achieved?

That's why "lateral accountability"—accountability to oneself and among one's peers[11]—is at the core of many successful interest-based communities. In contrast to hierarchical control, which is tough and expensive to monitor, lateral accountability often works as a positive externality of close collaboration. By being visible to the rest of the group, individuals have an incentive to not disappoint their peers; they develop an enlightened self-interest.

In some of the companies I've been involved in, we used weekly goals that were visible to the whole group: Every team member—including the founders and the CEO—updated their goals weekly, explained why they had or had not achieved them, and shared what they had learned in the process. This was good for morale, motivation, and self-regulation. It also helped us to connect the dots more effectively because we had a better idea of what the others were working on.

What This Means for Our Relationships

Successful people are often part of strong communities, or they develop a "tribe" around them with whom they go through life. Groups such as the

Young Presidents Organization have used these kinds of "circles" to enable trust-based conversations among members. In their case, a small number of their members interact regularly to support each other in their challenges. Ideally, these support and learning communities include people at similar life stages and with aligned values, but from different backgrounds.

And of course, our romantic relationships deserve a more conscious approach, too. Boston-based Natalya Bailey, an aerospace engineer and CEO of Accion Systems Inc., and her husband Christian Bailey, a community-builder and entrepreneur, practice three questions in their relationship. In the morning, they ask each other, "What do you want to achieve today?" and "How can I support you?" In the evening they ask each other, "What did you learn today?" The morning questions indicate an *other-focus*, and start the day with the feeling of having helped and being part of each other's lives. The question in the evening focuses on learning, on sharing observations. They are one of the most mutually trusting couples I have encountered and have created a beautiful family and tribe around themselves, and quite a few of my friends have adopted this exercise.

Sure, at the beginning it feels strange to ask your partner these kinds of questions. But while you will probably stop asking the exact questions after some time, the other-focus—and making sure that the other is an active part of our daily life—stays. I've tried it in different relationships, with varying results, but it certainly always increases both self- and other-awareness.

But the more important point here is that relationships of all types benefit from conscious rituals that enable meaningful interaction. What rituals could you implement in your own relationships or groups to foster trust and an open mind at the same time? The exact ritual matters less than the habit and the awareness you create.

Beware the Perils of Social Dynamics

Networks and communities can become serendipity accelerators. But there is a dark side to groups and relationships, too. As we've established, serendipity often relies on meaningful connection rather than hidden agendas. A female entrepreneur shared with me that men, often powerful men, would use these conversations to proposition her. The ambiguity of conversation can make it hard to call out this behavior as inappropriate— but an uncomfortable feeling remains. These potentially threatening settings are not only limiting the potential for serendipity (why would I want to connect the dots in a situation from which I would like to escape?), but also a stain on every other topic of conversation. Hidden agendas, biases, and inequalities can be found everywhere.

Serendipity can also skew our perception and deepen inequalities. For example, most democratic societies limit the ability of the police to stop and search people in the street. Even if the tactic might uncover some criminal activity and perhaps make others wary of breaking the law, it can be counterproductive because of the negative effect on innocent people who are stopped, particularly when the people being stopped are chosen by criteria having nothing to do with the crime, such as race.

In the UK, where three hundred thousand stop-and-searches were carried out in the 2016–2017 financial year,[12] black people were at least eight times more likely to be stopped by police than white people. Since police will always "coincidentally" find something illegal if they search enough people, this kind of serendipity can have all kinds of self-reinforcing and negative effects, from giving police more reasons to stop people of color to creating a social stigma that links black people to crime.*

---

* This negative serendipity and the social dynamics around it are often linked to racial bias or power structures. In some contexts, mafia-type structures render superficial support programs, for example via microfinance, meaningless.

Scottish novelist William Boyd has referred to the phenomenon of negative serendipity as "zemblanity" ("the faculty of making unhappy, unlucky, and expected discoveries by design"[13])—which can also be compounded. General Services Administration Counsel Richard Beckler supposedly assured the Trump transition team that any record requests from Special Counsel Robert Mueller's office would be directly referred to the transition team's attorneys. The only problem? He was hospitalized and died shortly thereafter. This "unpleasant surprise" compounded the Trump administration's problems.

And there are local cultures and belief systems.[14] In contexts that are marked by a high "power distance" (lower-ranking individuals accept and expect that power is distributed unequally), it might be harder to trigger serendipity, because hierarchical boundaries are more difficult to cross. In more age- or seniority-based cultures, it might be more difficult to spark serendipity between the old and the young. And in contexts with a low tolerance for unpredictability, risk management and accepting the "one truth" might curtail potential serendipity if the opinion of a teacher or senior executive is taken as given, there is not much space for unexpected solutions to emerge.

Of course, there are other conditions under which serendipity is curtailed, or where we do not need or want serendipity. In tightly controlled systems such as nuclear reactors or spaceships, focus is and should be on execution, rather than novelty.

Our Responsibility in (Amplifying) Serendipity

Inequality comes in many forms, even if we think that we have tackled it already. Take a less-privileged girl from a poor inner-city area. Even if she was fortunate enough to attend a very good school and gets exactly the same education as a girl from a middle-class background, she will still most likely have fewer positive coincidences.

Why? For one, much of what could potentially trigger or facilitate serendipity—such as a conversation over dinner with her parents about something related to what she had just learned in school—might happen less frequently. She might run into fewer people with whom she can experience serendipity. And she, in the end, will need to fight much harder to "make her own luck," given that her support systems might be limited.

Thus, in our design of school systems, apprenticeship systems, and the like, we need to keep in mind that it is less about content and direct access to opportunity, and more about helping build social opportunity spaces.

One way to do that is reclaiming areas of social deprivation, for example, involving arts organizations that can bring people together (and help bring crime down in the process). The idea is to move away from segregation by social group—parts of the population keeping their curtains down for fear of being detected is quite literally a sign of disconnectedness.

Stereotypes proliferate if we do not interact with each other. This applies across social, racial, tribal, and gender groups alike. But experiments in public services have shown promising signs already. Some city governments arrange a kind of professional speed-dating with young people and council members, connecting them with people they would usually not interact with. This shows them that unexpected opportunities are available, and connects them to a broader pool of ideas (more on these approaches in the next chapter).

Pairing people up in a more structured fashion with mentors who are close to their reality but now have access to different types of networks can be effective, too. It's great to have someone like Virgin founder Richard Branson visit a high school for an hour, but people relate better to someone who started out in similar conditions and shared similar struggles. Perhaps someone who came out of poverty now runs a successful business? Such a person would allow people to "visualize" themselves taking similar paths.

Perhaps there is even a way to go beyond one-hour catch-ups—enabling people to shadow their role models for a couple of days, to see what they really do every day? There is a reason many religious leaders have disciples—it is about learning over time, picking up non-codified, tacit knowledge that we cannot learn in school. We need exposure to it, we need to see different people in action, which can help us realize that there are different potential lives we can live and different routes that can be taken.

For education programs—including schools and incubators—the fact that ideas and people "pivot" and change over time needs to be integrated into them so they do not focus too much on structured content and particular mentors (e.g., per subject area). Instead, helping them develop a serendipity mindset that makes the best out of the unexpected becomes key, especially once they move away from the initial subject area. Rather than seeing changes as a weakness of the student or entrepreneur, they can be embraced as a sign of intelligence based on new information.

This approach can also include helping individuals develop their social skills for bridging different groups. Coupling people from varying backgrounds (including those of teachers, mentors, etc.) can be effective in this regard.[15]

Thus . . .

Compound serendipity works like compound interest: The higher the base level, the faster you can accelerate. But even if we start out with a low base serendipity potential, (almost) all of us can be more aware about the best kind of groups and people to connect to. We can start realizing our existing social capital—funnily enough, using it does not decrease it, but might even strengthen these relationships—and connect with the multipliers in our lives. We can join larger interest-based communities and leverage the proxy trust they give us.

If we develop a community ourselves, we can develop proxy trust in several ways, including via rituals and introducing peer-to-peer accountability and shared experiences. Then, weak ties either start to become strong ties, or they start working as if they were strong ties. Overcoming the boundaries of groups that might hold us back—and bridging to other groups—can be accomplished by reframing what we have in common and setting up our own small "tribes." This helps find a balance between cohesion and diversity—the engine of serendipity. The world is not fair, but we can tackle social inequalities by helping to develop social opportunity spaces that allow others to spot and connect the dots.

Until now, we have focused on what we as individuals can do to facilitate serendipity in our and other people's lives. But there's also the important role of facilitating nurturing conditions in organizations and in policy. The next chapter focuses on this from the perspective of company executives and policy makers—in case this is not your cup of tea, you can skip this chapter and directly go to chapter 9, which will focus on how you can increase your serendipity score.

But before getting there, the serendipity exercise in this chapter focuses on how we can increase our serendipity base level.

SERENDIPITY WORKOUT

1. Identify five people—existing contacts or people with whom you would like to develop a relationship—and do something together. Perhaps a book club or a circle of people interested in the same subject.[16] It matters less what exactly it is than just getting started. You can start by inviting them for coffee or brunch together. Ask one another what it is that you need at the moment to get lucky. If you get along as a group, ask if they would be interested in repeating it. Take it from there.

2. Identify the interest-based communities that help you bridge toward groups you haven't been in touch with. Perhaps join a local TEDx organizing team on the weekend?

3. At the next meeting of a group (for example, a local community group), ask people to share some of their core challenges (or if it's a more informal dinner, perhaps play "rose, bud, thorn"). Often, we go through very similar transitions as others; common touchpoints emerge and trust is built.

4. Map your professional network. Who are the multipliers you might have around you but never thought of? Reflect on how to develop meaningful relationships with them, for example, by inviting the local teacher for a coffee to learn more about each other. Focus on developing a meaningful relationship rather than a particular transaction.

5. If you organize events, ask yourself what the really important common denominator is. And what is a natural way that allows people to connect—rather than a "networking break"?

CHAPTER 8

FOSTERING THE CONDITIONS FOR SERENDIPITY

—

The way you deal with the unexpected defines who you are.
HUBERT JOLY, EXECUTIVE CHAIRMAN, BEST BUY

Our culture—the collective values, beliefs, and principles that guide us and our interactions—can play a powerful role in either nurturing or constraining serendipity.[1] Our culture is in a sense our collective mind, and if we want individual open minds, we must have a culture to match. How can we change an organization's base level of potential serendipity? How can we develop an environment in which constant improvement and learning can happen?

Earlier I mentioned the watercooler test. When visiting a new organization, I try to find the space where people connect during their breaks, where they catch up with each other. When listening in on some of the conversations while (pretending to) work on my laptop, after a while, patterns emerge from the conversations that signal a great deal about an organization's culture. In some organizations, conversations tend to focus on talking about people, often on what they did wrong ("Peter's a lousy presenter—why did they even hire him for that job?"). Of course, gossiping, at times and in measured doses, fulfills an important social function: It allows people to develop social bonds, exchange information, and remain entertained. But it can also come to dominate the conversation and thinking, and serendipity is less likely in an environment where, tomorrow, you could be the one being talked about. People are more cautious when they know they might be served up next on the gossip plate.

In other organizations, conversations might be more positive. ("I just came out of this meeting about the new project—why don't we do a related campaign as well?"; "Petra mentioned an idea about opening a new subsidiary in Mexico City—I just remembered I have an old friend there who might be interested in getting involved.")

Such exchanges focus on developing ideas, on looking toward a joint future. This always reminds me of a quote usually attributed to Eleanor Roosevelt: "Great minds discuss ideas; average minds discuss events; small minds discuss people."

At the core of an enabling culture is a willingness to share knowledge and ideas, and the understanding that it is OK to make the odd mistake without becoming the victim of the boss's wrath or the watercooler's verbal lynch mob. Recent research has shown that serendipity is higher in environments where blame is withheld, and where people are open to a range of ideas. In contrast, when open discussion is thwarted, serendipity is less likely.[2]

How can we foster a culture for serendipity in organizations?

Psychological Safety First

How safe we feel in our environment, whether that is with friends, family, or within the workplace, has a major impact on serendipity. A safe environment encourages people to speak up about the unexpected, for example, encounters or findings that might seem weird or crazy, or ideas and plans that are not fully thought through.

This is about psychological safety—the ability to show and employ ourselves without fear of negative consequences affecting self-image, status, or career.[3] Harvard professor Amy Edmondson has shown, in her exceptional work over the last decades, how psychological safety is at the core of a healthy corporate culture and of good performance.[4] Her work gained momentum in the 1990s with a study showing that better-performing teams are ones that talk more about mistakes. Initially, she was shocked: Do higher-performing teams make more mistakes? No, she realized. Those teams were not making more mistakes, they were just more open to talking about them and what they learned from them.

In lower-performing teams, mistakes are often swept under the carpet. I have witnessed this in many of the organizations I work with; projects that fail are silently buried, and with them the chance for others to benefit by learning from them. But encouraging people to discuss what they have learned from things that did not work promotes true knowledge sharing, learning, and increased trust.

In recent years, a number of studies, including at companies such as Google, have confirmed that the degree of psychological safety is a major difference between high- and low-performing teams. It unleashes latent talent, and, as we will see later, often facilitates serendipity.

Psychological safety is not about making everyone comfortable, nor is it about being unfailingly nice. Instead, as Edmondson highlights, it is about being direct, and about being willing to say when, and why, something did not work.

We have seen this play out earlier with Best Buy's chairman Hubert Joly, for whom the ability and willingness to ask for help is at the core of navigating today's fast-changing world. This is against many of our instincts, of course: A natural instinct often is to go at it alone, divert blame, look good in front of others, and to agree and to be agreeable.

This often leads us to self-censor, and that, in turn, leads to suboptimal outcomes. Edmondson discusses the example of Wells Fargo, a well-known financial services company. In 2015, the company focused on an aggressive cross-selling strategy: It tried to push additional products and services such as home loans to existing customers.

It turned out that many of their customers could not afford all these different services. But the top executives did not listen to the employees on the ground who had observed this trend. Instead, they aggressively pushed their people to sell as much as possible or risk losing their jobs. Can you imagine the psychological pressure this created? The salespeople started crossing ethical lines in order to appear competitive: They lied to clients and they invented customers to fool management. Ultimately, this illusion of success was exposed but not before much time and effort had been wasted and much goodwill sacrificed between staff and management, as well as between the company and its customers.

The problem here, apart from skewed incentives, was that people did not feel that it was safe for them to push back. In a psychologically safe setting, management would have asked, "What is it that holds people back? Let's ask them!" In the Wells Fargo setting, the mantra was closer to, "People are not trying hard enough. We must push harder!"

Conversely, Pixar created an environment of critical feedback and candor in which leaders such as cofounder (and former president) Ed Catmull openly acknowledged mistakes. He displayed humility, fallibility, and an infectious curiosity. To support that, meetings were set up to make it easier to critique and give candid feedback—for example, by starting from an admission that "Early on, all of our movies are bad!" This gave people the permission to push back, ask critical questions, and to feel safe doing so. It also allowed the company to recognize failed efforts quickly, to minimize losses, and to learn lessons from their mistakes—rather than to fall prey to an "escalation of commitment" (the tendency to invest additional resources into something that is a losing proposition due to a need to be or appear to be consistent).[5]

So, how can we increase psychological safety? Edmondson recommends three steps: *setting the stage, inviting participation,* and *responding productively.*

Setting the Stage

Setting the stage means formulating shared expectations and meaning. It focuses on making sure everyone understands that their voice is critical for success, thus decreasing the threshold for people to speak up. It is about conveying that a situation is complex, that it matters, that no one has it all figured out, and that everyone's contribution is crucial. If you are running a hospital, you know that delivering health care is error-prone. Administrators can be wrong, so having people speak up can literally save lives.

Edmondson's research suggests that because we believe we are supposed to know what to do in most situations, we focus on execution and hitting targets. But in reality, we often cannot know exactly what the right metrics are and must adjust as we go along. She admits that it appears more hard-nosed and decisive to just give a metric and pretend that's the only way to do it, but, in her words, "It's also out of touch with reality," especially in areas that are new territory for organizations. Instead, things often have to be tested and iterated.[6]

If showing empathy, curiosity, and an ability to listen were signs of weakness, then many of the dozens of *Harvard Business Review* "CEOs of the Year" that we covered in our Leaders on Purpose study would be considered "soft." As Brené Brown's work makes clear, it takes courage to be vulnerable.

Inviting Participation

This is all about giving people the confidence to believe that their voice is welcome by acknowledging gaps, practicing inquiry, and setting up structures and processes such as guidelines for discussion. This includes asking questions and actually listening to the answers. "What are your ideas, what are you seeing out there, what help can I offer you?" Careful listening portrays genuine interest, gives people space, and shows that you care.

This can include succinct questions that help people to feel comfortable naming and tackling larger issues. When faced with potential quality-control issues, the CEO of a children's hospital asked her staff, "Think about last week's experiences with your patients. Was everything as safe as you would like it to be?"

This approach makes the respective problem areas more tangible, especially for those who might feel that things are good as they are. It shows that there is always space for improvement. It focuses on tackling problems and learning rather than highlighting mistakes or assigning blame. This particular health-care CEO, Edmondson reports, turned her office into a "confessional," with people lining up to discuss what could be done better. This approach helps everyone focus on what *could be* rather than what *is*.

Responding Productively

This is all about an orientation toward continuous learning by expressing appreciation, destigmatizing failure, and sanctioning clear violations. For example, how should we respond once we hear about a mistake? Edmondson suggests signaling that the emphasis is on moving forward rather than dwelling on blame. It is important to make sure people are moving forward rather than standing still.

Imagine the nightmarish situation when someone has to admit, "I don't think I can make my deadline." A potential response can be, "Thank you for flagging the problem. What can we do to get it back on track?" When someone screws up—at least for the first time—the objective is to help them find their way out. (If they screw up repeatedly, then we need to get them more structural support, such as training or coaching. Or perhaps concede that this is not the right job for them after all.)

Does this inclusive approach work outside the United States or Canada, such as in societies where social hierarchies make it tough for employees to speak up? In fact, in more hierarchical societies such as Japan, concepts such as quality management emerged on the basis of the very idea that voices count throughout the organization. Edmondson highlights Toyota's physical example of this, the "Andon cord"—a pull cord or button that is activated by a worker whenever something goes wrong. Having a cord that people can pull is a subtle way to lower the threshold for people to contribute. It is a small design change that can help manifest psychological safety—and signal to people that their voice counts. In fact, Japanese companies in the 1980s and 1990s were leaders in innovation because they encouraged employees to contribute their hunches, knowledge, and intuitions.[7]

Going one step further, recent studies have shown that admitting small weaknesses or even volunteering them can be highly productive. One outstanding study focused on groups of people in brainstorming sessions. The researchers found that if members began by telling the group an embarrassing story about themselves, the group ended up being far more productive. In fact, groups that started their brainstorming by opening up to each other, even in a small way, generated 26 percent more ideas.[8] Embarrassing stories break the ice and create an atmosphere of mutual trust, where no one feels under attack or at a disadvantage.

The same applies when unconventional ideas are converted into practical action: Management research has shown that groups that have an open, honest culture of the type fostered by sharing embarrassing stories are more likely to succeed when implementing their new idea.[9]

This logic extends to other settings and often starts with baby steps. When the Project Alliance Leadership Team for the Sydney Olympics Northside Storage Tunnel project wanted to become more innovative, the organizational culture the team designed centered on the principle of a no-blame culture.[10]

And in our personal lives, we can create psychological safety with baby steps as well. Giving a brief justification before a question ("I know this is random, but . . .") signals to the other person that you are not a "threat." Most people want to interact with us, but we need to remove the barriers. In seminars, I often use the line, "Take the crazy German here as an excuse to ask the stranger next to you a question!" This allows people to ask questions they would usually not ask, and more importantly, removes the potential feeling of "invasion" that the other person might experience if someone they don't know asks a personal question. When we answer, it helps to actively listen, and to repeat back a key word or phrase that the other person has mentioned. It makes them feel heard, and invites them to say more about it.

Sometimes It Takes a Funeral

Unexpected or even puzzling insights, which are often the most valuable, are less likely to arise and certainly less likely to be aired if we start from a position of defensiveness or the fear that an unusual idea or argument will be ridiculed or exposed.

One method to help us increase psychological safety and the propensity for serendipity is the project funeral. Although the phrase sounds bleak, it describes an incredibly positive process. A project is laid to rest, and those involved get to open up about how they felt, what they learned, what they gained, and what they regret about the whole thing. Crucially, the funeral includes people who may not have been close to the project but who are, so to speak, paying their respects, such as project managers from other teams.

Project funerals can be a way to foster trust and serendipity, and sometimes even rebirth. A major nutrition and chemical company developed a coating for nonreflective picture frame glass. It is beautiful, but costs six times more than normal picture frame glass, and the team realized there was no market for it even though it was a great technology.[11]

During the funeral, when the project was "buried," someone asked if colleagues had considered the yield they might get on solar panels using this technology, given that so little light was reflected back off the glass. Presumably, this would have high yields, and the amount of additional electricity produced by the solar panel might be higher than the coating cost.

The project manager answered that they had never thought about this. They discussed the idea with solar panel specialists, started testing it, and found that it was very effective. The experts implemented it, and the company now has a strong business unit on solar. In the CEO's words, "It was totally unplanned, but there were a lot of good things which came together. Now, someone else will say: 'So this is pure luck.' But that's serendipity."

Small and large companies have experimented with this approach, which is not about celebrating failure. It is about celebrating learning and knowledge transfer in a safe environment. It not only facilitates serendipity, but also allows for true learning, which often happens when something doesn't work out, but only if we are honest with ourselves and others about what actually happened. However, for that to work, companies and communities must be open to new information and ideas, or people will not be as alert in noticing or making use of unexpected information.

We may try to create a feeling of safety by pretending to those around us that we have it all figured out, but this is often counterproductive. The best way to increase trust is often to combine a sense of confidence and direction with being true to the reality of a situation. We may prefer to tell stories in which rational processes lead to positive outcomes, but we might get better results if we were to promote the truth: that good ideas often come from strange corners, unexpected and unplanned encounters, or unintended screwups. The history of human, scientific, and technological progress is littered with accidents, slipups, and spillages. Clearly, it is essential to understand which element contributed to an unexpected outcome,[12] but many of the most interesting serendipitous discoveries happened only because people dropped or spilled substances.

John Wesley Hyatt's invention of celluloid (he was trying to make a billiard ball) and Hilaire de Chardonnet's invention of artificial silk following a chemical spillage are just two examples of breakthroughs derived from "intelligent mistakes."* Likewise, the microwave oven was not a result of someone looking for a faster or better way to cook.

During the Second World War, two scientists invented the magnetron—a tube that produced microwaves—for use in Britain's radar system to spot Nazi warplanes. Percy Lebaron Spencer accidentally discovered that microwave energy could be used to cook food when he saw that the radar waves melted a chocolate bar in his pocket. He connected the dots, and future experiments showed that microwave heating could raise the temperature of many foods far more rapidly than conventional ovens.

In the pharmaceutical industry, new ideas often come from the complex process of back and forth, trial and error. Novo Nordisk's former CEO Lars Sørensen, *Harvard Business Review*'s "CEO of the Year" in both 2015 and 2016, explained that he described to his staff the actual challenges of developing new ideas into commercial products, so that they knew what to expect when they were in the midst of it. He acknowledged the temptation to pretend everything is mapped out, "because then management looks smart. But that's not the way it works!" Lars discussed how in a company like Novo Nordisk—which is very regulated, hierarchical, and process-driven—along the way, it is necessary to capture a lot of information that needs to be structured so that the drug will be approved. However, there is also lots of cross-organizational project work, so people

---

* "Intelligent mistakes" are related to the principles of "limited sloppiness" (physician Max Delbruck) and "controlled sloppiness" (Salvador Luria). Like in artistic creations such as improvised jazz, we can create situations in which non-planned interactions are directed by a certain preparation. This creates an environment in which unintentional events can happen—and where they are celebrated. Intelligent mistakes are being enabled by this smart sloppiness. The comic cliché of a manic professor standing amid the rubble of an explosion and joyfully declaring his great discovery may contain a nugget of truth (De Rond, 2014; Mirvis, 1998; Napier and Vuong, 2013; Root-Bernstein, 1988).

tend to form informal networks from which they get their motivation, stimulation, and confirmation.

Lars gave people the space to operate in, and through, these informal networks while also time managing the process, in this case, taking an idea to pharmaceutical product. Enabling this interplay between clear direction and process, while also allowing for the actual experiences of the teams on the ground to unfold informally, made Lars one of the world's most successful CEOs.*

All this points us to an important aspect of serendipity: It often emerges based on teamwork.

You're Not Going to Play Every Position

Much of human progress has been driven by groups—even if we often attribute eureka moments to heroic individuals. But the understanding, and ultimate exploitation, of observations and connecting the dots often requires the resources and skills of several people. In a world where we rarely know what is coming next and which people and resources we might need, diverse groups often prove better at navigating our challenges.[13]

Take penicillin: The discovery of its applicability and importance was a team effort. The Oxford team was more than just its "hero" Alexander Fleming. People such as Ernst Chain and Howard Florey complemented Fleming on this journey. Deservedly, Fleming, Chain, and Florey received their Nobel Prize together. And Fleming would probably not have made his discoveries without the capital and laboratory provided by the University of Cambridge.[14]

Or think back to the example of Waqas's LinkedIn response. Whether

---

* Also see Sharp, 2018. Serendipitously, during our interview, Lars mentioned that he is interested in getting more involved in education. My colleague from Harvard, Leith Sharp, remarked that she was on the lookout for guest lecturers. A year later, Lars gave a lecture at Harvard.

or not his project works out, he created the opportunity space for potential serendipity by allowing someone else to connect the dots. His LinkedIn contact picked up on it and turned it into a valuable opportunity.

Walter Isaacson, whom we met in chapter 3, found that even the most successful, most innovative people cannot go at it alone. Rather, they put together a team with different styles, and different talents. He uses the example of Benjamin Franklin, whose greatest contribution as a U.S. founding father was not to be the smartest (that label went to Thomas Jefferson and James Madison) or the most passionate (that distinction goes to John Adams), or to possess the gravitas of George Washington. But he knew how to put together a team.

Famously, Steve Jobs, when asked what he considered to be his most successful product, did not answer "the Mac" or "the iPhone." No, putting together a team that will always turn out Macs and iPhones, that was the hard part. And Apple would not have emerged the way it did without the creativity, spirit, and temperament of Jony Ive and the business acumen of Tim Cook. In Jobs's words, "You're not going to play every position, so the question is, how do you get the right team around you?"[15]

Similarly, when Francis Bacon, the father of the scientific method, dreamed up his ideal research organization, it included pioneers, who tried new experiments; merchants of light, who kept up with the work of other organizations; mystery men, who collected earlier experiments into the state of the art; lamps, who directed experiments; inoculators, who executed experiments with high proficiency; and interpreters, who raised former discoveries into axioms.[16] Bacon realized that the understanding (and ultimate exploitation) of observations and their link to something else often requires the resources and skills of several people.

Leadership research and management models such as the Belbin model have long pointed out that a focus on just functional aspects, such as looking for "the marketing person" or "the HR person," misses the most important element: the traits, styles, and areas of application that complement each other in ways that make magic happen. If you have a Steve Jobs–type visionary, you need a Steve Wozniak–type executer to complement him. If you have a Nachson Mimran–type extrovert, you need an Arieh Mimran–type person to reflect with him on the potential value of discoveries. Tesla Motors, which accepts only around 3 percent of applicants, explicitly states that it is not looking for hard skills, even for its factories, but rather for soft skills and culture fit.

But the spark of an idea, the moment an unexpected connection is made, as an individual or in a team, is of course only the very beginning of the process that makes serendipity a real and valuable force.

For organizations, developing what management researchers call an "absorptive capacity"—being able to encounter new information, and then turn it into relevant knowledge and action—is paramount.[17] But existing cultures and related procedures can make the introduction of new ideas hard, and often it does not work out. In addition to bureaucracy and other potential hurdles, we are sometimes so busy with getting our job done that we don't allow for much serendipity. We're just too focused on being busy!

Even if we do encounter a new idea or insight, we need to integrate it into existing flows of knowledge, existing practices, and existing power structures. But once vested interests, power dynamics, or fear of change dominate—or there is disagreement on who owns a great idea—ideas can be quashed or interrupted.[18] And even more importantly, serendipity is often related to change and uncertainty. Many people don't feel comfortable with change. So, when we come up with new ideas, we often need to overcome resistance. How can we do that?

Organizations as Immune Systems

In a rapidly changing world, an open communal mind is not a nice-to-have, but a necessity. Procter & Gamble's CEO David Taylor runs the world's biggest consumer packaged goods company, serving over five billion people. To him it is clear that things often happen in unplanned ways. Staying still means moving toward obsolescence, and "every employee will need to think what can be improved. The idea is to train managers to not be in *evaluation mode* but in *developing mode*," he told me. This means creating an environment where people are seeking to learn as opposed to seeking to be right. In his view, if you don't have to be right all the time, then it becomes about *making connections*. "Trying to learn from others, and then help others, and then make connections that lead to new solutions to problems we couldn't solve earlier." Then, if things don't work but they inform something later on that does, he considers that an investment in future innovation—as opposed to a failure.

How does this play out in organizations?

We might assume that people are afraid of new ideas, and the related changes they might entail. But people are not inherently averse to change. It's the potential instability, risk, ambiguity, and threats to their power and influence that matter, and that need to be addressed. Research has shown that people think more about the potential costs of trying rather than the potential positive outcomes. Benefits can create impetus, but human nature tends to focus on risks, the potential costs of "unproductive accidents." These potential costs can prevent action even when the benefits could be substantial.[19]

This is linked to fascinating work on loss aversion—we are often more concerned about not losing than about winning. Salim Ismail, founding director of Singularity University in Santa Clara, California, compares it to an immune system: When you try to disrupt something in a big company, the immune system of the company will come and attack you.[20]

These costs depend heavily on the context—in a manufacturing company we try to minimize variation and experimentation, while in a graphic design company we might want to maximize it. Companies that I have worked with have addressed this challenge by articulating why *not* changing might actually be costlier or riskier than changing. They reframe the change so that the greater threat is defined as not changing. Then it is not about isolating people from change but instead supporting them in coping with change, and clearly articulating how that change affects them.

This prevents the ambiguity that creates situations in which everyone assumes the worst, and where the rumor mill is being fed. Ways to offer support include visualizing the consequences for the individual and formulating clear action steps. We can reason as much as we want but, in the end, we will need to overcome the self-serving bias—understanding what people really care about, and appealing to what they might win or lose. Many a senior leader I've worked with based their decision on new initiatives based on an observation related to someone they care about (e.g., their daughter's experiences), rather than what advisors told them. They would never admit this publicly—instead they provide lots of conventional justification for their decisions—but the fact does not change: Ideas become reality when they become personal, once we feel it's the right thing to do.

This relates to research on affective bias—people tend to believe in and care about their own ideas more than those of others. Interestingly, managers tend to overvalue their ideas by 42 percent, while frontline workers undervalue theirs by 11 percent.[21] Including relevant people, particularly multipliers and key "sponsors," early on in the idea development process can help overcome this bias.

Think back to the example of the Post-it Note that we encountered earlier.[22] Spencer Silver, the 3M researcher who was looking for strong adhesive, realized that his discovery had some merit. He asked others within 3M how they thought it could be used. Silver overcame the initial lack of enthusiasm for his discovery within 3M by winning over a couple of researchers who championed the idea, and by winning backing from people high up in the hierarchy, including a company vice president. Silver was the one who discovered the weak adhesive, but it was a collective effort, and 3M's absorptive capacity that allowed his coincidental discovery to be made valuable by connecting it to several potential uses and finding a place for it in the company's own process and strategy.

Finding these first adopters (and getting their buy-in) is key everywhere. One of my favorite videos on YouTube is "The Dancing Guy." Picture a festival park, where people sit around drinking and chatting, with music in the background. At some point, a "weird" guy starts dancing in the middle of the park. People look at him as if he's an alien. Then, a second person joins in, embraces him, and starts dancing. The second guy asks two others to join, and they invite more people. Soon, most of the surrounding crowd are running into the circle to dance. The out-group became the in-group, and the other way around. Now you are boring if you just sit around.

Most ideas seem crazy or weird at the beginning—and they have the power to become the "new normal" once there is a critical mass who support it.

How can companies ease the process, in addition to the cultural elements discussed earlier? Some companies minimize risk by, for example, breaking projects or problems into smaller steps that allow for rapid, and cost-effective, iteration. Or they use pliable materials that can be reused, or digitize as much as possible, making experimentation cheaper.[23] Or they expand the potential opportunity space by bringing in people from the outside.

Researchers Lars Bo Jeppesen and Karim Lakhani studied the crowdsourcing firm InnoCentive, showing that many problems that could not be solved internally were solved by individuals outside the company. The reason? The diverse group of people was able to open up a much broader potential solution landscape than any in-house team could ever do. This allowed for more potential "need-solution pairs."[24] They were also shielded from organizational politics—management history is full of examples of arrangements that allow people to experiment in less rigid environments before integrating ideas back into an organization (known as "skunk works" in business jargon).

However, in the end, much of it comes back to timing. Inflection points, such as crises, are often good contexts for implementing ideas. When Nike faced a major consumer backlash in the 1990s because of substandard practices by some suppliers, the firm used this as a prompt to increase supply chain accountability. It introduced more rigid codes of conduct and stricter third-party factory inspections. In 2013, Nike cut ties to several Bangladeshi suppliers whose factories were seen as unsafe, foregoing margins in the process. When a factory collapse in Dhaka happened soon afterward, Nike was not implicated. A short-term loss for a long-term gain—leveraging a crisis as opportunity to implement ideas. Also, you might recall Hubert Joly's earlier example about how Best Buy leveraged their reaction to the hurricane and the way they supported their employees and others in the process as a way to manifest their values, with positive long-term implications.

Crises are often the best moments to initiate change, and to show our true colors—in our own lives, and in our organizations.

Accelerating Interactions

These days, smokers are banished to the back steps of offices to indulge their habit. Still, they continue to form communities of their own that transcend the barriers of departments, hierarchies, or expertise. I know many smokers who will attest that it is while having a cigarette that they have made interesting connections that they would otherwise have missed. The smokers' corner is often a hotbed of gossip, but it may also be a breeding ground for ideas and insights.

While no responsible company would actively encourage its employees to smoke, thoughtful ones have found other ways to replicate the smokers' corner by creating reasons for a random range of people to meet and interact based on a shared interest. Companies that foster such shared activities (the karate group, the chess club, etc.) are making serendipity more likely.

Often those on the fringes of a process of problem solving may have a perspective that is hugely valuable. Research has shown that frontline workers often use informal contacts, trial and error, and heuristics (practical learning techniques), while managers at the center of an organization rely more on intelligence documents, deductive approaches, and formal reports, which potentially discourages serendipitous findings.[25]

Integrating cross-organizational responsibilities becomes particularly important after a merger or acquisition. When people fulfill a dual role in both the parent and subsidiary company, it helps link the different parts, and gives them the necessary standing in the parent organization to lobby for ideas that emerge from the acquired organization. We know that over 50 percent of the value in acquisitions can arise unexpectedly—the acquiring firm, for example, might come across a particular technology that it was not previously aware of.[26]

Remi Eriksen, CEO of DNV GL, one of Norway's largest international companies with operations in one hundred countries, told me how his company has people move around frequently, to have "the DNA of the organization pass through." This is based on the realization that not everything can be planned in advance and that strategy is about empowering people to tackle the unexpected proactively.

But all this does not help if people don't feel like interacting with others inside or outside the company. How can we incentivize people to practice networked intelligence and have more serendipity in their lives? LinkedIn founder Reid Hoffman and others have used subsidized lunches; Dharmesh Shah, cofounder of HubSpot, gave employees a budget for "learning lunches." The only criterion was to have lunch with someone smart from outside the organization. That's where usually the most valuable information is.

That way, serendipitous discoveries can be made, opening up new opportunities and fostering relationships. It also increases the feeling of autonomy, which has a positive effect on workplace happiness. Recent research has shown that more personal autonomy in the workplace has a clear correlation with lower turnover of workers, increased job satisfaction, and higher engagement at work. It also tends to alleviate negative emotions.[27] The learning lunch might well be the new golf-course meeting—especially helpful for people like me who don't play golf.

Diversity is important—in terms of both people and our own perspectives. I have used this in my own ventures, to get a fresh point of view. In some ventures, rather than working in the office with the team for a whole day, we sometimes do the heavier, conceptual things in the calmer office environment in the morning and then change location, working from a coffee shop in the afternoon, then a bar in the early evening. Doing the lighter, more interactive activities in an environment that gives us space to breathe makes us more receptive to new stimuli and ideas.

Diversity breeds serendipity. Why? Bisociations, those acts of connecting the dots, depend on combining previously unrelated information or ideas. Often, unsuspected connections or hidden analogies can then be revealed—we allow for "new ways of seeing."[28] Then, metaphorical leaps happen that unveil the true potential of an event or information. Take the apple falling from the tree: If we only look at it in the context of the tree, we see just an apple falling down. But if we see it in a broader context, we might realize that the apple represents and manifests gravity's pull on *any* object. We can often not understand this relevance ourselves and need people from other areas to help us appreciate the broader relevance of unexpected moments or encounters.

The more dispersed information is within an organization, the more difficult it becomes for these links to happen. As we have seen earlier, a simple focus on diversity and just bringing people together often leads to failure. We need to find a common denominator that incentivizes people to connect the dots. Philosopher-poet Johann Wolfgang von Goethe in his book *Wahlverwandschaften* ("Elective Affinities" or "Kindred by Choice") beautifully applied the logic of chemical reaction to social relationships. Using the metaphor of passions and interest being regulated by logics of chemical affinity, he built on Greek philosopher Empedocles: "People who love each other mix like water and wine. People who hate each other segregate like water and oil."

To really be able to mix water and wine, we need common denominators, such as a mutual cause, interest, experience, or even mutual enemy. Bisociations frequently arise when the two or more people in question have quite different perspectives[29] but are still willing to connect. It is easy to underestimate the importance of the trust needed to exchange ideas (see above).

It is not surprising that today's eminent management thinkers such as Henry Mintzberg are becoming more interested in "communityship" than "leadership." Ultimately, a sense of community is what matters when big things need to be done. Developing internal and external communities that help build expertise, transfer knowledge, and support elevating people becomes paramount, particularly in larger organizations.

This is all well and good, you might think, but how about if our corporate culture is competitive? Is this not too rosy a picture to paint?

Shifting a culture from competitive and taker-based to collaborative and enlightened-self-interest-based is not easy. In a context in which assholes rule, does it really pay to be community-oriented, generous, and collaborative?

In settings that are rooted in deep competition, people might pretend they care and then stab their rivals in the back when it matters. Research has shown that in these situations, companies are well advised to form new teams and communities of practice that break out of those established politics or processes that hamper the absorption of new thinking. Within these teams, we can set giving and collaboration as key principles, we can identify group rather than only individual targets, and we can base rewards on *both* collective and individual achievement.

And most important, we can not only reward collaboration but also take away the disincentives for being a positive contributor. Too often individuals with some ability or insight guard it as their preserve, their unique value from which they are determined to reap a reward. A culture that encourages individuals to give what they can, and that demonstrates to those individuals that it knows the value of that giving is a culture in which serendipity can thrive. It helps people rise to the occasion—however unexpected it is.

In many companies, people go through periods of competition and collaboration. Whenever two bigshot lawyers in a high-powered law firm are reminded of their friendship or a bigger cause that is worth fighting for, they help each other out, and their different personalities riff off each other. Whenever they are pitted against each other, they compete tooth and nail.

Many organizational cultures pit people against one another, but in another setting, those same people often could have collaborated. Effective cultures incentivize collaboration (and to some complementary degree, competition),[30] for example, by highlighting team accomplishments and how someone contributed to someone else.

Why does this matter for us as individuals? Vast research shows that giving tends to make us happier than taking. University of British Columbia researcher Elizabeth Dunn and her colleagues questioned 632 Americans about their level of income, how they spent their money, and their level of happiness. In their study published in *Science*, the authors found that regardless of income, those who spent money on others were considerably happier than those who spent money just on themselves.[31]

Yet, we often develop structures that incentivize the opposite. Fruitful environments remind people of this—incentivizing an enlightened self-interest and providing the soil in which serendipity can grow. But often, the culture is only the first step and we can leverage physical and virtual space design to accelerate serendipity.

Shaping Physical and Virtual Spaces for Serendipity

Countless studies have shown that the physical environment has a major influence on the likelihood of serendipity.[32] Remember Pixar's office design, which accelerates interactions between executives, animators, and computer scientists. Or take the Royal Society of Arts, which redesigned its central space into a coffeehouse, inspired by the Viennese coffeehouses that fueled many great—and not so great—ideas. In all of these, size does matter: Research has shown that employees who sit at cafeteria tables of twelve people tend to be more effective than sitting at those of four people—due to more serendipitous conversations and the larger network.[33]

Capitalizing on these potential benefits, companies such as Google and IBM's Accelerated Discovery Lab have designed their headquarters in ways that enhance the "cross-pollinations" of people and data across disciplines. In fact, Google, whose innovations such as Street View and Gmail came out of "positive collisions,"[34] designed its campus in Mountain View, California, to "maximize casual collisions." The buildings resemble bent rectangles, where employees within the complex will not be farther than a three-minute walk from one another. Rooftop cafés complement the design. This closes the structural holes between teams by connecting good ideas between groups that are usually disconnected.[35] Modern network analysis uses existing data to identify and map isolated teams and adjust space and structure accordingly.

Which small design changes can have a major impact? For starters, rooms with multiple types of seating encourage relaxed conversation.

Placing couches near doorways allows people to bump into each other when new people enter the room. Soon, sensors will allow us to develop offices that automatically reconfigure seats daily depending on where the system identifies structural holes.[36]

A more structural change is related to office design. Sharing an office with someone who is reasonably close to our area of interest but has a different perspective is a good way to facilitate serendipity. Seats2meet.com, a Dutch coworking company, has worked with a financial services company to repurpose their spaces in order to have people with different perspectives connect with each other. If you have a large reception area but nobody really uses it, they thought, why not offer entrepreneurs and others the opportunity to work from there? This helps develop buy-in with the local community and allows different areas of expertise to be available and new connections to emerge.

Employees can interact with people from the outside in a casual way—which research has shown is an effective way to actually develop interesting ideas and meaningful ties.[37] For example, joint events allow visitors to present ideas, to connect with each other, and to nurture collaborations. Seats2meet.com then facilitates interaction via a digital platform that allows people to share what they need and what they can offer.

Using a similar approach, RLabs has worked with banks and governments to rethink how their idle spaces could be used for training, coworking, and other purposes to make the best out of what is at hand, and develop effective community spaces.

However, often even community spaces do not feel like community. This is why Impact Hub, a coworking space and community for conscious entrepreneurs, has "hosts" that make you feel welcome when you enter. They introduce you to others. You can even make lunch together, if you feel like it, to feel less lonely within the crowd.

Research on computer-supported cooperative work (CSCW) has shown that we can replicate many of the above insights in the virtual world.

Platforms like InnoCentive open themselves up for unusual solutions, often creating unexpected connections. Similar to how physical proximity can increase the likelihood of serendipitous encounters, in virtual environments we can create more proximity between diverse people and ideas. Making it easier to communicate informally online, or have people receive updates of colleagues' social media activity, can increase serendipitous encounters.[38]

That's where the importance of filtering comes in again, especially in virtual environments, to rise above the "noise" these spaces hold and focus on the valuable ideas. And while virtual spaces can complement physical spaces, importantly, serendipity often happens locally rather than virtually. Companies such as Yahoo! have tried to get their employees back into the office, arguing that serendipity happens when impromptu meetings take place, not when you are home on your couch in your pajamas.

Why is that so? Humans have a strong preference for face-to-face interactions. New York University's Greg Lindsay aptly observed that often what's out of sight tends to be out of mind. Decades ago, studies showed that we are four times more likely to communicate with someone who sits six feet away than with someone who's sixty feet away—and almost never with those in separate buildings or floors.[39] This can be shown in our brain, too: People feel most creative when they are in motion and meet people, rather than when they sit at their desk in long stretches (the flipside of the maker schedule).

Networked Serendipity

The changing nature of tasks and approaches in a rapidly changing world also means that we need to rethink our approach to work. Once we might have gotten away with sitting in our office or cubicle, hiding away from interaction. Today, even in more stable industries such as pharmaceuticals, progress often depends on our ability to develop and leverage networks. For companies, this represents a shift from organization-centric initiatives to social and economic communities and networks (*ecosystems*).[40]

In our study of thirty-one of the world's leading CEOs, a key challenge that emerged for most of them was how to tackle uncertainty and the increased speed of change. Dan Schulman, CEO of PayPal, told me how PayPal partners with other companies, as they cannot meet every need at once, and only in such an integrated way are they able to maximize value. And who would have thought that former competitors such as BMW and Mercedes would set up a joint car-sharing service?

Or take Haier, which has shifted from being a product-driven company to what's called a "platform ecosystem." This is a shift that many leading companies are going through in their quest to disrupt before they are themselves disrupted. In a world where the future is unpredictable, these organizations have understood that they need to be more like starfish and less like spiders.[41]

What does this mean? Imagine the centralized organization as a spider, which will die if its head gets cut off. Conversely, a decentralized organization is a starfish that has no head. Cutting off a leg will lead to either direct regeneration or the emergence of a whole new starfish. Starfish organizations are more adaptable in today's rapidly changing business environment.

They can cultivate serendipity, not by planning centrally but by enabling multiple smaller parts to trial different solutions. While a quasi-starfish such as at MorningStar, a California-based agribusiness and food processing company where self-managing teams are supposedly delivering higher performance, is extreme, putting networks at the core of business has become paramount across the board.[42] That's where networked innovation comes into play.

History teaches us that new ideas and innovations, and societal progress more broadly, often arise from recombinations of existing ideas or technologies—the integration of which frequently happens through networks.[43] This can happen serendipitously, based on bringing together the knowledge of people who are exploring similarly unchartered territory.[44]

In the traditional models of innovation, the most important innovations came from central producers who planned them. In today's rapidly changing world, where we cannot know what people want or need tomorrow, customer-centric models are coming to the fore.[45] Advances in technology, such as the Internet of Things and Big Data, make it possible to create fully customizable products for even highly nuanced individual preferences. Consequently, being able to navigate the unexpected becomes a core capability for any organization that aims to stay fit for the future.

Together with Lloyd George Management's Alice Wang and Reading University's Jill Juergensen, I studied the fascinating transformation at Haier in more depth.[46] What Haier does is to leverage network effects. Network effects are all about networks becoming more valuable as we add (relevant) new people or organizations—nodes—to it.[47] It describes the exponential value curve that can result after a good or service achieves a critical mass of users—user acquisition becomes much less costly since the network offers utility beyond that point. Consequently, the good or service becomes much more valuable. What was true for the telephone system is as true for social media platforms such as Facebook. It wouldn't really be fun if you were the only user of Facebook, would it?

Haier has been reorganized into a platform ecosystem, incentivizing people within and outside the company to engage with emerging data and ideas. Hundreds of microenterprises—teams of people with an idea either based on an existing product such as a smart refrigerator or for something entirely new such as a games company—interact with them. Haier uses this model to place diverse bets, realizing that in ten years from now we might not even need refrigerators or washing machines anymore—so they prepare for the unexpected.

The empowered entrepreneurs can be more agile and closer to the needs of end users than a large organization could ever be, and the user-centric perspective allows for quick improvements.[48] Often this means we need to rethink how organizational structures look like.

At the Dutch conglomerate Philips, for example, a core question is on how to organize business units. CEO Frans van Houten shared with my research team the idea of changing traditional structures focused on a particular solution (e.g., tomography) to one focused on customer needs (e.g., a precision diagnosis) that could be tackled by different types of solutions. In formulating the challenge differently to their teams, the different types of business models potentially align closer with the actual customer need—and open up the potential "opportunity space" for new solutions to emerge. Technology orientation changes to a need-based clustering—it is being *reframed*.

We can see similar developments in areas such as the *makers movement*. "Maker spaces" often consist of a library of digital objects that "makers" can turn into physical ones using 3D printers. The large number of users in the highly modular 3D technologies environment enhances previously unsought variations. The fascinating thing here is that digital tools can help us turn atoms into bits. If we do not have to change a whole physical structure but only need to change something on the computer, transportation and sharing are easier—and the costs are lower.

In this way, maker spaces, innovative business units, and whole business ecosystems have a lot in common with biological ecosystems. They can adapt—change based on the initial function—but also *exapt*—use characteristics that evolved for other usages (or for no function at all) and co-opt them for their current role.[49] Companies increasingly structure research and development efforts in ways that allow for "exaptations"—driving serendipity. Makers that work in environments that are conducive to innovation habitually collect, organize, and store knowledge in ways that facilitate serendipity. At companies like IDEO, interesting ideas are being accumulated, often without a clear sense of how they could be used later. They are loosely organized and searched whenever something relevant comes along.[50] (Naturally, storing lots of data of customers comes with its own challenges, including those related to privacy and informed consent.)

Why Is That Relevant?

In the past, consistency, predictability, and large-scale production often made organizations successful. They became competitive through economies of scale, and it was possible to sacrifice individual nuance to meet the largest addressable market at the lowest possible price. But today's consumer is savvier and demands to be addressed as an individual with every opportunity to customize her or his own experience, often in cocreation with organizations.[51]

A customer survey is no longer enough. People's actions have always differed from how they say they act, which is why the unobtrusive observations in design thinking methodology are so popular, but in a fast-changing world, real-time responsiveness is key. When we put the customer and their evolving—and often unexpected—needs at the core, we design for serendipity. Just like when Haier's maintenance people who were called in for repairs found that many washing machine complaints concerned dirt and debris collection, they realized some rural customers were using washing machines to wash root vegetables.

Rather than dismiss these cases as invalid or as a worthless anomaly, Haier saw the potential value and developed a washing machine that could also process and filter vegetable dirt and debris. The potato washing machine was born—based on an active-listening approach and enabling individuals across the company to act on unexpected events by connecting the dots and turning them into opportunities.

How are these different people in an "ecosystem" glued together? At

Haier, it is a combination of events as well as super-nodes that become the connective tissue of the ecosystem. Haier hosts a WeChat group (a text-message-based app) for its micro-entrepreneurs, which facilitates casual and professional discussion. It also developed U+, a software platform that brings together customers, suppliers, employees, and entrepreneurs, facilitated by artificial intelligence and machine learning.

These ecosystems—which combine the logics of firm, market, and networks—can be effective vehicles for resource allocation. But more important, they allow for serendipity by providing space to new insights: by combining the ideas of collaboration and competition (coopetition). The juxtaposition of what we believed to be opposites allows for the creative friction that is frequently found at the core of serendipity. A basic assumption is that everything and everyone could be wrong, and can be improved.

Companies such as Haier benefit from this kind of coopetition, as it lets them be part of disruptive change. The microenterprises are relatively independent, they compete with others, including within Haier's ecosystem, but they often draw from this same ecosystem and cooperate with other entrepreneurial groups or Haier's headquarters. Within this ecosystem, a product can go from inspiration to being used by millions of consumers within weeks, something that could take months or even years for an isolated start-up. This is facilitated by an internal university, training center, and internal technology platforms.*

Sensor-based factories produce whatever is needed on demand—and in the same factory. This can be seen at BMW: Its modern vehicle architecture plant in Oxford can flexibly build different types, such as combustion engines or electric vehicles, depending on what the demand for BMWs in a country such as Russia will be in a year from now.

---

* Naturally, the question of who owns intellectual property and who owns our data is on top of the minds of many senior executives. The CEO of one of Sweden's leading banks, SED, Johan Torgeby, shared with us his idea to integrate a "code of conduct risk" into the balance sheet so to incentivize responsible approaches. *Social Physics* author Alex Pentland suggests a property right for personal information (Pentland, 2015).

This flexibility also spills over into the mindset of managers: They are being trained in how to react to volatility and uncertainty. Flexible working arrangements allow companies to keep employees even if times get tough.

Other leading companies, such as Baidu, a Chinese technology company, and Tencent, a Chinese investment conglomerate, have experimented with similar platform approaches. Tencent's WeChat services emerged after founder Pony Ma encouraged employees to compete internally to create a mobile messaging business. While some investors worried that this approach would duplicate efforts, Pony Ma's approach is rooted in the desire to build an organization that can disrupt itself and evolve before it gets disrupted from the outside.[52]

These approaches facilitate betting on randomly emerging ideas—and amplify work through providing new connections. They also act as a low-cost form of risk control. But they can also be challenging for those who have to navigate them by putting employees under pressure to constantly perform.[53]

Context Matters

Fostering serendipity, embracing uncertainty, and having flexible, open-ended goals are particularly valuable in entrepreneurial ventures, business divisions focused on innovation, and academic or scientific research. In more stable contexts with long project horizons, such as the pharmaceutical industry, companies often have to plan decades ahead. However, as we have seen with the example of Novo Nordisk, some degree of serendipity is found even in those industries.[54]

It is applicable more broadly and to all areas of life that we need to set ourselves up for success by expecting and leveraging the unexpected. In a world dominated by rigor and efficiency, overcoming the perception of serendipity as loss of managerial control and seeing it instead as a sign of an open mind and a positive corporate culture is crucial to avoid burying potentially valuable outcomes.

One might ask, "Do we—as an organization—have an incentive to encourage our employees to have more serendipity in their lives? Wouldn't that potentially make them leave the company once they stumble over something that 'changes their life'?"

Well, an old learning and development adage asks, "What if we train everyone and they leave the company?" To which a great rebuttal is, "Well, what if we don't train them and they stay?" There might be no other choice if we want to be fit for the future. The net benefit for an organization is high, including more motivated employees, and more and better ideas. It's like being in a marriage: If you are constantly afraid that your partner will leave you, there is a systemic problem that needs to be addressed. Holding your partner back from becoming their best self is counterproductive.

In this chapter, so far we have looked at the role of serendipity for and in organizations. But how does this play out in the places where we live— our cities and countries? What does it mean for governments and policymaking?

From Silicon Valley to Silicon Roundabout and Silicon Savannah to Chilecon Valley—and Back

Mayors, government ministers, and concerned citizens alike increasingly realize that in a world in which we cannot know what tomorrow will bring, we need to develop resilient communities and societies that can cope with the unexpected.[55] John Hagel, John Seely Brown, and Salim Ismail have been doing intruiging work on the importance of serendipity for organizations and cities.[56] They shift perspective from knowledge stocks—what we know—to knowledge flow, which is about always learning, always refreshing, always discovering. We need to pull ideas and knowledge from many people. The question becomes: How can we find things if we do not even know what's out there or what we're looking for?

Projects and programs are popping up worldwide. In Tokyo, Todd Porter, the TEDxTokyo curator and founder of EDGEof, has worked on developing a city ecosystem for serendipity. By starting an eight-story clubhouse with a companion country gateway hotel next door in a park—and with other nature-based locations in development—he aims to develop a meeting space where serendipity can flourish. In Chile, the leading technical and vocational education provider INACAP and the government agency CORFO have developed projects such as Start-Up Chile (CORFO) and Fab Lab (INACAP) to offer similar opportunities.

Felipe Lara, the innovation and entrepreneurship center manager at INACAP, explained how serendipity is at the core of his design principles. To tap into the potential of Chile's innovation ecosystem, Felipe and his team bring together people from across the country. This includes developing a network of labs across Chile that use interdisciplinary collaboration to make things happen. In Las Vegas, Tony Hsieh, founder of Zappos (an online shoe and clothing retailer), attempted to turn downtown Las Vegas into a center for innovation with a $350 million investment. The project has had its ups and downs, and if he could do it over again, he told CNBC in 2016, "he would have put 'collisions'—serendipitous encounters between individuals who can drive innovation—ahead of co-learning, connectedness and even return on investment."[57] Now Hsieh is actively focusing on creating "return on collisions."

But often these projects are bound to fail. Why? For starters, many cities and regional clusters have tried to copy clusters such as Silicon Valley (the area in Northern California where Facebook, Google, and other tech companies are based), in the belief that they can just be replicated. This underestimates the importance of the underlying culture. If you compare Silicon Valley to innovation clusters in Germany, it is clear that one is geared toward more radical innovation (Silicon Valley), the other (Germany) toward more incremental innovation (though as we have noted, the most radical of innovations often come out of resource-constrained settings in emerging markets). But both need people and mindsets that are equipped for it and complementary institutions such as schools nearby.

Silicon Valley entrepreneurship wouldn't have flourished without talent from universities such as Stanford (and initial government support). Copying only one element of an ecosystem usually fails—we need complementary elements such as culture and commitment.

Similar to how we look at companies, we need to look at cities and countries as ecosystems that nurture their dwellers or citizens—only if we can evolve can we sustain. This also means we need to facilitate spaces that allow for nurturing meaningful relationships rather than transactions. Ample research—for example in the context of investments into start-up enterprises—has shown that real buy-in takes time.

Management researchers Kathleen Eisenhardt at Stanford University and Benjamin Hallen at the University of Washington found that firms often form relationships effectively when executives engage in what the researchers call *casual dating*. This involves an informal but deliberate, repeated meeting with a few potential partners prior to attempting to form a formal relationship, while explicitly avoiding discussions solely focused on investments. This approach helps investors to familiarize themselves with a venture while avoiding the often-adversarial negotiations of formal relationships. Also, venture executives who ask for advice get closer to investors, as they develop buy-in.[58]

Sound familiar? In a way that's like dating in real life. In this case, we can develop environments that help nurture relationships without the pressure of having to develop informal spaces that bring diverse groups of people together.

The Power of Serendipity in Policymaking

Major political events that truly shape history are often serendipitous, and many modern societies are set up to embrace the unexpected at scale—for good or bad. Take democracies. They are based on the idea that citizens are free to choose their leaders and how their society is organized. This introduces uncertainty about what they think each time there are elections, and it's sometimes impossible to predict who will be the next leader, be it president, prime minister, or mayor. And it is nearly impossible to predict how people—investors, CEOs, borrowers, and lenders—will react when the Monetary Policy Committee of the Bank of England or the Federal Reserve in the United States increase interest rates.

We can estimate what will happen based on the past, but the nature of citizens' reactions often depends on variables we cannot predict. What is true for individuals and organizations is particularly true for government: In a rapidly changing world, we often don't know which questions to ask or which people or resources we might need in order to tackle constantly evolving, complex problems.

Governments around the world want to be seen as more "innovative"—more dynamic, more customer-centric—and yet they often try to plan everything out. But the best results often occur by accident, and effective governments mediate citizen reaction rather than trying to suppress uncertainty. So what then are ways that we can build serendipity into policy?

Traditional approaches such as the New Deal for Communities—a regeneration program of the UK government that tries to help turn around deprived neighborhoods—have often focused on improving specific local communities, so they concentrate on a particular geographic area. This might strengthen local identities and develop local social capital, but it can also reinforce isolation and weaken the ability and willingness to connect outside the community. This limits the bridging ties—relationships outside the community—that are crucial for serendipitous encounters and life opportunities.

This is why recent research has suggested that policymaking benefits from focusing less on simply reviving local areas, and more on developing bridges across economic and social divides. This can include focusing on cross-council cultural activities, developing communities of interest beyond local areas, communities of learning, or communities of cross-support.[59]

First attempts to cocreate—rather than simply hand over—public services, such as police-resident liaison groups or "friends of park" groups, have shown promising signs already.[60] And there is inspiration from other parts of the world.

In our research in Kenya and South Africa, we identified a number of ways for policymakers to develop effective ecosystems. First, policymakers and support organizations tend to devise support programs based on a central plan. Like most of us, they try to map out everything in advance. But local community members tend to know best what is needed and when. Developing a support infrastructure places the responsibility on locals, involving them early on in the process. Some governments use targeted and recurring roundtables across sectors to prompt discussion among citizens and help to form effective communities. People in the area/community are asked to share their current needs, and make "pledges" on how they aim to contribute to the bigger picture—ideally this will integrate with their present activities to make it more likely that projects are sustained. This can also help foster a more general sense of community on the local level, particularly if regions feel disconnected from the urban centers, or if there are high inequalities across districts and regions.

Second, identifying local informal leaders and legitimizing them with a stamp of approval from the government can be effective. Take the example of Gyan Shala, an education NGO that works in Bihar, one of India's most impoverished states. Gyan Shala's focus is on improving the education infrastructure. An organization like Gyan Shala—locally based and staffed, and in touch with local needs—can train a teacher in a couple of months. This is far faster than the government is able to. These kinds of initiatives constantly innovate in order to be relevant to the local communities. The government can benefit from this because, in a way, it is outsourcing the risk of experimentation—in other words, the things that can be difficult to explain to voters (it involves failures, after all!). But they can then cherry-pick the interesting parts that worked out—and potentially scale them up into national or regional programs. In India, this approach has helped reach thousands of people, particularly in low-income communities.

The role of local and global communities in catering to core human needs has important implications for how we think about safety nets. Current conversations tend to focus on economic considerations, such as a guaranteed minimum income and artificial intelligence. But Christian Vanizette, cofounder of the global social entrepreneurship movement MakeSense, witnessed in his work that in a globalized world, interest-based communities are key in enabling people to be ready for the unexpected. It is less about financial needs and more about communities that enable the individual to thrive. Then, governments do not need to fix everything, but can learn from movements such as MakeSense how people can get activated if they share a joint interest.

Thus . . .

In a fast-changing world, we often do not know what will come next and which people and resources we might need. We therefore need to enable ourselves, our companies, and our cities to be ready for the unexpected. Acknowledging the concept of serendipity and making it an acceptable part of our (organizational) lives becomes a core capability.

For serendipity to happen more often and with better outcomes, individuals and teams need to feel free and safe in their careers to pursue the unexpected and unusual—and have the legitimacy to do so. This can include setting the stage by indicating that nobody has figured it all out, and by inviting active participation with regard to what can be improved. Then, people become more alert and vigilant to unexpected encounters, and less likely to self-censor ideas.[61]

Organizations can highlight and celebrate the unexpected, give credit to those who encounter serendipity, and facilitate a culture that demonstrates that it is safe to pursue the unusual. Rituals such as project funerals can incentivize people to share more openly what did not work, and why, to allow for proper learning—and serendipity.

When we need to overcome barriers within organizations, de-risking, for example, by digitizing or using reusable materials, becomes important. We can develop more collaborative cultures by dis-incentivizing taking and incentivizing giving. And we can develop physical and virtual spaces in ways that make serendipity more likely, for example, by repurposing lobby spaces.

Policymaking can focus on providing nourishing environments, for example, by empowering local multipliers and helping them scale up their programs.

At the root of all of this is the need to overcome the perception that serendipity is about loss of control rather than a sign of a positive organizational culture. When that happens, the positive impact will follow—and this time, it will not be by accident.

This chapter's workout focuses on developing a serendipity-nurturing environment.

SERENDIPITY WORKOUT: NURTURING SERENDIPITY

1. Incentivize serendipity spotting. Ask in the weekly meeting: Did you come across something unexpected last week? If yes, does this change our assumptions (e.g., in terms of strategy)?

2. Capture incidences of serendipity. Highlight them. Make people see the potential trajectories. Highlight four of them in your next newsletter or event.

3. Facilitate psychological safety. At your next meeting, remind people that situations are complex and their voice is critical in getting it right. Say to your team, "Think about last week: Was everything as good as it could have been?" Make it easy for people to get back to you—be it in the meeting, or individually afterward.

4. Experiment with a project funeral, for example with regard to a recent project of yours that you felt had lots of potential but did not work out.

5. Install a "random coffee trial" or "random lunches" in your organization, such as pairing people from an acquired company with some from the acquiring company. Ask people to share their experiences at events and for the newsletter. Repeat four times to see the effect.

6. If you run a company, invite a group of young people to shadow your and your colleagues' activities. Afterward, ask them what they observed—which habits and routines seem superficial or even harmful? How might the company and its products be improved—or what could "destroy" you that you are not aware of?

7. If you had a (serendipitous) idea, identify three people within or outside your organization who could be champions for it.

Within your business, consider the informal power structure—who could help push it forward? Meet them for a relaxed conversation, explore what could be possible. Then identify three people who could stand in the way of your idea and think about ways either to win them over, or to circumvent them in a smart way. To find people outside your organization, visit places where multipliers hang out: for example, coworking spaces.

8. If you are an educator or policy maker: Develop an opportunity space in your area. Can you link a close-enough mentor to someone?

CHAPTER 9

EVALUATING SERENDIPITY

—

> *The best education is one that prepares you for your own venture into the unknown.*
>
> LEE C. BOLLINGER, PRESIDENT, COLUMBIA UNIVERSITY

After Helen Quilley is fired from her PR job, she leaves the office and drops an earring in the elevator. A man picks it up for her. She runs to the train on the London Underground and makes it—just. Or just misses it. The plot splits into two storylines, two parallel universes that unfold differently, depending on whether or not she catches that particular train. Helen—played by Gwyneth Paltrow in the movie *Sliding Doors*—experiences two very different alternative lives.

How many times have you wondered, "What if?" What would have happened if I had not accidentally run into the love of my life on that particular day? What would have happened if I hadn't coincidentally overheard that conversation that got me my new job?

An intriguing way to look at serendipity—and the degree to which it is malleable—is to look at counterfactuals: "What could have happened differently?"

If whatever happened was drawn from a pot of possible histories, luck in the realized world becomes just one of many options that could have happened.[1] If we go back in time and face the same situation again, how likely would an alternative history be? What was it about our own actions—if it was anything—that enabled it?

People tend to underestimate how life could have unfolded differently because of small lucky incidents.[2] It can be interesting to look at possible alternative histories that could have happened—was it smart luck (serendipity) or blind luck (luck of the draw) that played a role?

If you could simulate the different options, you might see that what actually happened was an improbable outlier among all the possible outcomes. Very small changes in the initial situation could lead to very different results. What happens next often compounds, and path dependencies emerge.[3]

What does that tell us? Take differences in skills: Initially, someone might simply have been in the right place at the right time.[4] This applies to sport as much as to social inequality.

For example, in every elite group of Canadian hockey players that was studied in a famous research project, at least 40 percent were born between January and March.[5] As the cutoff age for each hockey division is based on the calendar year, which resets on January 1, the players that are born in the first three months of the year usually have greater physical maturity. This makes them get chosen more often initially, giving them more game experience, potentially better training, and eventually better teammates.[6]

Their key advantage was not that they were better at hockey, but that they were stronger initially—and then, over the year, they ended up being better, given that they were put on a pathway to success. Their initial blind luck was amplified by path dependencies, which led to huge differences in long-term outcomes.

If history were to be rerun with a cutoff date of August 1st, the distribution of hockey players in the league would most probably be quite different. In alternative histories, the same hockey player would probably not have acquired the same skills and might have ended up in accounting instead of the hockey league, and vice versa.[7]

We can observe similar effects on social mobility and achievement—where small differences in zip codes at the beginning can make big differences over time. Take the hypothetical middle-class girl whose family could afford a great private tutor, who motivated her to study a particular subject. She goes on to win a Nobel Prize. In a counterfactual history, her father loses his job, tuition becomes unaffordable, and therefore she doesn't meet her tutor or acquire the same skills. Or perhaps a different tutor was chosen who failed to motivate her in the same way.[8] This one encounter—because of the path dependencies that it kick-starts—can produce huge differences in long-term outcomes. (Of course, as we have witnessed throughout the book, with a serendipity mindset she would probably have done something significant no matter what—she would have become a different fig on the fig tree.)

This is true in other areas as well, from technology adoption to wealth accumulation to status hierarchies—where an initial distortion leads to very different long-term outcomes because of path dependencies.[9] If you inherit four hundred million dollars from your father (a "small million-dollar loan," as Donald Trump would say), it would be difficult not to become a billionaire, even if you just put the money in the bank and enjoyed the (compound) interest.

That's why we shouldn't be too impressed by people who appear to excel exceptionally. They often enjoyed early luck of the draw, and exceptional performance often reflects random context. Then, from a good baseline, they become disproportionally more successful. This "the rich get richer and the poor get poorer" dynamic is captured by a phenomenon known as the Matthew Effect. It is based on the idea of accumulated advantage: Those who have more—for example, status or money—tend to be placed in situations where they can gain more.*

---

* The term was coined by sociologist Robert K. Merton (1968) and takes its name from the biblical Parable of the Talents (Matthew 25: 14–30). In addition, someone like Donald Trump, who had "luck of the draw," goes big—or goes home. There is often no middle way when it comes to extremes, which

However—and this is one of the biggest problems with tales from the trenches at conferences, in classrooms, and over grandpa's dinner—as with smart luck or serendipity, people's perceptions and narratives often do not properly reflect this blind luck. Trying to imitate their successful behavior can be counterproductive. It might not have had a lot to do with actual performance, and potentially only worked because of contextual factors.

Research across disciplines has shown that people tend to create stories that emphasize their intellect and intention and consciously or subconsciously overlook difficulty, uncertainty, and randomness.[10] But as we know, a good story is often less probable than a less satisfactory one.

Getting Lucky, and the Deceit of Survivors

Mistaking blind luck for skill thus happens more often than we might think—often, based on survivor bias. We do not see what Nassim Nicholas Taleb calls the "silent grave"—the many lottery ticket holders who did not win. We have a natural tendency to focus on survivors, and disregard failures.[11] We draw lessons from lucky survivors—which often can be dangerous, as their context is usually not ours. If we over-attribute success to things done by the successful person rather than to randomness or blind luck, we learn false lessons. We study the victors without seeing the accompanying losers who acted in the same way but were not lucky enough to succeed.

This can be frustrating when listening to conference tales, but it becomes outright lethal in other contexts. Disasters are often precipitated by many near-misses—successful outcomes that averted failure, shortly before the actual disaster. People often fail to consider how the same

---

is why there is little to learn from them in terms of success tactics if we are not as open to risk-taking and didn't have similar luck of the draw.

decision that led to a positive outcome could have led to disaster. This often nurtures risk-taking and a false sense of security, as in 2003 when the *Columbia* space shuttle disintegrated during atmospheric entry and killed everyone aboard.[12] Foam debris had detached from the shuttle on several missions before the disaster. Luckily, it had never hit a sensitive portion of the orbiter. Given that no failure had occurred, NASA officials interpreted the near-misses as successes, and saw the foam detachment as ordinary incidence with no serious repercussions. They normalized (negative) deviance. They were *lucky* that nothing negative had happened—until it did. The accident killed all seven crew members.

We often interpret near-misses as success, rather than realizing how quickly they can or could have turned into disaster. Why is this important?

Biased responses to such near-misses mean that organizations and systems that experience them remain vulnerable when they should be using a near-miss as a warning sign that something needs to be fixed.[13] I have been guilty of this myself: When I got my first car at the age of eighteen, I had many, many near-misses (scratched cars, knocked trash cans, etc.), and I took them as signs that I could get away with such behavior. Instead I should have realized that at some point my antics might get me killed. And they almost did.

What can we do to avoid this? Research has shown that it can be effective to take an outside view and to imagine alternative histories. Once we become aware of our implicit biases and start to simulate alternative histories, we can improve risk management, learning—and the "right" actions.[14]

I have tried to put this into practice nowadays on my bike rides—with varying degrees of success. When I cross a street in a risky fashion, I try to tell myself that yes, nothing happened in this case, but next time I might not be as lucky.

Should something happen—like a car hitting me—it would seem like bad luck to the observer. But given all the previous near-misses, the probability of it happening might have been quite high (I conveniently skipped sending this part of the book draft to my family).*

Beware the High Achiever

Being inspired by giants such as Michelle Obama, Richard Branson, Bill Gates, or Oprah Winfrey is great, but it can lead to disappointment. Even if you could copy exactly every step they took, you would not be able to replicate their initial conditions—and how precisely their path unfolded. Extreme performers are usually outliers, which means they are less likely to be successfully followed—there is a high probability that chance or privilege played a major role.[15] A popular software billionaire started out in a wealthy family who sent him to a private school with computers, enabling him to develop his hobby of programming. Then, his parents connected him to a major company's president—and he later received a contract with that company.

This is why it is more effective to look at patterns rather than individual stories—and at role models who are closer to our living reality. For example, consider the inspiring shop owner or the principled consultant at Boston Consulting Group. They can be helpful to understand possible trajectories. This is particularly true in more "linear" contexts such as banking, law, or consulting, where career tracks are laid out relatively clearly.[16] The counterfactual histories of the senior partner in a consultancy might be closer to the other possible alternative histories than those of an entrepreneur who had the right product at the right time after lots of missed shots before that, or who might have taken an excessive risk.

---

* This builds on *probabilistic thinking*: The world is often dominated by probabilistic outcomes (rather than deterministic ones). We cannot predict the future with much certainty, but we can ascribe odds to less or more probable events. You might have done that yourself when crossing the street and trying to ascribe the odds of being hit by a car.

Management scholars Chengwei Liu and Mark de Rond in their research convincingly argue that the more extreme a performance is, the less one can usually learn from it. Why? Because this outlier is more likely to indicate unreliability—for example, excessive risk-taking or cheating—and it could easily have unfolded very differently.[17]

Donald Trump, when debt-ridden in the 1990s, famously (and abhorrently) said that a homeless person had a higher net worth than him. Given Trump's excessive risk-taking, his alternative history might well have led him to debt-ridden failure, rather than to the U.S. presidency. Learning from his "success" might lead to failure as much as it might lead to success. It is extremely idiosyncratic.

In fact, often the second-best performers are the ones we can learn from the most. Outstanding performances in many fields tend to be followed by less outstanding ones because extreme performances are often associated with extreme luck. But extreme luck is unlikely to persist, and performances usually regress to the mean.[18] Then, people usually try to come up with some kind of explanation for the performance change—rather than realizing that it's just that their blind luck has been running out!

This book will help you not to rely on that one shot of blind luck—but rather, to develop a high base level of serendipity, which will remain at a high level no matter what.

Are We Fundamentally Wrong?

This leads us to one of the most fascinating phenomena out there: attribution bias.

People tend to attribute outcomes to one of four factors: luck, effort, skill, and task difficulty. The more the cause of the outcome is considered to be uncontrollable and external, the more people tend to attribute it to luck.[19]

Much of this book has focused on how we can create our own smart luck by cultivating a serendipity mindset (and the related serendipity field), which is a skill in itself. However, there are occasions where good or bad luck can be utterly undeserved—and we often wrongly attribute it.

We often consider failure to be due to bad luck, while we attribute success to effort or skill. This leads to overlearning from (pseudo-) successes, and under-learning from failure—giving us an illusion of control.[20] But research has shown that people tend to misinterpret outcomes that involve randomness. As we saw in earlier chapters, we might see patterns where there are none and then attribute lucky outcomes as due to our personal characteristics and our own effort rather than blind luck.[21]

This can backfire, particularly when we evaluate others or are being evaluated. Take performance evaluations. We often adjust our aspirations based on performance feedback and interpret success or failure based on whether our performance was below or above expectations, which is why evaluations are so important. They are often based on the final outcome—rather than the context and quality at the time when the decision was made. This is where the *fundamental attribution error* comes into play—the tendency to over-attribute success to skill, rather than situational factors such as luck.[22]

Nobel Prize winner Daniel Kahneman has shown that people in these situations tend to apply cognitive shortcuts—for example, substituting a difficult question such as "What is the unobserved level of skill of this person?" with an easy one such as "What is the observed level of performance of this person?"[23]

This heuristic can save time, and it can be correct because high performers are generally more skilled—unless they are extreme outliers who have benefited from blind luck.[24] But errors can be costly, so this particular heuristic is not always recommended. It depends on the difference in cost of two potential errors: a false negative (mistaking skill for luck), and a false positive (mistaking luck for skill).[25]

When evaluating performance, people tend to err toward false positives—we often attribute luck to skill.* This might be good for employee motivation since we might sustain an appetite for taking risk and further develop our skills if we feel our recent success was based on skill rather than luck.[26]

However, if erring toward false negatives implies inaction, that usually is costlier than action—which suggests that we might make more false positive mistakes. This can lead to very costly errors—such as the financial crises that resulted, at least in part, from rewarding traders' luck and excessive risk-taking. Or the *Columbia* space shuttle disaster, which was a result of evaluating lucky near-misses as "successes." These errors can quickly spiral out of control.[27] This can also lead us to draw the wrong conclusions about why someone was successful. Perhaps the "nasty boss" didn't only make it because they were nasty? It's very likely that many other factors—sometimes even including luck of the draw—played a role.

However, more often than not, blame and praise—and the related promotions and pay—are associated with the unintended consequences of our or others' actions. We might post-rationalize and create stories, but in reality, many things happen unintentionally. Intentions are all well and good but unpredictable factors often produce consequences unrelated to our initial intentions.

Sufficiently skilled managers are likely to be promoted, but the difference in skills between one level and the next is usually small or even negative. Because many exceptional performances are random, those promoted tend to be people who have been lucky a couple of times, and therefore have attracted attention, rather than those who might be higher-skilled but seem average.[28]

One way to deal with this is to try to reduce noise. We can abstract performance pay from external events, or from overly subjective evaluations that focus on particular areas that had a high probability of randomness

---

* This can backfire on a societal level because it can lead to less social spending based on the belief that people are responsible for their own fate—potentially leading to lower social mobility.

interfering. Or we can take inspiration from the ancient Greek and Venetian republics: They used random selection as a "leveler." Political leaders were selected at random.[29] And they might not have been far off: Recent studies have shown that random selection outperforms more sophisticated mechanisms of governance in financial markets and politics, because it is more resistant to nepotism, more robust, overcomes stereotypes, and is perceived as fairer.[30] But this approach can undermine confidence in the abilities of leaders, and can have a negative effect on motivation. What to do about it? Research suggests that the potential candidates should be preselected from a clearly defined pool of contenders who performed well.[31] This mix between performance and random selection can help level the playing field.

The Power of Unintended Consequences

But even if we try to level the playing field, good intentions do not necessarily lead to good outcomes, especially when it comes to social problems. I have witnessed this firsthand in development projects. The related outcomes are often uncertain and have unintended consequences.

When you educate a fourteen-year-old boy in Nairobi's impoverished Kibera district, that might sound wonderful on paper. Your organization will be lauded by donors—you have helped a young person acquire knowledge! You are excited—until you learn that your focus on individuals might just have destroyed a family or community structure. Perhaps the boy was the family's only breadwinner. Now that you have taken him away all day to "get him an education," his sister must bring in the money instead. And there are not many options in impoverished areas for a girl to bring in money.

An alternative approach would have been to think about the effect your actions could have on the whole family. Perhaps then you might decide it is more important to help develop a new income stream for the family first, and also consider educating the whole family rather than just one member, which might not only create a financially precarious situation for the family, but also stir up resentment: If the boy becomes "so much smarter" than the rest of the family they might drift apart.

Take this slightly provocative example that a senior executive shared with me: "I was in a meeting with an African president, who said, 'All this bloody food help of you Western white-faces is not helpful. In the past, people were at least dying in my country. Now you keep them alive with your carbohydrates and your stupid food help and all that stuff. And since the food help is carbohydrate-rich and not rich of vitamins and minerals, my people become ill but stay alive. Then my country becomes poorer every year. Thank you very much.'"

Good intention, bad and unintended outcome. This serendipitous encounter between the executive and the president actually made the company rethink its strategy, and it now focuses on a more holistic approach that takes into account the complexity of the situation.

Whether good intentions lead to good outcomes or bad, people tend to determine blame and praise based on results. What does this mean? Often ill-intended actions or incompetent managers are rewarded for their "achievements" when circumstances outside their control result in a poor decision having an unforeseen beneficial outcome, while well-intended actions or competent executives are blamed for failures that are equally outside their control. Sometimes we even make moral judgments of people who intended well, yet had bad luck.[32] Been there, done that.

This is due to the fact that we infer from unlucky instances that the person might have been negligent, or had false assumptions.[33] As decisions are often based on gut feeling or intuition, the negative outcome might be blamed on the decision maker "not having been rigorous enough"—even though they might have been more rigorous than a comparable person with a positive outcome.

That's particularly relevant when it comes to rewarding people for success based on factors beyond their control—which is not only a fairness problem, but can also make us less motivated.[34] For example, executives are often aware that they could be made scapegoats if performance declines even if it was mostly due to external factors—and so extremely high compensation packages are often considered as insurance for those situations.

We tend to treat executives whose actions resulted in success as heroes, while those whose decisions resulted in failure are treated as villains— even though their decisions might have been identical![35]

Take large-scale failures such as nuclear plant disasters, financial crises, and oil spills: They are often blamed on executives—even though they frequently result from outside factors hitting a fragile system. Catastrophes such as the 1977 Tenerife air disaster, in which two Boeing 747 passenger jets collided on the airport runway and led to the highest number of casualties in aviation history (583), often have a number of situational factors coming together, such as weather, airport conditions—and in this case, terrorism (the threat of a terrorist strike at a nearby airport prompted both planes to be diverted to Tenerife).[36]

We usually derive our perception of the quality of the person from the quality of the outcome. The issue then is when "unlucky" people get fired, but the system remains fragile—which is just awaiting the next normal accident.[37]

In a community organization that I was involved in, we used to dramatically substitute leadership teams after each crisis without addressing the core root problem, such as misalignment between community and company. This led to a constant repetition of the same tensions and problems, just in different manifestations.[38] Many a conflict could have been avoided by fixing the root cause rather than the symptoms and leadership.

The *magnitude* of failure, or success, often says less about the skill of the executive and their luck and more about system characteristics.[39]

Of course, there is the role of individual skill in prompting or avoiding errors. Poorly trained executives can make situations worse and make the collapse of systems more likely. Mindful executives, in turn, can develop resilience into tightly coupled systems before additional damage occurs.[40]

But there is also a much simpler explanation why people attribute bad luck to failure and skill to success: People enjoy being associated with skill for good performance, and bad luck for bad performance. So, the polite thing to do is to give credit to the person for it, even if it is not merited.

As we know, the world is indeed not always fair—hard work might sometimes lead to positive outcomes, but so might contextual factors such as blind luck, inherited wealth, or social connections masquerading as skill.[41] But that is precisely the difference between this blind luck that just happens *to* us and active, smart luck (serendipity) that we can shape ourselves. Once we develop a serendipity mindset, it is not about luck versus skill—cultivating serendipity becomes a life skill in itself.

Given that many of the most important skills in the next years will be related to this mindset, individuals and employers alike are likely to look out for their serendipity score. How can we capture it?

Calculating Our Serendipity Score

Previous research in the information sciences, psychology, management, and related areas has started to identify and validate measures that can help us develop a serendipity score. Essentially, we can look at each step of the process (serendipity trigger, connecting the dots, sagacity, tenacity), and find questions that help us measure it. The questions below are drawn from recent research.[42]

You can start rating yourself on a scale of 1–5, where strongly agree = 5 and strongly disagree = 1:

Score

1. I sometimes chat to strangers when in line in public spaces such as the supermarket or bank.   _____

2. I try to understand what the underlying dynamic behind a problem is.   _____

3. I often see the value in unexpected information or encounters.   _____

4. I can get excited about a broad variety of topics.   _____

5. I have a strong sense of where I want to go.   _____

6. I am not easily discouraged when faced with a tricky problem.   _____

7. I tend to be "mentally present" in situations.   _____

8. I try to understand people's deeper motivation.   _____

9. Good things always seem to happen to me.   _____

10. I often listen to gut feeling and hunches.   _____

11. I trust my judgment.   _____

12. I tend to try to get what I want from life.   _____

13. I expect most people I meet to be nice, pleasant, and helpful.   _____

14. I tend to look on the bright side of life.   _____

15. I believe that errors can be turned into something positive (e.g., learning).   _____

16. I don't tend to dwell on bad things that happened to me.   _____

17. I try to learn from mistakes that I made in the past. _____

18. I consider myself to be lucky. _____

19. I often meet the right person at the right time. _____

20. I regularly go to events where I speak to strangers. _____

21. I am well-connected within the groups and organizations that I am part of. _____

22. I am part of three or more diverse groups. _____

23. I often host other people. _____

24. When someone tells me about a problem, I think about how I or someone else could be of help. _____

25. I put myself into another person's shoes to try to understand a situation. _____

26. I am grateful for the small things in life. _____

27. I often reflect on my actions and how they affect others. _____

28. I surround myself with people who make me feel comfortable to explore ideas. _____

29. People around me feel that they can share their ideas and challenges with me. _____

30. I ask people for help when I need it. _____

31. I often follow up on interesting associations between topics or ideas. _____

32. I tend to be tenacious about following through with ideas even if it takes time. _____

33. I am comfortable in uncertain situations. _____

34. I believe that nothing is set in stone. _____

35. I often use humor to lighten the tone of a
    conversation.   _____

36. I do not feel that I have to be perfect in any
    situation.   _____

37. I tend to ask a lot of questions.   _____

38. I live a life that feels true to my values. _____

TOTAL   _____

Add up your numbers. The maximum score is 190, and the closer you get to that, the closer you are to achieving the serendipity mindset.

Many people find that their scores fall somewhere in the range of 80–100 and that by tweaking their life step by step, they will find that over time their scores will improve to around 140–160, which is fantastic.

Don't worry about how your score compares to others'; what's important is how your serendipity score today compares with your answers and your scores in a week or a month from now. You should make a point of asking yourself these questions regularly and taking note of your scores so that you can chart your improvement over time.

I have used these questions in my seminars, and already after a single week people start to report back that by changing their approach, serendipity is happening more often, for example, high-profile people responding to the participants' "cold" emails, people unexpectedly meeting exactly the person they in hindsight felt they needed to meet ("I just met the best friend I never knew I had"), and people feeling more joyful and "getting back an enthusiasm for life."

This is first and foremost an exercise for individuals, but it can also be practiced in teams—people asking each other these questions can be a playful way to develop relationships and awareness of serendipity—and eventually, for finding innovation and solutions to societal challenges. Depending on the context, some of the questions can be helpful for internal practices such as performance reviews or recruitment, to focus on hiring and rewarding people who make the organization more able to be lucky, and to cope with a fast-changing world.

Why is this important? Because it starts working like a self-fulfilling prophecy: The more we focus on something, the more we learn about it, and the more we will want to do it. Companies such as Zappos have picked up on this idea and included questions such as, "On a scale of one to ten, how lucky are you?" in their interviews. Founder Tony Hsieh explains that Zappos "aims to hire the lucky people that bring more good luck to Zappos."[43] In Zappos's case, this was inspired by Richard Wiseman's studies on luck—showing that people who self-report as being lucky are more likely to pick up on cues, and tend to be luckier in the future than those who self-identify as unlucky.

What Wiseman and Hsieh understood is that it's not about people being inherently lucky or unlucky in life—but that smart luck is about being open to opportunity beyond how the situation or task presents itself. Unlucky people tend to blame fate—lucky people tend to go through life with open eyes. I have seen this in my own work as well: A week or so after a workshop on serendipity, participants tend to send feedback along the lines of "since I've been opening my eyes to serendipity, it's happening all the time now!"

Thus . . .

Reflecting on counterfactuals can help us understand what it was about a situation that might have caused us to be lucky or unlucky. Was it our own effort or just blind luck? If it was your own effort, can it be repeated? Unintended consequences can be avoided by trying to understand the longer-term outcomes rather than short-term consequences. A core challenge for individuals and organizations is to evaluate people who will also be lucky in the future—rather than those who just had blind luck once. The serendipity score can help us with estimating where we are on this journey—and make us more conscious of what we can focus on. It is not set in stone.

SERENDIPITY WORKOUT: REFLECT AND SCORE

1. Reflect on the incidents in your life that shaped you. What could have happened differently? What was your role in them? Were they examples of blind luck or smart luck? What can you learn from them?
2. Who are the people in your life who create smart luck wherever they go? What are three things you can learn from them?
3. How are evaluation systems set up in your organization? Can you improve them so to abstract from random events and focus on the actual effort (*how* someone reached their goal)?
4. Repeat the serendipity score exercise once a month to check in. Which areas can you improve, using the exercises in this book?

CHAPTER 10

THE ART AND SCIENCE OF CULTIVATING SERENDIPITY

‒

I'm a great believer in luck, and I find the harder I work, the more I have of it.

F. L. Emerson

S erendipity can be a profound source of joy and wonder, of those magical moments that make life meaningful and interesting. It can be a key part of our journey, of living a fulfilled and successful life. In short, it can give us back an enthusiasm for life—it can turn the unexpected from a potential threat into a source of delight. If a good life is the accumulation of good days, serendipity can fill our days with joy and with meaning.

This book aims to give hope—and strategies for creating a good life—in an era of polarization. It gives a shared narrative on how we can shape our own smart luck. It's not only the Richard Bransons, J. K. Rowlings, Oprah Winfreys, Michelle Obamas, and Bill Gateses of the world who can be lucky, and who can set up environments for others to be lucky—all of us can do it in our own ways.

While blind luck plays a major role in life, there are ways in which we can shape our own destiny and create conditions, for ourselves and for others, that make "smart" luck more likely over time and with better outcomes. Every missed flight becomes an opportunity—for love, meeting an investor, making a friend, you name it—if you speak to the person next to you.

It is time to let go of the old idea that success results only from either blind luck or skill. Instead, we can work hard to develop the mindset and conditions for active and smart luck to happen.

Developing a serendipity mindset is all about how we frame the world—establishing a core motivation, seeing and connecting the dots, turning them into opportunities, and (potentially) accelerating and amplifying them. It is also about always having an eye out for the potential biases that we all have. (This book is no exception—while I have tried to minimize my own biases, I'm sure there are bits of hindsight or survivor bias here and there, and a story that I would tell one way today, I would probably tell very differently twenty years from now!)

In a time when uncertainty pushes many people to rely on dogma as an anchor, this book offers an alternative: to develop a serendipity mindset and related serendipity field that helps us to cope with whatever life throws at us. And that puts relationships and a sense of meaning and belonging at the core of our existence.

Perhaps this is a new way for you to look at the world. If so, I hope this framework poses important questions that, when you answer them, will help you and those around you to live more joyful, fulfilled, and successful lives. It is a process rather than a destination, a dynamic skill rather than a static solution. And like a muscle, with appropriate training it will become stronger and stronger and part of your natural way of life. Unless you have always intuitively operated like this! In which case, this book is an opportunity to tweak some strategies, to reflect and make sense of how you approach life already. In this case, I hope it might give additional legitimacy to your way of life, especially if you have sometimes had to make up "linear stories" in order to appear more credible. I hope it gives you an active language and shows that there is agency in cultivating serendipity—that it is not a loss of control, but indeed, the only way to get rid of an illusion of control.

But beware the optimizer dilemma! If we strive too much for something, we might never reach it. As with happiness and love, serendipity is not something that can be excessively searched out; rather it is something we can be ready for—and get in shape for. Similar to the fear of missing out (FOMO), the fear of missing serendipity (FOMS) is something best avoided.

But if you are in the right state of mind, are ready and willing, and open to the unexpected, serendipity of all kinds (including true love) is more likely to occur. Then, we embrace rather than take the magic out of "surprises."

By definition, we cannot know or program serendipitous outcomes, or they wouldn't be serendipitous.[1] But what we can do is make some of the unforeseen come to us more often, and with better outcomes. It's not only about showing up, it's about *how* we show up. If you go to the gym and run into someone who could have been the love of your life but neglected to shower for a couple of days or are in a foul mood, your probability of ending up together might be lower than if you are in a better place.

And if we want a happy ending, it often depends on when we stop the story, from which (and whose) perspective we look at it, and how we feel at that moment. Then, a love relationship that ends in a breakup can still be seen to have been a "success".

For organizations, it is vital to develop a "collective mindset," or perhaps even a dynamic capability,[2] that allows for the integration, building, and reconfiguring of internal and external competencies to facilitate an environment in which unexpected discoveries are enabled and nurtured.

We simply cannot know what people will want or need tomorrow—and people will probably not know it themselves, either. Henry Ford, at the dawn of the motor age, was probably right when he said that if he had asked people what they wanted, they would have asked for faster horses. He offered them cars instead, and they were delighted. In organizations, we need to be aware that we cannot predict the future, and that it pays to reward those who create the conditions in which serendipity can happen.

Social and environmental problems, in particular, can be hard to disentangle, and outcomes of interventions are often impossible to predict. That means that we need to develop policies not only around what we know or pretend to know, but also around what we don't know. We have to focus more on social opportunity spaces, and less on prescriptive ideas, which means investing in basic science and training for serendipity mindsets. Inspiring minds can attract criticism for sending the message that individuals themselves can change their circumstance. Instead, the critics argue, we need "systems change." But guess what? Behind systemic change there are usually individuals, often from unexpected places. Waiting for government to fix every problem means submitting to a passive mindset. As long as we keep in mind that there are systemic problems, and that we cannot kid ourselves that small changes can help tackle the real problems, there is much to be said for living life as if it is rigged in our favor, whatever our background.

Developing structural resilience, social mobility, and innovation in the twenty-first century is not about trying to plan everything. The best we can do is to set ourselves and others up to create conditions that make the best out of whatever might happen. Serendipity becomes a powerful mechanism for unleashing human potential. As Joe Kaeser, CEO of Siemens, shared with our Leaders on Purpose team, "The future is uncertain. It's pretty fast in the way it changes, so we've got to create an adaptive mindset. And this adaptability is actually the right element to foster change actively."

But of course, cultivating serendipity is not a panacea. There are structural dynamics, particularly related to power structures, that make it easier for some than for others to develop this mindset and the related serendipity field, and to benefit from the outcomes. The lottery of birth does not distribute access to wealth, education, and skills equally, and there are complex structural issues such as poverty that are and will always be difficult to overcome.

However, across social strata and cultural contexts, cultivating serendipity can be an effective path to escape the confines of "destiny" and create our own luck by setting ourselves up for success. For educational institutions—and parents, for that matter—supporting children in their development of a serendipity mindset and a related serendipity field will be at the core of producing a generation able to navigate an uncertain world. This mindset and skill set will set us apart from robots. It's no longer about merely teaching knowledge, it's about learning how to *be* in a world that makes us different from machines.

I certainly do not have all the answers. Serendipity has been much discussed but little studied, and the embryonic research that has been done is scattered across many different disciplines. I have tried to integrate wherever possible and used analogous thinking for areas where we do not yet have much evidence. I don't make many causal claims, and we need to experiment—there is much to be learned, and this book is not without its own challenges. Had I written it ten years ago or ten years from now, my sense-making process would probably have been very different. I would interpret my own story differently in light of my interest and my feelings at that time. It's quite literally survivor bias (and a number of others, including confirmation bias).[3] But for now, this is the best I can do, and I am looking forward to seeing this as a journey of learning and cocreation with you.

I hope that this book is just the start of a journey and, perhaps, a movement. I'm looking forward to joining you on your own personal serendipity journey. To me, this book has been a wonderful excuse to question many of my own beliefs and biases (of which there are many), and to rethink things such as success and what I take for granted.

For the future, we might want to ask whether there are any emotional, physical, or mental "fundamentals" without which we can't cultivate serendipity. Can people specialize? How much can we rely on a serendipity mindset, and to what degree will we need other forms of learning and discovery that are more "predictable"?

This book is grounded in a "rational optimism," with a plea to stay optimistic even when you're surrounded by cynics. Viktor Frankl's insight that we need to start as optimists to then become the real realists was inspired by Goethe's thought that if we take someone as they are, we make them worse, but if we treat them as who they could be, we enable them to become who they could be.

I hope that this book can be a part of helping us develop ourselves, our friendships, and our organizations to become who we are truly capable of becoming. Not a particular end point or "best self," but trying out variations of our whole selves. Exploring the potential of who we could be with a framework that guides us on this journey.

The world is for many parts socially constructed—once we start questioning existing structures and ideas, we open up a whole new world for ourselves and for others. Perhaps this can make us be part of shaping a new, healthier type of "enlightened self-interest"—based capitalism, in which those who were luckier in the initial birth lottery open up opportunity spaces for those less initially fortunate. To enable everyone to be an agent of their own smart luck, rather than a passive recipient. This is the real sixth sense: the serendipity sense.

This book is a reminder that we do not have to have it all figured out—a serendipity mindset will allow us to navigate the future. Then the answer to "What am I doing with my life?" could be something like, "I am setting myself up for serendipity."

ACKNOWLEDGMENTS

—

This book stands on the shoulders of giants, both of fascinating research papers and beautiful minds that shared their stories and observations. It brings together the last fifteen years of my life, and many of the people that are dearest to me have been part of this process. My editor tells me to keep it short, so this section focuses on the wonderful minds and souls without whose love, support, and patience this book would not have happened. No acknowledgment chapter could ever do justice to them and the trust they put into me, but hopefully it's a start.

Ulla, Rainer, and Malte Busch have been my rocks throughout my life, have made me feel that everything is possible, and gave me the foundations for living a conscious and joyful life. My grandmother Leni, who did not live long enough to see this book come to fruition, has been a role model particularly with regard to resilience and making the best out of what life throws at us.

Grace Gould made me believe in myself again after a tough period, and I cannot thank her enough for her encouragement, making me laugh so much, and reminding me to focus again on those things that I enjoy doing the most. Sophie Johnsson has been by my side during the most difficult period of my life, and I am very grateful for her having been an emotional rock.

Gail Rebuck has been a truthful guide, inspiration, and sounding board throughout this journey, and I cannot thank her enough for her wisdom, encouragement, and to-the-point advice.

My agents Gordon Wise and Kristine Dahl have moved mountains. My publishers at Penguin Life (Emily Robertson and Marianne Tatepo) and at Riverhead (Jake Morrissey) have used their editorial brilliance to help turn my ideas into a (hopefully!) readable book. My publicists Shailyn Tavella and Julia Murday have brought it to light.

My colleagues at NYU's Center for Global Affairs and at LSE's Marshall Institute have provided me with the most nurturing of home grounds I could wish for. My academic collaborators, especially Harry Barkema, Saul Estrin, and Susan Hill, have introduced me to the joy of combining science with a meaningful impact. My Leaders on Purpose team, and in particular Christa Gyori, Tatjana Kazakova, Leith Sharp, Maya Brahman, and Nicole Belleslie, have energized me throughout.

Carolin Krenzer, Stephan Chambers, Michael Hastings, Gerry George, Steven D'Souza, Michael Mayernick, and my cofounders at Sandbox have been a great inspiration throughout the last years. Phil Kaye and Fabian Pfortmüller have inspired and sensitized me especially regarding underlying structural dynamics such as racial and other implicit biases that often manifest in day-to-day interactions. Jessica Carson—the embodiment of a serendipitor—has been a wonderfully inspiring mirror for my thoughts and ideas. Andrew Hill and the Bracken Bower Prize jury supported this idea when it was still in its embryonic stages, for which I am deeply grateful.

Tuukka Toivonen, Paolo Rigutto, Karin King, Noa Gafni, Tatjana Kazakova, Matthew Grimes, Jim de Wilde, Tim Weiss, Arieh and Nachson Mimran, Marlon Parker, Christoph Seckler, Willem Büchler, Archish Mittal, Edward Goldberg, and Christopher Ankersen gave their time (and most probably, nerves!) to go through early drafts. I cannot thank them enough for their pertinent feedback and advice. Simon Watkins and Shane Richmond were of great support in helping me shape the ideas and content. Brad Gyori opened my eyes to the role of arts in understanding orchestrating serendipity.

The Sandbox Network, Nexus Summit, World Economic Forum, Performance Theatre, MakeSense, Royal Academy of Arts, and Global Shapers communities have been a constant inspiration. Simon Engelke and Seredy.org—a platform facilitating serendipitous connections—introduced me to fantastic people.

Alice Wang, Alexa Wright, Jill Juergensen, Kelsey Beuning, and Michael Junga were of great help in data collection and analysis.

Last but absolutely not least, my heartfelt thank you goes to all the brilliant minds who shared their thoughts and stories with me. While we were not able to integrate all of the stories into the book, I am looking forward to helping highlight the most inspiring stories in other ways.

This book integrates the ideas, thoughts, and insights of a broad variety of beautiful minds and souls, and while I tried my best to integrate them as truthfully as possible, I'm sure that there are occasions where I wasn't able to do full justice to the brilliance of an idea. I will make sure to sharpen this over time, seeing this as the start of the conversation. There are many other people who have been close to me and who have shared their support, and I will find other ways to thank them.

This book is the result of an intense search for meaning. I have, of course, been lucky regarding the people I have met and the ideas I have encountered. But what has turned those moments into a coherent whole is something far more intriguing than plain chance—serendipity. Thank you for being part of this journey.

GLOSSARY

Blind luck: Success or failure brought about simply by chance rather than through our own actions

Compound serendipity: A process where each new instance of serendipity has greater potential because of the ones that have gone before

FOMS: Fear of Missing Serendipity

Hub ambassador: Local representative

JOMO: Joy of Missing Out

Lateral accountability: Accountability to oneself and among peers

Opportunity space: The potential dots that could be there or that could be connected

Serendipitor: Someone who cultivates serendipity

Serendipity field: The opportunity space that holds all the potential bisociations/(connections of) dots that could happen, and our capacity to do something with it

Serendipity mindset: Both a life philosophy and a method and a skill set that we can develop to cultivate more positive coincidences in our own and other people's lives

Smart luck: Luck that we bring about with our own actions; "active" luck

Social capital: The benefits of social relations (e.g., resources, emotional support, etc.)

Tie strength: Combination of the amount of emotional intensity, time, and reciprocal services that characterize the tie. Ties to friends are "strong ties" while ties to casual acquaintances are "weak ties."

Zemblanity: The faculty of making unhappy, unlucky, and expected discoveries; the opposite of serendipity

NOTES

___

INTRODUCTION

1. Denrell et al., 2003; Dunbar and Fugelsang, 2005.
2. Burt, 2004; de Rond and Morley, 2010. Serendipity has been understood as either a quality or a process (McCay-Peet and Toms, 2018). Serendipity is all about seeing "pairs" of observations that may have nothing in common apart from that they are meaningfully related—and so definitions that frame it as pure "blind luck" appear inaccurate (de Rond, 2014). The observation might just be chance, but it is in the response to it, the sagacity of the observer, that births serendipity from chance. This is why I refer to "smart luck" instead of "blind" luck.
3. I conducted a literature review based on search terms such as "serendipity," "chance," "coincidence," "luck," and used a snowballing approach to integrate papers from other fields as I came across them (Flick, 2009). I focused on those that appeared to be meaningfully related, and complemented them with observations, archival information, and interviews. In the interviews and observations, I looked for emerging patterns, and aggregated emerging insights into themes (see Flick, 2009; Yin, 2003). The book integrates a number of my research projects and recent papers and studies, including insights from a Leaders on Purpose study, in which my colleagues Christa Gyori, Leith Sharp, Maya Brahman, and Tatjana Kazakova and I interviewed thirty-one of the world's leading chief executives, including of companies such as BMW, Haier, MasterCard, PayPal, and Philips (also see Busch, 2019; Gyori et al., 2018; Kazakova and Gyori, 2019; Sharp, 2019). I followed a similar coding logic throughout projects to identify underlying patterns. I complemented these different data collection efforts with my own experiences during fifteen years of cultivating serendipity, as well as conversations with inspirational people around the world.
4. Brown, 2005; de Rond, 2014; Napier and Vuong, 2013.

CHAPTER 1: SERENDIPITY

1. See Merton and Barber, 2004. Serendipity researcher Pek van Andel (1984) simply calls it "the art of making an unsought finding." Other definitions demarcate serendipity as "search leading to unintended discovery" (Dew, 2009) or "the unique and contingent mix of insight coupled with chance" (Fine and Deegan, 1996). I use a broad definition of serendipity based on its original definition, including possibilities such as initial search for something else as well as non-search (not actively looking for anything specific) (see Napier and Vuong, 2013). For Horace Walpole's initial correspondence, see Lewis, 1965.

2. Depending on a number of considerations (including potential "pseudo-serendipity"), researchers tend to differentiate three to five forms. The three types that I discuss cover the whole spectrum. "Normal," non-serendipitous problem solving would be to have a clear intent and a presupposed solution—you go from A to B. While some researchers have differentiated between "real" and "fake" serendipity, others (e.g., Dew, 2009) have predefined aspects such as search (and thus implicitly decided on particular types). Based on the assumptions that the value of unexpected encounters comes in all shapes and forms, this book covers all types (see e.g., de Rond, 2014; Napier and Vuong, 2013; and Yaqub, 2018, for excellent discussions).

3. Of course, the serendipity journey is not limited to one serendipitous encounter, but often includes a string of unexpected events—in this case, I focus on the key parts of the process (which could be further deconstructed).

4. Busch, 2019; Gyori et al., 2018.

5. Some researchers have argued that examples such as Fleming's are *pseudo-serendipitous*. In their view, pseudo-serendipity encapsulates the situation where you are looking for something already, and then come across something coincidentally that helps reach your initial goal (so, essentially, a coincidental way to reach the same goal). "Real" serendipity then refers to something completely unexpected. In this logic, the discovery of DNA, for example, would count as pseudo-serendipity because the original target was relatively clear, but chance events enabled unraveling the molecule. And in the case of penicillin, Fleming was somewhat prepared for his observation, as he was already interested in the antibiotic effects of substances. Following the logic of those researchers, "true" serendipity would have demanded a change in objective (Roberts, 1989). Most researchers (including myself) do not share this narrow notion and consider incidences such as the discovery of DNA as serendipity in the broader sense: a trigger via a bisociation led to a surprising positive outcome. Else, almost all serendipity would count as pseudo-serendipity (also see Copeland, 2018; Sanger Institute, 2019).

6. The Conversation, 2015.

7. The exact labeling differs, but recent papers focus on the process and the key parts. Makri et al. (2014), for example, look at the process as: Unexpected circumstances + insight > make connection > project value > exploit value > valuable outcome.

Others pronounce the "connecting the dots" part (e.g., Pina e Cunha et al., 2010; de Rond, 2014). Some of the most interesting insights in this regard come from studies in the context of information sciences and ICT technology. Stephann Makri and colleagues, for example, showed how in an information technology environment, the likelihood of serendipity can be increased by tackling different parts of the process, particularly by seizing the emerging opportunities. Just an unexpected encounter is not enough (Makri et al., 2014).

8. Simonton, 2004.

9. Busch, 2018; Busch and Barkema, 2020; McCay-Peet and Toms, 2018; Napier and Vuong, 2013; Van Andel, 1992.

10. de Rond, 2014; Fine and Deegan, 1996; McCay-Peet and Toms, 2018; Merton and Barber, 2004. Naturally, this process is not always completely "linear." For example, trigger and bisociation often happen at the same time, or there can be feedback effects—but by looking at the different steps we can derive important insights.

11. For (accelerating) serendipity in combinatorial chemistry, see for example Mc-Nally et al., 2011; for qualitative methods, see for example Glaser and Strauss's (1967) work on grounded theory and Merton's (1949) work on social theory and social structure.

CHAPTER 2: BECOMING ATTUNED

1. Borja and Haigh, 2007; McKinney, 1966. I am indebted to Mattan Griffel for making me aware of the paradox and for being my first partner in crime when using it as an exercise.

2. Pina e Cunha et al., 2010. We also tend to miss smaller coincidences, as we are usually attracted by the big surprising ones.

3. Wiseman, 2003.

4. For work on missing serendipity, see for example Barber and Fox, 1958; and Napier and Vuong, 2013. A related concept is that of "social failures" (e.g., Piskorski, 2011), which refers to social interactions that do not occur but that would make people better off if they did.

5. Napier and Vuong, 2013.

6. Katz et al., 2017.

7. Surowiecki, 2004.

8. Denrell et al., 2003.

9. Busch, 2019; Sharp, 2019.

10. Coad, 2009; Fildes et al., 2009; Geroski, 2005.

11. Cohen et al., 1972; Hannan et al., 2003; Herndon et al., 2014. Also, often the ones who have the greatest stories based on one or two "lucky choices"—like predicting a stock market crisis—are surprisingly bad at making similarly good choices. They were often lucky in the sense of blind luck. In those cases, we mistake blind luck for

skill, and in the long run, top performers become average performers. But in the short run, those blind luck profiteers can take advantage of the situation by presenting their luck as talent and demanding additional rewards for it (Denrell et al., 2019).

12. Liu and de Rond, 2014; McGahan and Porter, 2002; Rumelt, 1991; also see Denrell, 2004; Denrell et al., 2015; Henderson et al., 2012.

13. Roese and Vohs, 2012; Sharp, 2019.

14. Hadjikhani et al., 2009; Jaekel, 2018; Sagan, 1995; Svoboda, 2007; Voss et al., 2012. For the Virgin Mary in grilled cheese sandwiches, see http://news.bbc .co.uk/1/hi/world/americas/4034787.stm.

15. Also see Conrad, 1958; Mishara, 2010. A related concept is that of "patternicity"— the tendency to find meaningful patterns in meaningless noise. In contrast, "randomania" refers to the phenomenon of attributing something to chance that is apparently related to data or patterns. This includes fascinating areas such as dream precognition.

16. An overview on Leith Sharp's work on ideas flow can be found on www.flowleader ship.com. Also see Leaders on Purpose 2019 CEO study.

17. LSE book reading (2019) by Deborah Levy.

18. Adamson and Taylor, 1954; Duncker, 1945.

19. Allen and Marquis, 1964; Arnon and Kreitler, 1984.

20. Dane et al., 2011; also see Arnon and Kreitler, 1984.

21. Ritter et al., 2012.

22. D'Souza and Renner, 2016; also see German and Barrett, 2005; German and Defeyter, 2000.

23. Marsh, 2019.

24. For an overview of potential models, see: https://fs.blog/mental-models/.

25. Additional sources that informed this chapter: Asch, 1951; Kirzner, 1979; Lorenz et al., 2011; Merton and Barber, 2004; Pina e Cunha et al., 2010; Schon, 1983; Spradlin, 2012; von Hippel and von Krogh, 2016.

26. I thank Rey Buckman for the suggestion.

CHAPTER 3: THE OPEN MIND

1. Merton and Barber, 2004; Pina e Cunha et al., 2010.

2. Busch and Barkema, 2019; Kirzner, 1979; Merton and Barber, 2004; Pina e Cunha et al., 2010. Also see Dew, 2009.

3. These insights are incorporated from Busch and Barkema, 2017. Using qualitative methods, we collected data for a period of five years. We visited the locations several times, and conducted observations, interviews, and archival data analysis.

4. Busch and Barkema, 2017.

5. Wiseman, 2003.

6. Making the abstract concrete often gives us a feeling of control. I still remember the tedious time I spent working on my PhD: five years of research and writing to tackle one broad question. It was a scary and seemingly uncontrollable period of my life. But discussions with friends allowed me to break it down into actionable items, including four concrete papers that I treated as distinct "projects" with clear outcomes. This made it all feel more manageable and made it easier for me to sleep better. Once I felt in control, the emerging sense of direction made it easier to navigate life.

7. Busch, 2012; Leaders on Purpose 2019 CEO study.

8. This relates to the "bicycle theory" that a Fortune 500 CEO shared with my Leaders on Purpose team. In his eyes, the key to get the organization going is to mobilize the energy with a view that energy is not a finite quantity, but something that you can create. It's like being on a bicycle: If you try to direct a bicycle at a standstill, you fall. The key is for the bicycle to get going. It doesn't matter if the bicycle is going exactly in the right direction, but the key is to keep going and then you adjust course. If you're moving, you can change the direction of the bicycle.

9. www.theguardian.com/news/oliver-burkeman-s-blog/2014/may/21/everyone-is -totally-just-winging-it.

10. Leaders on Purpose 2019 CEO study.

11. This resonates with previous work on modeling humility (e.g., Owens, 2012). Anand Mahindra, CEO of the Mahindra Group, one of the world's leading conglomerates active in almost every industry, told me how his waste-to-energy business emerged serendipitously in this way—and that "what has been consuming us after that is how do we institutionalize serendipity, even though that's an oxymoron."

12. Dweck, 2006.

13. Doidge, 2007; Kolb and Gibb, 2011. For companies, it has been shown that an understanding of one's market needs, purpose, and self-conscious inquiry is crucial to capture opportunities in constantly changing environments (see Danneels, 2011; Leaders on Purpose 2019 CEO study).

14. Scholars from Henry Mintzberg and Saras Sarasvathy onward have discussed that "emergent strategy" or "effectuation" might be more realistic portrayals of reality than strategic planning—though that still is what most business schools focus on. In the context of entrepreneurship, this is spelled out convincingly by Saras Sarasvathy's theory of *effectuation*. Effective entrepreneurs, she showed, often do not work out their target destination and then design the steps to reach it. They do the opposite: They look at what they have in front of them—the resources, skills, connections, and the marketplace—and build something based on them. Then, they often iterate (Sarasvathy, 2008). Effectuation is based on the idea of non-predictive control—that is, the better firms can control the future, the less they will need to predict it. It is especially relevant for those individuals that need to cope with dynamic environments that do not allow them to predict the future.

15. Also see Merrigan, 2019.

16. Van Andel, 1994; Williams et al., 1998.

17. See Diaz de Chumaceiro, 2004; Napier and Vuong, 2013; van Andel, 1994.

18. Wharton Business School, 2017.

19. For example, research has shown that inexperienced start-up founders are often alert and have an intense appetite for information—but their search is less focused. In contrast, more experienced managers tend to stay on track (Busenitz, 1996).

20. Pina e Cunha et al., 2010. Also see Kornberger et al., 2005; Miyazaki, 1999.

21. Miyazaki, 1999; also see Kornberger et al., 2005.

22. Business is replete with models for this kind of approach. For example, *fishbone diagrams* that trace cause and effect allow us to look beyond the initial surface problem toward the underlying causes. Some problems can be preempted by *fault tree analysis* that looks for the events that would cause a problem and set in place measures to avoid them. This is particularly important in fields with very low failure tolerance. In a nuclear reactor or an airplane, you do not have the luxury of waiting until a symptom occurs and only then look for a cause—it's better to work out what could go wrong and prevent that happening in the first place. (Every time I fly, I take great comfort from the fact that this kind of analysis has—hopefully!—been carried out.) (Also see Ishikawa, 1968; von Hippel and von Krogh, 2016.)

23. See von Hippel and von Krogh, 2016.

24. See, for example, Kurup et al., 2011; Smith and Eppinger, 1997; Thomke and Fujimoto, 2000; Volkema, 1983; von Hippel and von Krogh, 2016.

25. Emirbayer and Mische, 1998; Schwenk and Thomas, 1983; von Hippel and von Krogh, 2016.

26. Then, a main challenge is to identify the efficiency and effectiveness of search strategies—the "economics of search"—which are usually based on *satisficing* rather than *optimizing* algorithms given that resources (such as a doctor's time) are limited, and problems complex (see Fleming and Sorenson, 2004; Garriga et al., 2013; Laursen and Salter, 2006).

27. Simon, 1977.

28. Here, a well-structured problem statement is articulated, then a solution landscape (potential solutions to the problem) is searched by casting rough-mesh digital nets over the whole solution landscape to discover the approximate location of potentially desirable solution "peaks." In progressive steps, finer-mesh networks are hovered over the most promising areas, aiming to discover the most satisfactory solution. Depending on the respective rules that are specified (e.g., breadth first or depth first), potential results can be identified within given constraints (see Ghemewat and Levinthal, 2008; Levinthal and Posen, 2007; von Hippel and von Krogh, 2016).

29. Stock et al., 2017; von Hippel and von Krogh, 2016.

30. Tyre and von Hippel, 1997; von Hippel and Tyre, 1996; von Hippel and von Krogh, 2016.

31. Gronbaek, 1989; Thomke and Fujimoto, 2000; von Hippel and von Krogh, 2016. For similar approaches focusing on trial and error, see: Hsieh et al., 2007; Kurup et al., 2011; Nelson 2008.

32. E.g., Ferre et al., 2001; von Hippel and von Krogh, 2016; see Conboy, 2009, for a review.

33. Toms, 2000; also see Dew, 2009; Graebner, 2004; McCay-Peet and Toms, 2010; Stock et al., 2017.

34. Stock et al., 2017; also see Cosmelli and Preiss, 2014; Schooler and Melcher, 1995.

35. Klein and Lane, 2014.

36. Stock et al., 2017; also see Cosmelli and Preiss, 2014; Schooler and Melcher, 1995.

37. See, e.g., Cosmelli and Preiss, 2014; Pelaprat and Cole 2011; Topolinski and Reber, 2010.

38. Example adapted from von Hippel and von Krogh, 2016.

39. von Hippel and von Krogh, 2016. Naturally, as some have argued (e.g., Felin and Zenger, 2015), often what is new to us might not be new to others, and others might have gone through a more "step by step" process already.

40. Among others, in addition to the suitcase example, von Hippel and von Krogh use the following two helpful examples. 1) If you are a parent, picture the following situation: You notice a baby carrier for a bicycle in the window of a store—it looks very safe and sturdy. Until now you had used the car to take your daughter to daycare. You are also, however, an avid bike rider. Suddenly, you think, "I didn't think I needed a baby carrier, but this one could actually be very effective in my day-to-day life: using my bike to carry my daughter to nursery instead of using the car!" (This may be more likely in a Nordic country than it would be in London or New York!) 2) Imagine you are at a trade show, aiming to see "what's out there." You might have an idea of what you're interested in, but you're mostly there to explore. By chance, you encounter a company stand offering a new payroll-processing software that, it claims, addresses particular needs and problems better than existing rivals. You are not looking to change payroll systems, but nevertheless you take a look. As you do, you realize this payroll is designed to be excellent for organizations with large numbers of staff working very flexible hours. This happens to be the employment strategy your company is planning to adopt. Then it dawns on you—actually your existing payroll package will not be able to cope with that employment strategy.

41. See, e.g., Bradley et al., 2012; Krumholz et al., 2011.

42. Merrigan, 2019.

43. The *lead user approach* and its developments are inspired by innovation expert von Hippel. Lead users are the people, often but not always early adopters of some system or technology, who are pressing the boundaries of its use. They tend to identify the limitations and the risks lurking in a system or technology long before

the wider group of users. The lead user may even have formulated solutions before you even knew there was a problem (Churchill et al., 2009; von Hippel, 1986).

44. I thank Georgie Nightingall, founder of Trigger Conversations, for this thought. Her related TEDx talk can be found here: www.youtube.com/watch?v=ogVL BEzn2rk; she also recommends this TED talk to have better conversations: www .ted.com/talks/celeste_headlee_10_ways_to_have_a_better_conversation/dis cussion?quote=1652.

CHAPTER 4: THE STIMULATED MIND

1. For a fantastic related discussion, see von Hippel and von Krogh, 2016.
2. Leaders on Purpose 2019 CEO study.
3. For more background reading on intrinsic and extrinsic motivation, see Ryan and Deci, 2000.
4. Leaders on Purpose 2019 CEO study. This also applies to firms: Firms develop a unique firm-specific theory of value creation—revealing an architecture and bundle of problems that deserve attention. This then guides the strategic direction and allows it to filter. The central vehicle for value creation, then, lies in composing and updating the firm's theory and using it to formulate problems, organize a solution search, and select from among available need-solution pairs—it is something that is unique to them (Felin and Zenger, 2015). A reason why we can charge more for new products is that in existing markets, there is a clear idea of how to price products. When it comes to novel problems or novel uses, markets for novel problem/solution pairs can lead to value creation opportunities that are unforeseen by others—and for which a theory can be created (including a justification for higher prices!).
5. Grant, 2015; also see Engel et al., 2017.
6. Businesses have used a number of approaches to do so, including the real options analysis, in which decisions are broken down into multiple smaller ones, with the commitment to a later phase depending on the outcome of former stages (Mc-Grath, 1999). Bayesian updating—wherein we take into account all prior probabilities and update them as and when we get new information—is an interesting related concept in this regard as well.
7. Cohen et al., 1972. The idea is that in decision situations such as meetings, participants dump problems and solutions into the bin—and chance often determines which solutions get attached to which problems. But of course, here the assumption is that we use already formulated problems and solutions—while in a rapidly changing world, questions and answers are often more emergent.
8. Many large organizations have started placing bets different ways, be it by using more decentralized structures (e.g., at AIG) or internal incubators (e.g., at Siemens) that turn their companies into platforms, and, like at BMW, train their people in how to navigate a world full of uncertainty (for example, by retraining

current employees rather than hiring new people). At Inditex, CEO Pablo Isla structures work in ways that people "conceive the company as if it was a small company, as if it was the first day."

9. Collectivism is about the emphasis on cohesiveness and prioritization of group over self (Hofstede, 1980; Schwartz, 1990). Collectivistic societies tend to be more trust- and relationships-based, while more individual societies tend to be more contract- and deal-based. In one of my summer-school courses that consists of students that are usually around eighteen to twenty-five years of age, I often get asked by students from more "deal-focused" cultures (e.g., Germany) if the relationship-building with more collectivistic cultures (e.g., Kenya) wouldn't be a "waste of time." I usually respond with an example from my work in Kenya: It took me a long time to develop a couple of deep friendships; but now, whenever I go, I have access to everyone, because in the words of a Kenyan friend of mine, "everyone is the brother or sister of someone." And because I am introduced by someone they trust, everything gets done quite quickly. More importantly though, it showed me (coming from a very individualistic background) that business can be much more fun when you see it as a social setting rather than a purely commercial setting. I've learned much more about Kenya because of it; and in the long run, it has paid off in many other ways, too.

10. www.npr.org/sections/health-shots/2019/05/25/726695968/whats-your -purpose-finding-a-sense-of-meaning-in-life-is-linked-to-health.

11. This beautifully relates to Simon Sinek's work. Sinek, whose work on "why" has inspired individuals and organizations around the world, asks: Why do we keep score in general? He points to the fact that from a very early age on, most people have the desire to "win." But which score do we use? For some it is fame, for others, it is money, power, or family. The score helps us to feel that we progress—a relative account of how things are going. Sinek uses the example of a billionaire who loses a million and gets depressed. The change in money does not really have an impact on her lifestyle—but she might feel she lost. Going back to the "why" helps us to ground in what it was about in the first place. The beauty of a serendipity score? It is about who we can become in relation to ourselves.

12. AoK Fehlzeiten Report, 2018.

13. See, e.g., Dunn et al., 2008.

14. Preethaji and Krishnaji, 2019.

15. There is a well-known, perhaps apochryphal story of John F. Kennedy asking a cleaner in the NASA operations center why she seemed so happy: "I'm part of putting a man on the moon!" she replied. I've seen similar effects with receptionists who become the key communication-people, or with cleaners who are addressed as equals. At the end of the day, dignity, social connectedness, and feeling linked to a higher purpose go a long way.

16. Mandi et al., 2013.

17. Leaders on Purpose 2019 CEO study.

18. Wiseman, 2003.

19. Busch and Barkema, 2019.

20. Quote adjusted from Nelson Mandela. See www.theguardian.com/lifeandstyle /2012/feb/01/top-five-regrets-of-the-dying. This episode also made me realize that actions often have unintended consequences, and that conflicts can be good—as my cofounder Fabian Pfortmüller remarked during our recent debriefs, "Forests need to burn from time to time, to rejuvenate soil and for new trees to grow." In the case of one of our organizations, it allowed a new generation of leaders to emerge organically.

21. For a great interview on these themes, see: https://medium.com/@farnamstreet /adam-grant-on-intentional-parenting-4e4128a7c03b.

22. Other companies that have tried to integrate values at scale include Mars, where the "Five Principles" are being used to guide decisions in meetings and unite employees across cultures based on the core values of mutuality, quality, responsibility, efficiency, and freedom.

23. Laloux, 2014.

24. This is closely linked to the reciprocity principle (see Cialdini, 1984).

25. Grant, 2014; Grant, 2017.

26. See, for example, Dunn, Aknin, and Norton, 2008.

27. Laloux, 2014.

28. Please note that this is not the same as the willingness to take risks. As Adam Grant has pointed out nicely in *Originals*, many original people are actually very risk averse. For deeper reading into the respective areas, see Erdelez, 1999; Heinstroem, 2006; Stock et al., 2016.

29. Proactive behavior refers to self-initiated and future-oriented action that aims to change and improve the situation or oneself (Grant, 2000; Parker et al., 2006). It concerns a domain of behavior in which individuals are agentic and anticipatory in their actions—they are thinking, planning, calculating, and acting in advance with foresight about future events before they occur (Bandura, 2006; Bindl et al., 2012; Parker et al., 2006).

30. Grant, 2017. Also see Simonton, 2003.

31. Brian Little at Cambridge University has done excellent work on this; for a short summary, see his TEDx Talk: www.youtube.com/watch?v=NZ5o9PcHeL0.

32. Extroversion is one of the "big five traits" defined by OCEAN: O for Openness, C for Conscientiousness, E for Extroversion, A for Agreeableness, and N for Neuroticism.

33. Cain, 2013; her wonderful TED Talk can be found here: https://ed.ted.com/les sons/susan-cain-the-power-of-introverts.

34. Wiseman, 2003; McCay-Peet et al. (2015) show the same for extroversion.

35. Wiseman, 2003.

36. Baron, 2008; Helfat and Peteraf, 2015. Work on organizational creativity has shown that positive affect makes it easier for people to make new associations in

their minds, as it boosts the fluidity of their thinking across different topics (see, for example, Isen et al., 1987).

37. These approaches have sometimes been described as being pseudo-scientific (see Lederman and Teresi, 1993; https://plato.stanford.edu/entries/pseudo-science/#NonSciPosSci).

38. Preethaji and Krishnaji, 2019.

39. Pinker, 2017.

40. See, for example, Pershing, 2015; Walia, 2018.

41. The Law of Attraction—the belief that negative or positive thoughts bring negative or positive experiences into one's life—has attracted both a lot of followers and a lot of critics, who have described it as non-science posing as science or quantum mysticism. For a short overview, see www.wikizero.com/en/Law_of_attraction_(New_Thought)#cite_note-gazette-1.

42. Beitman, 2016.

43. Preethaji and Krishnaji, 2019.

44. Jennifer Hawthorne's estimate as cited in Preethaji and Krishnaji, 2019.

45. In fact, suspending judgment, and especially the thought of how others will judge us, is often at the core of core themes such as creativity (Amabile et al., 1996).

46. Preethaji and Krishnaji, 2019; clip on www.youtube.com/watch?v=E8aprCNnecU. Some of these premises are related to the idea of emotivism—namely, that moral judgments are not statements of fact but expressions of someone's feelings (see, e.g., www.britannica.com/topic/Language-Truth-and-Logic).

47. Chopra, 1994.

48. Schermer, 2007; also see https://plato.stanford.edu/entries/pseudo-science/#NonSciPosSci.

49. For the general importance of humility and managing errors, see Seckler et al., 2019.

50. Kahneman (2011) differentiates between System 1—an often unconscious and fast way of thinking—and System 2—a slow but controlled way of thinking.

51. Porges, 2009; Porges, 2011. This can, for example, play a major role with regard to healing trauma (Van der Kolk, 2014).

52. For the relationship between alertness and serendipity, see Pina et Cunha et al., 2010.

53. Adapted from Preethaji and Krishnaji, 2019.

54. See www.newyorker.com/magazine/2019/01/21/the-art-of-decision-making.

55. Recent research has shown that focusing on (agile) habits rather than specific goals can be effective—as long as they do not constrain us. Warren Buffett did not become a billionaire by setting himself the goal to become a billionaire—he became a billionaire by developing wisdom and knowledge and making reading a daily habit (Buffett purportedly tries to avoid meetings, and spends most of his day reading). Rather than focusing on goals only (e.g., "I want to spend ten hours with my fiancé

per week"), we can focus on a habit (e.g., "I want to have dinner with my fiancé every second evening"). Goals are often imbued on us—extrinsic—while habits can become an important heuristic. For some inspiring nuggets of wisdom on these questions, see www.farnamstreetblog.com/2017/06/habits-vs-goals/ and www .farnamstreetblog.com/2013/05/the-buffett-formula-how-to-get-smarter/.

CHAPTER 5: ENABLING AND SPOTTING SERENDIPITY TRIGGERS

1. Pirnot et al., 2013.
2. See McNally et al., 2011. Another example is computer scientists introducing systems that increase chance elements in information retrieval by using data-mining in ways that offer unexpected links to new interesting information (Beale, 2007; Liang, 2012).
3. A nice short clip on this: www.youtube.com/watch?v=U88jj6PSD7w.
4. Or take the internet, where embedded search results or "suggested pages" can all be prompts of serendipity—there's a whole industry (and dozens of research papers) now focused on increasing chance elements by embedding unexpected links to new interesting information (Beale, 2007; Liang, 2012).
5. www.politico.com/magazine/story/2018/01/20/henry-kissinger-networking -216482.
6. Creating serendipity triggers becomes natural once we start putting ourselves out there. A more radical example is entrepreneur Cara Thomas, who decided to travel solo through Southeast Asia for three months based on the adventures that friends suggested. She was terrified about it, but opening herself up to the unknown allowed for magic experiences to happen—and her business, which focuses on everyday serendipity experiences, emerged from it. Or take Keyun Ruan, whom we have already met, who during her studies in Germany would take a random train on Fridays, curious to speak with strangers wherever she ended up. Her approach reminded me of Jack Reacher, author Lee Child's character who solves the most unexpected cases by taking random buses across the United States.
7. Aknin et al., 2013; Dunn et al., 2008.
8. Dew, 2009; McCay-Peet and Toms, 2010; Napier and Vuong, 2013.
9. Busch and Mudida, 2018; Granovetter, 1973.
10. Burt, 2004; Yaqub, 2018. However, not in all cultures; see for example Xiao and Tsui (2007) for a good study on why brokerage might not work (the same way) in the collectivistic context of China.
11. However, introductions are also a responsibility (we will be attached to it, if we want it or not). And in the midst of a hectic day, we might feel like directly introducing people—but it's vital to first ask the other person if they mind being introduced.
12. This includes the work task environment, and the type of the work itself (McCay-Peet and Toms, 2010).

13. Catmull, 2008; Lehrer, 2011.
14. Catmull, 2008; Lehrer, 2011.
15. See, for example, https://blog.websummit.com/engineering-serendipity-story-web -summits-growth/ and https://blog.websummit.com/why-you-shouldnt-attend -web-summit/.
16. Busch and Lup, 2013.
17. Busch and Barkema, 2017.
18. http://www.nytimes.com/2012/06/10/opinion/sunday/friedman-facebook -meets-brick-and-mortar-politics.html.
19. http://graphics.wsj.com/blue-feed-red-feed/.
20. Busch and Mudida, 2018.
21. Brown, 2005; Pina e Cunha et al., 2010, Merton and Barber, 2004.
22. http://news.bbc.co.uk/1/hi/magazine/8674539.stm Thanks to Paolo Rigutto for pointing me to this story.
23. Merton and Barber, 2004.
24. Merton, 1968.
25. Merton and Barber, 2004.
26. Hargadon and Sutton, 1997; Garud et al., 1997.
27. See www.businessinsider.com/salesforce-ceo-marc-benioff-beginners-mind-2018-9.
28. Super-encounterers (Erdelez, 1999) face unexpected data and information more often than others as part of the information acquisition process. This builds on findings in the philosophy of science literature (e.g., van Andel, 1994) that show that unexpected discoveries are facilitated by a questioning mind.
29. de Bono, 1992. De Bono developed the *six thinking hats* system, a decision-making method that helps groups think more effectively—each hat represents a certain way of thinking. Also see Birdi, 2005.
30. See, for example, de Bono, 2015.
31. Gyori, 2018.
32. As with everything, taking it to the extreme ("extreme disjunction") can lead to pattern blindness, in which audiences are bewildered and overwhelmed by disjointed information. Sometimes artists might want to cause this effect, though over time and with longer works, it might strain attention and build exhaustion (Gyori, 2018).
33. The potential of the disjunctive is to shatter expectations, with four types that are relevant for serendipity: Spatial disjunction preserves the continuity of time but shifts the viewer's perspective to a new location. In film, a scene would be filmed from different angles. In work environments, it would be changing locations (e.g., coffee shop 1 to coffee shop 2), to get a freshening up. Temporal disjunction involves leaps in time, for example by removing a bit of footage from a single shot of film, so that a jump occurs. Spatiotemporal disjunction is about shifting both time and space. For example, a novel shifting from a diary entry written in the evening

in the city shifts to a letter written in the morning in the countryside. Authorial disjunction is about shifting between authorial perspectives (e.g., the surrealists' "exquisite corpse" experiment), where multiple artists create collaborative poems and drawings. And last but not least, syntactic disjunction is about shattering symbolic continuity—for example, the cut-up novels of William S. Burroughs, where pages of linear prose are sliced into sections and assembled in nonlinear fashions.

34. Gyori, 2018; Lessig, 2008; Navas et al., 2014.

35. For a great overview of interest-based negotiations, see Fisher et al., 2011.

36. Marx and Engels as quoted in Gyori, 2018. See for example Marx and Engels, 1998.

37. Eisenstein, 1969; also see Gyori, 2018.

38. Gyori, 2018.

39. The same is true in academia, where we often find unexpected associations and patterns when looking at a larger structure with fresh eyes. *Grounded theory* and other qualitative methodologies such as the *Gioia method*, for example, allow for ideas to emerge organically. When I worked on the RLabs study, for example, I went into it with a very broad research question. Then, I tried to look out for surprising insights that were different from what I (and current research) would expect, and started to make sense out of them. I reshuffled them until some interesting themes emerged that could be relevant beyond that context (in this case, that bricolage is scalable). As ever with serendipity, it is about controlling a process, rather than the outcome—and to keep our eyes open to the unexpected, like Sherlock Holmes would do (Busch and Barkema, 2019). Also, abduction—the creative act of constructing explanations to account for surprising observations in the course of experience—can be an effective approach to generate new theses. Abduction helps synthesize existing concepts with new insights.

40. Gyori, 2018; Lessig, 2008; Navas et al., 2014.

41. Mintzberg et al., 1996; Pascale, 1996. However, this story has been debated over decades, some arguing it was emergent, others that it was planned, so we need to take it with a grain of salt.

42. Procter, 2012.

43. Gyori, 2018.

44. Derrida, 1982; Gyori, 2018.

45. Take the example of fan-edits: Fan-edits are trailers or cinematic scenes that are recut to create genre-jumping deconstructions. *The 40-Year-Old Virgin* reboots from farce to psychological thriller; the horror movie *The Shining* becomes the feel-good movie *Shining*. In a similar vein, Derrida took Plato's *Phaedrus* and deconstructed it, with appropriate devotion (Gyori, 2018).

46. Gyori, 2018; also see Delanty et al., 2013.

47. This can unsettle and create opportunities for oppressed people. Outcasts can become heroes, and the spotlight goes to the revolutionary—history is full of

examples from x to "post" (*post-colonialism, post-modernism*, etc.)—propelling mankind forward (Gyori, 2018).

48. See https://fs.blog/2016/04/munger-operating-system/.

49. Davis, 1971.

50. Gyori, 2018.

51. Gentner and Markman, 1997; Gick and Holyoak, 1980; also see Stock et al., 2017. Given the still relatively rare research related to serendipity, I partly use analogical thinking in this book, too. This type of reasoning can be prompted by unplanned events such as the serendipitous observation of a particular event or artifact. Associative thinking or analogy is a process for the navigation of complex opportunity spaces. However, this approach is only possible if the target domain is known—which often is not the case with newly emerging serendipitous matters.

52. Gick and Holyoak, 1980. This type of thinking often favors experts, because they tend to aggregate specific domain knowledge, which tends to be well organized and highly accessible (Bedard and Chi, 1992; Ericsson and Staszewski, 1989). This can potentially allow experts to identify more connections between their respective current state and previous (or future) experiences (Stock et al., 2017). You can only identify an anomaly if you have an understanding of what is "normal." Experts are thus more likely to engage in analogical transfer as they are better able to see parallels between their expertise domain and the respective situation. Expert knowledge tends to be more abstract and conceptual (not like the surface-level knowledge that laymen tend to show), and thus allows for drawing parallels and inferring missing information. However, as discussed in chapter 2, it might also lead to "functional fixedness."

53. de Bono, 1992.

54. Gummere, 1989.

55. Koestler, 1964.

CHAPTER 6: **TURNING SERENDIPITOUS**
ENCOUNTERS INTO OPPORTUNITY

1. Burgelman, 2003.

2. Barber and Fox, 1958.

3. Christoff et al., 2009; Mason et al., 2007; also see Stock et al., 2017.

4. Ritter and Dijksterhuis, 2015; Van Gaal et al., 2012.

5. Busch et al., 2019; Gyori et al., 2018.

6. McCay-Peet and Toms, 2010.

7. Gilhooly and Murphy, 2005.

8. Sio and Ormerod, 2009.

9. Also see Stock et al., 2017.

10. Safi Bahcall has some interesting thoughts on these questions: https://podcast notes.org/2019/03/16/bahcall/.

11. "Citizenship in a Republic," Speech at the Sorbonne, Paris, April 23, 1910.

12. Busch and Barkema, 2019; Napier and Vuong, 2013.

13. See https://mastersofscale.com/ev-williams-never-underestimate-your-first-idea/.

14. https://hbr.org/2016/05/people-favor-naturals-over-strivers-even-though-they-say -otherwise.

15. Duckworth, 2016.

16. Source: Robyn Scott and www.huffingtonpost.com/robyn-scott/from-prison-to -programmin_b_6526672.html.

17. See www.youtube.com/watch?v=7COA9QGlPDc.

18. Runde and de Rond, 2010.

19. See, for example, Gilbert and Knight, 2017.

20. Why intervention often leads to worse outcomes: www.farnamstreetblog.com /2013/10/iatrogenics/.

21. Taleb, 2012.

22. David, 2016.

23. Kahneman, 2011; also see www.farnamstreetblog.com/2017/09/adam-grant/.

24. White et al., 2016; also see "What would Batman do? Self-distancing improves executive function in young children," White and Carlson, 2015. For a short write-up, see www.weforum.org/agenda/2017/12/new-research-finds-that-kids-aged-4-6 -perform-better-during-boring-tasks-when-dressed-as-batman.

25. Patterson and Mischel, 1976.

26. www.newyorker.com/science/maria-konnikova/struggles-psychologist-studying -self-control.

27. Turkcell's outgoing CEO Kaan Terzioğlu shared with me how his company used a digital dashboard, which monitors and uses artificial intelligence to filter ideas and run the business. For example, basic artificial-intelligence/recognition tools helped filter the best ideas of idea competitions; the best idea was implemented, and the winner got a percentage of the profits. This created a culture of ideas and stewardship, and according to Kaan turned out to be one of its partnering consulting firm's most successful projects globally. This technology allowed employees to contribute, at scale, and to filter, at scale. These digital dashboards can also be used to create more transparency and accountability, so that performance is more visible and it is visible which results are being achieved.

28. McKay-Peet and Toms, 2018.

29. Felin and Zenger, 2015; Schultz, 1998.

30. Felin and Zenger, 2015; Zenger, 2013. Firms develop a unique firm-specific theory of value creation—revealing an architecture and bundle of problems that deserve attention. This then guides the strategic direction and allows it to filter. The central

vehicle for value creation, then, lies in composing and updating the firm's theory and using it to formulate problems, organize a solution search, and select from among available need-solution pairs. It is something that's unique to them. Take Apple (Isaacson, 2011): Steve Jobs stumbled over bit-mapping technology, the "mouse," and graphical user interface, all of which were key to the Macintosh. Jobs needed a theory to recognize the potential uses of the solutions. Xerox was aware of the value of these technologies, too—indeed it was given the opportunity to invest in Apple in return for the chance to look at the solutions and technologies. However, only Jobs's theory, and bundles of competences, brought real value. His and his team's sagacity made the difference. This is closely related to a concept that has been prominent in research on serendipity: *generative doubt*. Generative doubt can help us to critically assess which triggers might be worthwhile, and to connect the dots that could become valuable opportunities. Then, if you run into something or someone unexpectedly, you ask, "Is there a meaningful association with something I am excited about—and are the two aligned?" Generative doubt can help us synthesize different pieces of information and leverage coincidences (Pina e Cunha et al., 2010).

31. Iyengar and Lepper, 2000.
32. Many organizations have used approaches such as "Go/No-Go" before beginning a project or launching a product. They evaluate opportunities using methods such as Discounted Cash Flow and Net Present Value. But this fixates on targets, usually in relatively stable environments where people try to avoid failure and focus on what worked in the past, not on what might work in the future. This can be fatal, particularly in rapidly changing environments in which uncertainty prevails, and is not ideal for making the most of serendipity. Forecasting things such as cash flows becomes almost impossible in more dynamic environments, even if we succumb to an illusion of control.
33. Guy et al., 2015; McKay-Peet and Toms, 2010.
34. Guy et al., 2015; McKay-Peet and Toms, 2018.
35. Fan et al., 2012; Pariser, 2001.
36. Andre et al., 2009; Benjamin et al., 2014.
37. Huldtgren et al., 2014.
38. McCay-Peet and Toms, 2010; Toms et al., 2009.
39. This includes emails from Nigerian princes. Have you ever wondered why those random emails that offer you millions of dollars are written so poorly that it's clear to most people that they are a scam? Well, one possible explanation is that it's a filter: It takes a lot of effort to get a person to a point that is actually useful for scammers—such as a willingness to part with their credit card details. So they try to filter out skeptics at the outset, to save effort. They use a "hard filter," which only those naïve enough to believe that a Nigerian prince would actually want them to

inherit millions will be captured by. This reduces the pool to only those ultimately likely to give you their credit card details—keeping "recruitment costs" low.

40. Pina e Cunha et al., 2010.
41. Meyers, 2007.
42. www.paulgraham.com/makersschedule.html.
43. Cain, 2013.
44. Davis et al., 2011; Pejtersen et al., 2011.
45. Depending on the cultural context, this can manifest differently. In more mono-chronic cultures (e.g., Northern Europe), in which planning is key and where clear starting and ending times prevail, this can play out differently than in more polychronic cultures (e.g., much of Africa, Latin America), where a more flexible concept of time leads to more flexible agendas, simultaneous task solving, and—presumably—a different approach to time.
46. Frank, 2016.

CHAPTER 7: AMPLIFYING SERENDIPITY

1. Busch, 2014.
2. Eagle et al., 2010.
3. Rowson et al., 2010; also see Bacon et al., 2008.
4. Busch and Barkema, 2019. For the whole story, see www.youtube.com/watch?v= M1qsexQYAsc&t=9s.
5. Granovetter, 1983.
6. Busch and Barkema, 2020; Busch and Mudida, 2018.
7. For community builders, this raises the question of community boundaries. It is hard to develop trust or proxy trust in a group where everyone can just be a member. A community is often only as strong as its "weakest" link (in a non-Darwinian way). If there are too many people who are not trustworthy, the whole community dynamic is at stake, especially if there are no effective mechanisms to resolve conflict (e.g., a community council or grievance committee). Trust and belonging are at the core for a number of reasons, and could be important for broader themes such as tackling the "loneliness epidemic" (https://hbr.org/cover-story/2017/09 /work-and-the-loneliness-epidemic).
8. www.gsb.stanford.edu/insights/how-invest-your-social-capital?utm_source =Stanford+Business&utm_medium=email&utm_campaign=Stanford -Business-Issue-160-4-21-2019&utm_content=alumni. Thank you to Mustard Seed's Alex Pitt for the suggestion!
9. Russell, 2012 (1912). Scholars such as Karl Popper subsequently used it as an effective metaphor to discuss that even the right assumptions can lead us to the wrong conclusions—in this case, yes, the turkey thought it got fed every morning

at the same time, but was not aware that it would indeed be killed for Christmas (Chalmers, 1982). Taleb later adopted this metaphor to talk about Black Swan moments—those unexpected moments that lie outside the realm of our usual expectations; that carry an extreme impact on our lives; and that can be explained only after they happened (here, from the turkey's—not the butcher's—perspective).

10. Busch and Barkema, 2019.

11. Busch and Lup, 2013.

12. See, for example, http://www.independent.co.uk/news/uk/home-news/police-stop-search-cannabis-marijuana-smell-drug-policy-guidance-hmic-report-a8105061.html.

13. Boyd, 1998.

14. See, e.g., GLOBE study (House et al., 2004); Hofstede, 1980.

15. Some schools, for example, explicitly focus on integrating a diverse range of children from different socioeconomic classes and cultural backgrounds, which appears to be one of the few strategies that actually improves test scores.

16. Luck circles are particularly interesting: Lucky breaks often come from casual acquaintances, so luck circles can be effective: http://www.artstrategies.org/downloads/CCFMaterials/LuckCircle.pdf.

CHAPTER 8: FOSTERING THE CONDITIONS FOR SERENDIPITY

1. de Rond, 2014; Pina e Cunha et al., 2010. In a globalized world, we sometimes assume that people are more alike than they are—and many pitfalls restrict us from serendipity because things get lost in translation. That's where national background comes into play—a major shaper. (National) culture shapes our values, which in turn shapes our attitudes and behaviors. It is a pattern of shared basic assumptions—which then translates into values and observable artifacts such as behavior, clothing, and symbols such as logos, physical structures (e.g., open office spaces), jargons, rituals, etc. But importantly, while culture is something that is shared by all or almost all members of some social group (e.g., school, organization, family, country, professional group, etc.), it is not static and not monolithic. Cultural misunderstandings happen all the time, even if we are not aware of it. What seems like a small misunderstanding happens everywhere, anytime. What can we do to train ourselves? We can increase our cultural intelligence by increasing cognitive knowledge and developing a metacognitive ability of monitoring ourselves, and to revise and adjust based on experience.

2. de Rond, 2014; Napier and Vuong, 2013; Pina e Cunha et al., 2010.

3. Kahn, 1990.

4. Edmondson, 1999; also see https://hbr.org/ideacast/2019/01/creating-psychological-safety-in-the-workplace.

5. Catmull, 2008.
6. https://hbr.org/ideacast/2019/01/creating-psychological-safety-in-the-work place.
7. Nonaka, 1990.
8. https://hbr.org/2017/10/research-for-better-brainstorming-tell-an -embarrassing-story.
9. Meyers, 2007; Sutton, 2001.
10. Clegg et al., 2002; Pitsis et al., 2003.
11. Busch, 2019; Gyori et al., 2018.
12. Merton and Barber, 2004.
13. Busch and Barkema, 2019.
14. Pina e Cunha et al., 2010; Meyers, 2007.
15. Isaacson, 2011; also see https://heleo.com/conversation-the-one-key-trait-that -einstein-da-vinci-and-steve-jobs-had-in-common/17410/.
16. Yakup, 2017.
17. Zahra and George, 2002.
18. Czarniwaska, 2008.
19. Austin et al., 2012.
20. https://deloitte.wsj.com/cio/2015/06/02/singularitys-ismail-on-disruptive -exponentials/.
21. Sting et al., 2019.
22. Pina e Cunha et al., 2010.
23. Austin et al., 2012.
24. Jeppesen and Lakhani, 2010; von Hippel and von Krogh, 2016.
25. Regner, 2003.
26. Graebner, 2004.
27. https://work.qz.com/1174504/why-its-smart-to-let-employees-lunch-with -competitors-and-pay-for-it/.
28. Hargadon and Bechky, 2006; Napier and Vuong, 2013.
29. Foster and Ford, 2003.
30. Bunge, 1996.
31. Dunn et al., 2008.
32. This includes the work task environment, and the type of the work itself (McCay-Peet and Toms, 2010).
33. www.nytimes.com/2013/04/07/opinion/sunday/engineering-serendipity.html.
34. Silverman, 2013; www.nytimes.com/2013/04/07/opinion/sunday/engineering -serendipity.html.
35. Burt, 2004.
36. www.nytimes.com/2013/04/07/opinion/sunday/engineering-serendipity.html.
37. Hallen and Eisenhardt, 2012.

38. Guy et al., 2015; McKay-Peet and Toms, 2018.
39. www.nytimes.com/2013/04/07/opinion/sunday/engineering-serendipity.html.
40. For example, Adner and Kapoor, 2010; Kapoor and Agarwal, 2017; Nambisan and Baron, 2013.
41. Brafman and Beckstrom, 2006.
42. For a balanced perspective, see https://hbr.org/2016/07/beyond-the-holacracy-hype.
43. www.wsj.com/articles/SB118841662730312486.
44. Hagel et al., 2012.
45. Baldwin and von Hippel, 2011; Stanek et al., 2017.
46. The Economist Intelligence Unit, 2016.
47. Alstyne et al., 2016. However, there often is a tradeoff between size and cohesion; often, we can only develop trust with a smaller number of people.
48. Previous research on innovation tends to posit two types of innovation: *incremental innovation*, which tends to benefit most from strong ties to the parent organization, and *radical innovation*, which tends to benefit most from breaking away from the parent organization and adding new and more heterogeneous contacts to their network. Since the resources required for both are different, the central organization's role becomes to support incremental innovators to *exploit* resources within the firm, while helping radical innovators *explore* resources outside the firm. Weaker ties tend to be more effective for idea/opportunity generation, whereas strong ties tend to be more effective for resource exploitation (Elfring and Hulsink, 2012). Negative network effects, such as congestion, occur when there are too many users on a good or service.
49. Gould and Vrba, 1982.
50. See Gould and Vrba, 1982; also see Andriani and Cattani, 2016; Austin et al., 2012.
51. Ernst and Young, 2016. Naturally, innovation can also happen the other way round—driven by a company, but in a rapidly changing world, often customers are driving innovation.
52. Chen, 2016.
53. The experimentation approach can apply to whole markets. Carlos Brito, CEO of one of the world's largest fast-moving consumer goods companies, AB Inbev, shared with our Leaders on Purpose team how the growth of a brand in a particular market is often the customer telling them which one to bet on—"you have to listen, they know better than us." This often depends on the ability of employees to spot things—in the words of Anand Mahindra, "My first lesson on organizational behavior was that you can draw up all the boxes, but who you put into the box will shape it. The person will redefine that job. I never believed that organizations are as hierarchical as we think. They are always flexible enough to let that shape emerge, it is not immutable—there is constant movement."

54. In some contexts where there is extremely low failure tolerance, such as nuclear reactors, routines are there for a reason. But even in those contexts, serendipity can be important, especially in crisis moments. The same is true for different cultures: In some cultures, hierarchies might be more important than in others; in those settings, employees expect to receive orders rather than to take their own initiative. Similarly, in more "masculine" societies, there are particular gender expectations (Gesteland, 2005; Hofstede, 1984; House et al., 2004).

55. Also see www.centreforpublicimpact.org/the-serendipity-of-impact/.

56. Hagel et al., 2012.

57. http://www.cnbc.com/2016/08/09/zappos-ceo-tony-hsieh-what-i-regret-about
-pouring-350-million-into-las-vegas.htm.

58. Hallen and Eisenhardt, 2012; Westphal and Zajac, 1998.

59. Rowson et al., 2010.

60. Also see Chanan and Miller, 2010.

61. Meyers, 2007; Pina e Cunha et al., 2010.

CHAPTER 9: EVALUATING SERENDIPITY

1. Durand and Vaara, 2009; Liu and de Rond, 2014.

2. Byrne, 2005; Kahneman and Miller, 1986.

3. Denrell et al., 2013; Liu and de Rond, 2014.

4. See Pritchard, 2005; Pritchard and Smith, 2004; Teigen, 2005.

5. Barnsley et al., 1985; Gladwell, 2008.

6. Pierson et al., 2014.

7. Liu and de Rond, 2014; Pierson et al., 2014.

8. See Liu and de Rond, 2014.

9. Gould, 2002; Lynn et al., 2009; Samuelson, 1989.

10. March, 2010.

11. Denrell, 2003.

12. Madsen and Desai, 2010; Tinsley et al., 2012; also see Liu and de Rond, 2014.

13. Liu and de Rond, 2014.

14. Cornelissen and Durand, 2012; Durand and Vaara, 2009; Tsang and Ellsaesser, 2011.

15. Liu and de Rond, 2014.

16. Levy, 2003.

17. Liu and de Rond, 2014.

18. Harrison and March, 1984; Liu and de Rond, 2014

19. Liu and de Rond, 2014. For writings on attribution theory, see Hewstone, 1989; Weiner et al., 1971.

20. Camerer and Lovallo, 1999; Hogarth and Makridakis, 1981. For the self-serving bias and similar attribution biases, see Miller and Ross, 1975.

21. Ayton and Fischer, 2004; Maltby et al., 2008; Tversky and Kahneman, 1974.
22. Gilbert and Malone, 1995; Liu and de Rond, 2014.
23. Kahneman, 2011.
24. Goldstein and Gigerenzer, 2002.
25. See Liu and de Rond, 2014. Though, as we have seen, this might of course not be an either/or question.
26. Benabou and Tirole, 2006; Gromet, Hartson, and Sherman, 2015; Liu and de Rond, 2014.
27. Dillon and Tinsley, 2008; Hilary and Menzly, 2006; Liu and de Rond, 2014.
28. Barnett, 2008; March and March, 1977.
29. Zeitoun, Osterloh, and Frey, 2014.
30. Biondo et al., 2013; Pluchino et al., 2010; Thorngate et al., 2008.
31. Liu and de Rond, 2014.
32. Liu and de Rond, 2014; Pritchard, 2006; Williamson, 1981.
33. Young et al., 2010.
34. Bebchuk and Fried, 2009; Wade, O'Reilly, and Pollock, 2006.
35. Dillon and Tinsley, 2008; for the HALO effect, see Rosenzweig, 2007.
36. Liu and de Rond, 2014; also see Perrow, 1984.
37. Liu and de Rond, 2014; *Normal Accident Theory* (Perrow, 1984) suggests that failed executives tend to be over-blamed.
38. Merrigan, 2019.
39. Alesina et al., 2001; Liu and de Rond, 2014; also see Dillon and Tinsley, 2008; Vaughan, 1997.
40. Weick and Sutcliffe, 2006; Langer, 1989.
41. Piketty, 2014.
42. Serendipity is a complex process, and this score is of course not the last word on measuring serendipity—it merely serves as a guiding star on our serendipity journey. Many researchers have looked at the challenge of measuring serendipity in terror: It is tough to measure a process. In fact, students often get told they should not inquire about serendipity, as it's "too complex." However, similar to how a business model canvas appeared "too broad" when I started my PhD, a serendipity field will be difficult but not impossible to explore, and ultimately, to measure. I hope that this book can prompt fruitful future measurements and operationalizations. For promising first attempts at conceptualizing and/or measuring serendipity and related concepts (some of whose measures I integrate), see Erdelez, 1995; McCay-Peet and Toms, 2012; Makri and Blandford, 2012; McCay-Peet, 2013; Wiseman, 2003;. Future scales could take inspiration from absorptive capacity (e.g., Zahra and George, 2002), unexpectedness (e.g., Adamopolos and Tuzhilin, 2014), originality (e.g., Koh et al., 2007), interestingness (Andre et al., 2009), and novelty (Toms, 2000). Some are objective, some perceptive.
43. Tjan, 2010.

CHAPTER 10: THE ART AND SCIENCE OF CULTIVATING SERENDIPITY

1. van Andel, 2014.
2. Busch and Barkema, 2019; de Rond et al., 2011.
3. The tendency to favor, search for, interpret, and recall information that confirms one's preexisting beliefs (for example, Plous, 1993). I tried to minimize this by using quality criteria that were developed for qualitative methods (see, e.g., Flick, 2009).

BIBLIOGRAPHY

Adamson, R. E., and Taylor, D. W., 1954. Functional Fixedness as Related to Elapsed Time and to Set. *Journal of Experimental Psychology*, 47(2): 122–26.

Adner, R., and Kapoor, R., 2010. Value Creation in Innovation Ecosystems: How the Structure of Technological Interdependence Affects Firm Performance in New Technology Generations. *Strategic Management Journal*, 31(3): 306–33.

Aknin, L. B., Dunn, E. W., Sandstrom, G. M., and Norton, M. I., 2013. Does Social Connection Turn Good Deeds into Good Feelings? On the Value of Putting the 'Social' in Prosocial Spending. *International Journal of Happiness and Development*, 1(2): 155–71.

Alesina, A., Glaeser, E., and Sacerdote, B., 2001. Why Doesn't the US Have a European-Style Welfare System? *Brookings Papers on Economic Activity*, 3(1): 1–66.

Allen, T. J., and Marquis, D.G., 1964. Positive and Negative Biasing Sets: The Effects of Prior Experience on Research Performance. *Administrative Science Quarterly*, 35(4): 604–33.

Alstyne, M., Parker, G., and Choudary, S., 2016. Pipelines, Platforms and the New Rules of Strategy. *Harvard Business Review*, 22 April.

Altshuller, G., 1998. *40 Principles: TRIZ Keys to Technical Innovation*. Worcester, MA: Technical Innovation Center.

Amabile, T., Conti, R., Coon, H., Lazenby, J., and Herron, M., 1996. Assessing the Work Environment for Creativity. *Academy of Management Journal*, 39(5): 1154–84.

Andre, P., Cazavan-Jeny, A., Dick, W., Richard, C., and Walton, P., 2009. Fair Value Accounting and the Banking Crisis in 2008: Shooting the Messenger. *Accounting in Europe*, 6(1): 3–24.

Andriani, P., Ali, A., and Mastrogiorgio, M., 2017. Measuring Exaptation and Its Impact on Innovation, Search and Problem Solving. *Organization Science*, 28: 320–38.

Andriani, P., and Cattani, G., 2016. Exaptation as Source of Creativity, Innovation and Diversity: Introduction to the Special Section. *Industrial and Corporate Change*, 25(1): 115–31.

AoK Fehlzeiten Report, 2018 (WIdO, Universitaet Bielefeld, Beuth Hochschule fuer Technik); www.wiwo.de/erfolg/beruf/fehlzeiten-report-sinnlose-arbeit -macht-krank/22993760.html.

Arnon, R., and Kreitler, S., 1984. Effects of Meaning Training on Overcoming Functional Fixedness. *Current Psychological Research and Reviews*, 3(4): 11–24.

Asch, S. E., 1951. Effects of Group Pressure Upon the Modification and Distortion of Judgments, in H. Guetzkow (ed.), *Groups, Leadership and Men*. Pittsburgh, PA: Carnegie Press, 222–36.

Austin, R. D., Devin, L., and Sullivan, E. E., 2012. Accidental Innovation: Supporting Valuable Unpredictability in the Creative Process. *Organization Science*, 23(5): 1505–22.

Ayton, P., and Fischer I., 2004. The Hot Hand Fallacy and the Gambler's Fallacy: Two Faces of Subjective Randomness? *Memory and Cognition*, 32(8): 1369–78.

Bacon, B., Daizullah, N., Mulgan, G., and Woodcraft, S., 2008. *Transformers: How Local Areas Innovate to Address Changing Social Needs*. London: NESTA.

Baldwin, C., and von Hippel, E., 2011. Modeling a Paradigm Shift: From Producer Innovation to User and Open Collaborative Innovation. *Organization Science*, 22(6): 1399–417.

Bandura, A., 2006. Toward a Psychology of Human Agency. *Perspectives on Psychological Science*, 1(2): 164–80.

Barber, B., and Fox, R. C., 1958. The Case of the Floppy-Eared Rabbits: An Instance of Serendipity Gained and Serendipity Lost. *American Journal of Sociology*, 64(2): 128–36.

Barber, R. K., and Merton, E., 2006. *The Travels and Adventures of Serendipity: A Study in Sociological Semantics and the Sociology of Science*. Princeton, NJ: Princeton University Press.

Barnett, W. P., 2008. *The Red Queen Among Organizations: How Competitiveness Evolves*. Princeton, NJ: Princeton University Press.

Barnsley, R. H., Thompson, A. H., and Barnsley, P. E., 1985. Hockey Success and Birth-Date: The Relative Age Effect. *Canadian Association for Health, Physical Education and Recreation Journal*, 51(1): 23–28.

Baron, R. A., 2008. The Role of Affect in the Entrepreneurial Process. *Academy of Management Review*, 33(2): 328–40.

Beale, R., 2007. Supporting Serendipity: Using Ambient Intelligence to Augment User Exploration for Data Mining and Web Browsing. *International Journal of Human-Computer Studies*, 65: 421–33.

Bebchuk, L. A., and Fried, J. M., 2009. Paying for Long-Term Performance. *University of Pennsylvania Law Review*, 158: 1915–59.

Bédard, J., and Chi, M. T. H., 1992. Expertise. *Current Directions in Psychological Science*, 1(4): 135–9.

Beitman, B., 2016. *Connecting with Coincidence: The New Science for Using Synchronicity and Serendipity in Your Life*. Boca Raton, FL: Health Communications.

Bénabou, R., and Tirole, J., 2006. Incentives and Prosocial Behavior. *American Economic Review*, 96(5): 1652–78.

Benjamin, D. J., Heffetz, O., Kimball, M. S., and Szembrot, N., 2014. Beyond Happiness and Satisfaction: Toward Well-Being Indices Based on Stated Preference. *American Economic Review*, 104(9): 2698–2735.

Bindl, U. K., Parker, S. K., Totterdell, P., and Hagger-Johnson, G., 2012. Fuel of the Self-Starter: How Mood Relates to Proactive Goal Regulation. *Journal of Applied Psychology*, 97(1): 134–50.

Biondo, A. E., Pluchino, A., Rapisarda, A., and Helbing, D., 2013. Reducing Financial Avalanches by Random Investments. *Physical Review*, 6, September.

Birdi, K. S., 2005. No Idea? Evaluating the Effectiveness of Creativity Training. *Journal of European Industrial Training*, 29(2): 102–11.

Borja, M. C., and Haigh, J., 2007. The Birthday Problem. *Significance*, 4(3): 124–7.

Boyd, W. 1998. *Armadillo: A Novel*. New York: Vintage.

Bradley, S. E. K., and Casterline, J. B., 2014. Understanding Unmet Need: History, Theory and Measurement. *Studies in Family Planning*, 45(2): 123–50.

Brafman, O., and Beckstrom, R., 2006. *The Starfish and the Spider: The Unstoppable Power of Leaderless Organizations*. New York: Penguin.

Bridgman, T., Cummings, S., and Ballard, J., 2019. Who Built Maslow's Pyramid? A History of the Creation of Management Studies' Most Famous Symbol and Its Implications for Management Education. *Academy of Management Learning and Education*, 18(1): 81–98.

Brown, S., 2005. Science, Serendipity and Contemporary Marketing Condition. *European Journal of Marketing*, 39: 1229–34.

Bunge, M., 1996. *Finding Philosophy in Social Science*. New Haven, CT: Yale University Press.

Burgelman, R. A., 2003. Practice and You Get Luckier. *European Business Forum*, 1(16): 38–39.

Burt, R., 2004. Structural Holes and Good Ideas. *American Journal of Sociology*, 110(2): 349–99.

Busch, C., 2012. Building and Sustaining Impact Organizations. TEDxLSE; www .youtube.com/watch?v=mfGb1qZ7bW0.

———. 2014. Substantiating Social Entrepreneurship Research: Exploring the Potential of Integrating Social Capital and Networks Approaches. *International Journal of Entrepreneurial Venturing*, 6(1): 69–84.

———. 2018. How to Make Serendipity Happen at Work. Geneva: World Economic Forum; www.weforum.org/agenda/2018/07/how-to-make-serendipity -happen-at-work/

———. 2019. Fit for the Future: Integrating Profit and Purpose at Scale. In Gyori, C., Gyori, B., and Kazakova, T. (eds), *Purpose-Driven Leadership for the 21st Century: How Corporate Purpose Is Fundamental to Reimagining Capitalism*. London: Leaders on Purpose.

Busch, C., and Barkema, H. G., 2016. How and Why Does the Network of Social Entrepreneurs in Low-Income Contexts Influence Performance? *Academy of Management Proceedings*, 2018(1).

———, 2017. Scaling Bricolage in the Context of Deep Poverty. *Academy of Management Proceedings*, 2017(1).

———, 2019. Social Entrepreneurs as Network Orchestrators. In George, G., Tracey, P., Baker, T., and Havovi, J., (eds.), *Handbook of Inclusive Innovation*. London: Edward Elgar, 464–86.

———, 2020. Planned Luck: How Incubators Can Facilitate Serendipity for Nascent Entrepreneurs through Fostering Network Embeddedness. *Entrepreneurship Theory & Practice* (forthcoming).

Busch, C., and Lup, D., 2013. The Role of Communities in Social Innovation. Paper presented at the International Social Innovation Research Conference, Said Business School, University of Oxford.

Busch, C., and Mudida, R., 2018. Transcending Homophily: Navigating Institutional Change in Ethnically Fragmented Societies. *Academy of Management Proceedings*, 2018(1).

Busenitz, L. W., 1996. Research on Entrepreneurial Alertness. *Journal of Small Business Management*, 34(4): 35–44.

Byrne, D., 2005. Complexity, Configurations and Cases. *Theory, Culture and Society*, 22(5): 95–111.

Cain, S., 2013. *Quiet: The Power of Introverts in a World That Can't Stop Talking*. New York: Broadway Books.

Camerer, C., and Lovallo, D. A. N., 1999. Overconfidence and Excess Entry: An Experimental Approach. *American Economic Review*, 89(1): 306–18.

Carpenter, E., 2015. *Art of Creation: Essays on the Self and Its Powers* (Classic Reprint). London: Forgotten Books.

Catmull, E., 2008. How Pixar Fosters Collective Creativity. *Harvard Business Review*, September.

Chalmers, A., 1982. *What Is This Thing Called Science?* (2nd ed.) St Lucia: University of Queensland Press.

Chanan, G., and Miller, C., 2010. The Big Society: How It Could Work: A Positive Idea at Risk from Caricature. PACES; http://www.pacesempowerment.co.uk /pacesempowerment/Publications.html.

Chen, L. Y., 2016. Tencent Using Internal Competition in App Push: www.bloom berg.com/news/videos/2016-09-14/tencent-using-internal-competition-in -app-push.

Chopra, D., 1994. *Seven Spiritual Laws of Success*. San Rafael, CA: Amber-Allen.

Christoff, K., Gordon, A. M., Smallwood, J., Smith, R., and Schooler, J. W., 2009. Experience Sampling During fMRI Reveals Default Network and Executive System Contributions to Mind Wandering. *Proceedings of the National Academy of Sciences*, 106(21): 8719–24.

Churchill, J., von Hippel, E., and Sonnack, M., 2009. Lead User Project Handbook: A Practical Guide for Lead User Project Teams; https://evhippel.files.word press.com/2013/08/lead-user-project-handbook-full-version.pdf.

Cialdini, R. B., 1984. *Influence: The Psychology of Persuasion*. New York: Harper-Business.

Clegg, S. R., Vieira da Cunha, J., and Pina e Cunha, M., 2002. Management Paradoxes: A Relational View. *Human Relations*, 55(5): 483–503.

Coad, A., 2009. *The Growth of Firms: A Survey of Theories and Empirical Evidence*. Cheltenham: Edward Elgar.

Cohen, M. D., March, J. G., and Olsen, J. P., 1972. A Garbage Can Model of Organizational Choice. *Administrative Science Quarterly*, 17(1): 1–25.

Conboy, K., 2009. Agility from First Principles: Reconstructing the Concept of Agility in Information Systems Development. *Information Systems Research*, 20(3): 329–54.

Conrad, K., 1958. *Die beginnende Schizophrenie. Versuch einer Gestaltanalyse des Wahns* [*The Onset of Schizophrenia: An Attempt to Form an Analysis of Delusion*]. Stuttgart: Georg Thieme Verlag.

Copeland, S. M., 2017. Unexpected Findings and Promoting Monocausal Claims, a Cautionary Tale. *Journal of Evaluation in Clinical Practice*, 23(5): 1055–61.

———, 2018. "Fleming leapt upon the unusual like a weasel on a vole": Challenging the Paradigms of Discovery in Science. *Perspectives on Science*, 26(6): 694–721.

Cornelissen, J. P., and Durand, R., 2012. Moving Forward: Developing Theoretical Contributions in Management Studies. *Journal of Management Studies*, 51(6): 995–1022.

Cosmelli, D., and Preiss, D. D., 2014. On the Temporality of Creative Insight: A Psychological and Phenomenological Perspective. *Frontiers in Psychology*, 5(1184): 1–6.

Crant, J., 2000. Proactive Behavior in Organizations. *Journal of Management*, 26(3): 435–62.

Crawford, L., 1984. Viktor Shklovskij: Différance in Defamiliarization. *Comparative Literature*, 36(3): 209–19.

Czarniawska-Joerges, B., 2014. *A Theory of Organizing*. Cheltenham: Edward Elgar.

D'Souza, S., and Renner, D., 2016. *Not Knowing: The Art of Turning Uncertainty into Opportunity*. London: LID Publishing.

Dane, E., 2010. Paying Attention to Mindfulness and Its Effects on Task Performance in the Workplace. *Journal of Management*, 37(4): 997–1018.

Danneels, E., 2011. Trying to Become a Different Type of Company: Dynamic Capability at Smith Corona. *Strategic Management Journal*, 32(1): 1–31.

David, S., 2016. *Emotional Agility: Get Unstuck, Embrace Change, and Thrive in Work and Life*. New York: Avery.

Davis, M. S., 1971. That's Interesting! Towards a Phenomenology of Sociology and a Sociology of Phenomenology. *Philosophy of the Social Sciences*, 1: 309–44.

Davis, M. C., Leach, D. J., and Clegg, C. W., 2011. The Physical Environment of the Office: Contemporary and Emerging Issues. In Hodgkinson, G. P., and, J. K. Ford (eds.), *International Review of Industrial and Organizational Psychology*, 26: 193–237.

De Bono, E., 1985. *Six Thinking Hats: An Essential Approach to Business Management*. London: Little, Brown.

———, 1992. *Serious Creativity: Using the Power of Lateral Thinking to Create New Ideas*. New York: HarperBusiness.

————, 2015. *Serious Creativity: How to Be Creative Under Pressure and Turn Ideas into Action*. London: Random House.

De Rond, M., 2014. The Structure of Serendipity. *Culture and Organization*, 20(5): 342–58.

De Rond, M., Moorhouse, A., and Rogan, M., 2011. Make Serendipity Work for You; https://hbr.org/2011/02/make-serendipity-work.

De Rond, M., and Morley, I., 2009. *Serendipity*. Cambridge: Cambridge University Press.

Delanty, G., Giorgi, L., and Sassatelli, M. (eds.), 2013 (reprint). *Festivals and the Cultural Public Sphere*. London: Routledge.

Denrell, J., 2003. Vicarious Learning, Undersampling of Failure, and the Myths of Management. *Organization Science*, 14(3): 227–43.

Denrell, J., Fang, C., and Liu, C., 2015. Chance Explanations in the Management Sciences. *Organization Science*, 26(3): 923–40.

————, 2019. In Search of Behavioral Opportunities from Misattributions of Luck. *Academy of Management Review* (in press).

Denrell, J., Fang, C., and Winter, S. G., 2003. The Economics of Strategic Opportunity. *Strategic Management Journal*, Special Issue 24(10): 977–90.

Denrell, J., Fang, C., and Zhao, Z., 2013. Inferring Superior Capabilities from Sustained Superior Performance: A Bayesian Analysis. *Strategic Management Journal*, 34(2): 182–96.

Denrell, J., and March, J., 2001. Adaptation as Information Restriction: The Hot Stove Effect. *Organization Science* 12(5): 523–38.

Derrida, J., 1982. *Margins of Philosophy* (1st British ed.). Belfast: Prentice Hall/Harvester Wheatsheaf.

Dew, N., 2009. Serendipity in Entrepreneurship. *Organization Studies*, 30(7): 735–53.

Diaz de Chumaceiro, C. L., 2004. Serendipity and Pseudoserendipity in Career Paths of Successful Women: Orchestra Conductors. *Creativity Research Journal*, 16(2–3): 345–56.

Dillon, R. L., and Tinsley, C. H., 2008. How Near-Misses Influence Decision Making Under Risk: A Missed Opportunity for Learning. *Management Science*, 54(8): 1425–40.

Doidge, N., 2007. *The Brain That Changes Itself: Stories of Personal Triumph from the Frontiers of Brain Science*. New York: Viking.

Duckworth, A., 2016. *Grit: The Power of Passion and Perseverance*. New York: Scribner.

Dunbar, K., and Fugelsang, J., 2005. Causal Thinking in Science: How Scientists and Students Interpret the Unexpected. In Gorman, M. E., Tweney, R. D., Gooding, D., and Kincannon, A., (eds.), *Scientific and Technological Thinking*. Mahwah, NJ: Lawrence Erlbaum, 57–79.

Duncker, K., 1945. On Problem Solving. *Psychological Monographs*, 58(5): i–113.

Dunn, E. W., Aknin, L. B., and Norton, M. I., 2008. Spending Money on Others Promotes Happiness. *Science*, 319(5870): 1687–88.

Durand, R., and Vaara, E., 2009. Causation, Counterfactuals and Competitive Advantage. *Strategic Management Journal*, 30(12): 1245–64.

Dweck, C., 2006. *Mindset: The New Psychology of Success*. New York: Random House.

Eagle, N., Macy, M., and Claxton, R., 2010. Network Diversity and Economic Development. *Science*, 328(5981): 1029–31.

Edmondson, A., 1999. Psychological Safety and Learning Behavior in Work Teams. *Administrative Science Quarterly*, 44(2): 350–83.

Eisenstein, S., 1969. *Film Form: Essays in Film Theory by Sergei Eisenstein*. New York: Harcourt.

Elfring, T., and Hulsink, W., 2003. Networks in Entrepreneurship: The Case of High-Technology Firms. *Small Business Economics*, 21(4): 409–22.

Emirbayer, M., and Mische, A., 1998. What Is Agency? *American Journal of Sociology*, 103: 962–1023.

Engel, Y., Kaandorp, M., and Elfring, T., 2017. Toward a Dynamic Process Model of Entrepreneurial Networking Under Uncertainty. *Journal of Business Venturing*, 32: 35–51.

Erdelez, S., 1999. Information Encountering: It's More Than Just Bumping into Information. *American Society for Information Science*, 25: 25–29.

Ericsson, K. A., and Staszewski, J. J., 1989. Skilled Memory and Expertise: Mechanisms of Exceptional Performance. In Klahr, D., and Kotovsky, K. (eds.), *Complex Information Processing: The Impact of Herbert A. Simon*. Hillsdale, NJ: Erlbaum, 235–67.

Ernst and Young, 2016. The Upside of Disruption: Megatrends Shaping, 2016 and Beyond; https://assets.ey.com/content/dam/ey-sites/ey-com/en_gl/top ics/disruption/ey-megatrends-final-onscreen.pdf.

Fan, J., Zhang, J., and Yu, K., 2012. Vast Portfolio Selection with Gross-Exposure Constraints. *Journal of the American Statistical Association*, 107: 498, 592–606.

Felin, F., and Zenger, T. R., 2015. Strategy, Problems and a Theory for the Firm. *Organization Science*, 27(1): 207–21.

Ferré, J., Brown, S. D., and Rius, F. X., 2001. Improved Calculation of the Net Analyte Signal in Inverse Multivariate Calibration. *Journal of Chemometrics*, 15(6): 537–53.

Fildes, R., Goodwin, P., Lawrence, M., and Nikolopoulos, K., 2009. Effective Forecasting and Judgmental Adjustments: An Empirical Evaluation and Strategies for Improvement in Supply-Chain Planning. *International Journal of Forecasting*, 25(1): 3–23.

Fine, G. A., and Deegan, J. G., 1996. Three Principles of Serendip: Insight, Chance and Discovery in Qualitative Research. *International Journal of Qualitative Studies in Education*, 9(4): 434–47.

Fisher, R., Ury, W. L., and Patton, B., 2011. *Getting to Yes: Negotiating Agreement Without Giving In*. New York: Penguin.

Fleming, L., and Sorenson, O., 2004. Science as a Map in Technological Search. *Strategic Management Journal*, 25(8–9): 909–28.

Flick, U., 2009. *An Introduction to Qualitative Research* (4th ed.). London: Sage.

Foster, A., and Ford, N., 2003. Serendipity and Information Seeking: An Empirical Study. *Journal of Documentation*, 59(3): 321–40.

Frank, R., 2016. *Success and Luck: Good Fortune and the Myth of Meritocracy*. Princeton, NJ: Princeton University Press.

Garriga, H., von Krogh, G., and Spaeth, S., 2013. How Constraints and Knowledge Impact Open Innovation. *Strategic Management Journal*, 34(9): 1134–44.

Garud, R., Hardy, C., and Maguire, S., 2007. Institutional Entrepreneurship as Embedded Agency: An Introduction to the Special Issue. *Organization Studies*, 28(7): 957–69.

Gentner, D., and Markman, A. B., 1997. Structure Mapping in Analogy and Similarity. *American Psychologist*, 52(1): 45–56.

German, T. P., and Barrett, H. C., 2005. Functional Fixedness in a Technologically Sparse Culture. *Psychological Science* 16(1): 1–5.

German, T. P., and Defeyter, M. A., 2000. Immunity to Functional Fixedness in Young Children. *Psychonomic Bulletin and Review*, 7(4): 707–12.

Geroski, P. A., 2005. Understanding the Implications of Empirical Work on Corporate Growth Rates. *Managerial and Decision Economics*, 26(2): 129–38.

Gesteland, R. R., 2005. *Cross-Cultural Business Behavior*. Copenhagen: Copenhagen Business School Press.

Ghemawat, P., and Levinthal, D. A., 2008. Choice Interactions and Business Strategy. *Management Science*, 54(9): 1638–51.

Gick, M. L., and Holyoak, K. J., 1980. Analogical Problem Solving. *Cognitive Psychology*, 12(3): 306–55.

Gilbert, D. T., and Malone, P. S., 1995. The Correspondence Bias. *Psychological Bulletin*, 117(1): 21–38.

Gilbert, J., and Knight, R., 2017. *Dirt Is Good: The Advantage of Germs for Your Child's Developing Immune System*. London: St Martin's Press.

Gilchrist, A., 2009. *The Well-Connected Community* (2nd ed.). Cambridge: Polity Press.

Gilhooly, K. J., and Murphy, P., 2005. Differentiating Insight from Non-Insight Problems. *Thinking and Reasoning*, 11(3): 279–302.

Gladwell, M., 2008. *Outliers: The Story of Success*. London: Allen Lane.

Glaser, B. G., and Strauss, A. L., 1967. *The Discovery of Grounded Theory*. Chicago: Aldine.

Goldstein, D. G., and Gigerenzer, G., 2002. Models of Ecological Rationality: The Recognition Heuristic. *Psychological Review*, 109(1): 75–90.

Gould, R. V., 2002. The Origins of Status Hierarchies: A Formal Theory and Empirical Test. *American Journal of Sociology*, 107(5): 1143–78.

Gould, S. J., and Vrba, E. S., 1982. Exaptation—A Missing Term in the Science of Form. *Paleobiology*, 8(1): 4–15.

Graebner, M. E., 2004. Momentum and Serendipity: How Acquired Leaders Create Value in the Integration of Technology Firms. *Strategic Management Journal*, 25(89): 751–77.

Granovetter, M. S., 1973. The Strength of Weak Ties. *American Journal of Sociology*, 78(6): 1360–80.

Grant, A., 2014. *Give and Take: Why Helping Others Drives Our Success*. New York: Penguin.

———, 2015. No, You Can't Pick My Brain, But I'll Talk to You Anyway; www.huffingtonpost.com/adam-grant/no-you-cant-pick-my-brain_b_8214120.html.

———, 2017. *Originals: How Non-Conformists Move the World*. New York: Penguin.

Gromet, D. M., Hartson, K. A., and Sherman, D. K., 2015. The Politics of Luck: Political Ideology and the Perceived Relationship Between Luck and Success. *Journal of Experimental Social Psychology*, 59: 40–46.

Grønbæk, K., 1989. Rapid Prototyping with Fourth Generation Systems: An Empirical Study. DAIMI Report Series 17(270).

Gummere, R. M., 1989. *Seneca Epistulae Morales*. Boston: Loeb.

Guy, J. H., Deakin, G. B., Edwards, A. M., Miller, C. M., and Pyne, D. B., 2014. Adaptation to Hot Environmental Conditions: An Exploration of the Performance Basis, Procedures and Future Directions to Optimise Opportunities for Elite Athletes. *Sports Medicine*, 45(3): 303–11.

Gyori, B., 2018. Creating Kismet: What Artists Can Teach Academics About Serendipity. In Goggin, M. D., and Goggin, P. N. (eds.), *Serendipity in Rhetoric, Writing and Literacy Research*. Louisville, CO: Utah State University Press, 247–56.

Gyori, B. Gyori, C., and Kazakova, T. (eds.). Leaders on Purpose Study 2019: Purpose-driven Leadership for the 21st-Century—How Corporate Purpose Is Fundamental to Reimagining Capitalism. London: Leaders on Purpose.

Gyori, C., Sharp, L., Busch, C., Brahmam, M., Kazakova, T., Gyori, B. (eds.). Leaders on Purpose CEO Study 2018: Purpose-Driven Leadership for the 21st Century—North Star. Washington, DC: Leaders on Purpose.

Hadjikhani, N., Kveraga, K., Naik, P., and Ahlfors, S. P., 2009. Early (M170) Activation of Face-Specific Cortex by Face-Like Objects. *Neuroreport*, 20(4): 403–7.

Hagel III, J., Brown, J., and Davison, L. 2012. *The Power of Pull*. New York: Basic Books.

Hall, E. T., 1976. *Beyond Culture*. New York: Anchor Books/Doubleday.

Hallen, B. L., and Eisenhardt, K. M., 2012. Catalyzing Strategies and Efficient Tie Formation: How Entrepreneurial Firms Obtain Investment Ties. *Academy of Management Journal*, 55(1): 35–70.

Hannan, M. T., Pólos, L., and Carroll, G. R., 2003. Cascading Organizational Change. *Organization Science*, 14(5): 463–82.

Hargadon, A. B., and Bechky, B. A., 2006. When Collections of Creatives Become Creative Collectives: A Field Study of Problem Solving at Work. *Organization Science*, 17(4): 484–500.

Hargadon, A., and Sutton, R. I., 1997. Technology Brokering and Innovation in a Product Development Firm. *Administrative Science Quarterly*, 42(4): 716–49.

Harrison, J. R., and March, J. G., 1984. Decision Making and Postdecision Surprises. *Administrative Science Quarterly*, 29(1): 26–42.

Heinstroem, J., 2006. Psychological Factors Behind Incidental Information Acquisition. *Library and Information Science Research*, 28: 579–94.

Henderson, A. D., Raynor, M. E., and Ahmed, M., 2012. How Long Must a Firm Be Great to Rule Out Chance? Benchmarking Sustained Superior Performance Without Being Fooled by Randomness. *Strategic Management Journal*, 33(4): 387–406.

Hernando, A., Villuendas, D., Vesperinas, C., Abad, M., and Plastino, A., 2009. Unravelling the Size Distribution of Social Groups with Information Theory on Complex Networks. *The European Physical Journal B*, 76(1): 87–97.

Herndon, T., Ash, M., and Pollin, R., 2014. Does High Public Debt Consistently Stifle Economic Growth? A Critique of Reinhart and Rogoff. *Cambridge Journal of Economics*, 38(2): 257–79.

Hewstone, M., 1989. *Causal Attribution: From Cognitive Processes to Collective Beliefs*. London: Wiley-Blackwell.

Hilary, G., and Menzly, L., 2006. Does Past Success Lead Analysts to Become Overconfident? *Management Science*, 52(4): 489–500.

Hofstede, G., 1984. *Culture's Consequences: International Differences in Work-Related Values*. Newbury Park, CA: Sage.

Hogarth, R. M., and Makridakis, S., 1981. Forecasting and Planning: An Evaluation. *Management Science*, 27(2): 115–38.

House, R. J., Hanges, P. J., Javidan, M., Dorfman, P. W., and Gupta, V., 2004. *Culture, Leadership and Organizations: The GLOBE Study of 62 Societies*. Thousand Oaks, CA: Sage.

Hsieh, C., Nickerson, J.A., and Zenger, T. R., 2007. Opportunity Discovery, Problem Solving and a Theory of the Entrepreneurial Firm. *Journal of Management Studies*, 44(7): 1255–77.

Huldtgren, A., 2014. Design for Values in ICT. In van den Hoven, J., Vermaas, P., and van de Poel, I. (eds.), *Handbook of Ethics, Values and Technological Design*. Dordrecht: Springer, 1–24.

Huldtgren, A., Mayer, C., Kierepka, O., and Geiger, C., 2014. Towards Serendipitous Urban Encounters with SoundtrackOfYourLife. *Proceedings of the 11th Conference on Advances in Computer Entertainment Technology*. New York: ACM.

Isaacson, W., 2011. *Steve Jobs*. New York: Simon and Schuster.

Isen, A. M., Daubman, K. A., and Nowicki, G. P., 1987. Positive Affect Facilitates Creative Problem Solving. *Journal of Personality and Social Psychology*, 52(6): 1122–31.

Ishikawa, K., 1968. International Electrotechnical Commission, 2006. Fault Tree Analysis (FTA), International Standard IEC 61025. Geneva: IEC, Geneva.

Iyengar, S. S., and Lepper, M. R., 2000. When Choice Is Demotivating: Can One Desire Too Much of a Good Thing? *Journal of Personality and Social Psychology*, 79(6): 995–1006.

Jaekel, P., 2018. Why We Hear Voices in Random Noise; http://nautil.us/blog/why-we-hear-voices-in-random-noise, retrieved August 2018.

Jeppesen, L. B., and Lakhani, K. R., 2010. Marginality and Problem-Solving Effectiveness in Broadcast Search. *Organizational Science*, 21(5): 1016–33.

Jung, C. G., 2010. *Synchronicity: An Acausal Connecting Principle*. (From Vol. 8 of *The Collected Works of C. G. Jung*). Princeton: Princeton University Press.

Kahneman, D., 2011. *Thinking, Fast and Slow*. London: Penguin.

Kahneman, D., and Miller, D. T., 1986. Norm Theory: Comparing Reality to Its Alternatives. *Psychological Review*, 93(2): 136–53.

Kapoor, R., and Agarwal, S., 2017. Sustaining Superior Performance in Business Ecosystems: Evidence from Application Software Developers in the iOS and Android Smartphone Ecosystems. *Organization Science*, 28(3): 531–51.

Kasarda, J., and Lindsay, G., 2012. *Aerotropolis: The Way We'll Live Next*. London: Penguin.

Katz, D. M., Bommarito II, M. J., and Blackman, J., 2017. A General Approach for Predicting the Behavior of the Surpreme Court of the United States. *Plos One*, 12(4): 1–18.

Khan, W., 1990. Psychological Conditions of Personal Engagement and Disengagement at Work. *Academy of Management Journal*, 33(4): 692–724.

Kirzner, I., 1979. *Perception, Opportunity, and Profit*. Chicago: University of Chicago Press.

Klein, G., and Lane, C., 2014. *Seeing What Others Don't*. Grand Haven, MI: Brilliance Audio.

Kolb, B., and Gibb, R., 2011. Brain Plasticity and Behaviour in the Developing Brain. *Journal of the Canadian Academy of Child and Adolescent Psychiatry*, 20(4): 265–76.

Kornberger, M., Clegg, S. R., and Rhodes, C., 2005. Learning/Becoming/Organizing. *Organization*, 12(2): 147–67.

Krumholz, H. M., Curry, L. A., and Bradley, E. H., 2011. Survival After Acute Myocardial Infarction (SAMI) Study: The Design and Implementation of a Positive Deviance Study. *American Heart Journal*, 162(6): 981–87.

Kurup, U., Bignoli, P. G., Scally, J. R., and Cassimatis, N. L., 2011. An Architectural Framework for Complex Cognition. *Cognitive Systems Research*, 12(3–4): 281–92.

Laird, J. D., Wagener, J., Halal, M., and Szegda, M., 1982. Remembering What You Feel: Effects of Emotion on Memory. *Journal of Personality and Social Psychology*, 42(2): 646–57.

Laloux, F., 2014. *Reinventing Organizations: A Guide to Creating Organizations Inspired by the Next Stage of Human Consciousness*. Millis, MA: Nelson Parker.

Langer, E. J., 1989. *Mindfulness.* Cambridge, MA: Addison-Wesley Reading.

Laursen, K., and Salter, A. J., 2006. Open for Innovation: The Role of Openness in Explaining Innovation Performance Among UK Manufacturing Firms. *Strategic Management Journal,* 27(2):131–50.

Leaders on Purpose, 2019. The CEO Study; www.leadersonpurpose.com/the-ceo -study.

Lehrer, J., 2011. Steve Jobs: "Technology Alone is Not Enough." *New Yorker,* October 7.

Lederman, L., and Teresi, D., 1993. *The God Particle: If the Universe is the Answer, What Is the Question?* Boston: Houghton Mifflin.

Lessig, L., 2008. *Remix: Making Art and Commerce Thrive in the Hybrid Economy.* New York: Bloomsbury Academic.

Levinthal, D., and Posen, H. E., 2007. Myopia of Selection: Does Organizational Adaptation Limit the Efficacy of Population Selection? *Administrative Science Quarterly,* 52(4): 586–620.

Levy, M., 2003. Are Rich People Smarter? *Journal of Economic Theory,* 110(1): 42–64.

Lewis, W. S., 1965. Foreword to Remer, T. G. (ed.), *Serendipity and the Three Princes, from the Peregrinaggio of 1557.* Norman: University of Oklahoma Press.

Liang, R. H., 2012. Designing for Unexpected Encounters with Digital Products: Case Studies of Serendipity as Felt Experience. *International Journal of Design,* 6(1): 41–58.

Liu, C., and de Rond, M., 2014. Good Night and Good Luck: Perspectives on Luck in Management Scholarship. *Academy of Management Annals,* 10(1): 1–56.

Lorenz, J., Rauhut, H., Schweitzer, F., and Helbing, D., 2011. How Social Influence Can Undermine the Wisdom of Crowd Effect. *Proceedings of the National Academy of Sciences,* 108(22): 9020–25.

Luke, D., 2011. Experiential Reclamation and First Person Parapsychology. *Journal of Parapsychology,* 75: 185–99.

Lynn, F. B., Podolny, J. M., and Tao, L., 2009. A Sociological (De)Construction of the Relationship Between Status and Quality. *American Journal of Sociology,* 115(3): 755–804.

Madsen, P. M., and Desai, V., 2010. Failing to Learn? The Effects of Failure and Success on Organizational Learning in the Global Orbital Launch Vehicle Industry. *Academy of Management Journal,* 53(3): 451–76.

Makri, S., and Blandford, A., 2012. Coming Across Information Serendipitously— Part 1. *Journal of Documentation,* 68(5): 684–705.

Makri, S., Blandford, A., Woods, M., Sharples, S., and Maxwell, D., 2014. "Making My Own Luck": Serendipity Strategies and How to Support Them in Digital Information Environments. *Journal of the Association for Information Science and Technology*, 65(11): 2179–94.

Maltby, J., Day, L., Gill, P., Colley, A., and Wood, A.M., 2008. Beliefs Around Luck: Confirming the Empirical Conceptualization of Beliefs Around Luck and the Development of the Darke and Freedman Beliefs Around Luck Scale. *Personality and Individual Differences*, 45(7): 655–60.

Mandi, A., Mullainathan, S., Shafir, E., and Zhao, Z., 2013. Poverty Impedes Cognitive Function. *Science*, 341(6149): 976–80.

March, J. C., and March, J. G., 1977. Almost Random Careers: The Wisconsin School Superintendency, 1940–1972. *Administrative Science Quarterly*, 22(3): 377–409.

March, J. G., 2010. *The Ambiguities of Experience*. Ithaca, NY: Cornell University Press.

Marsh, C., 2019. How *Chef's Table* Turned Food TV into Mouthwatering Art. *Vulture*, May 1; www.vulture.com/2019/05/chefs-table-food-tv-mouth-watering-art.html.

Marx, K., 2009. *Das Kapital: A Critique of Political Economy*. Washington, DC: Regnery Publishing Inc.

Marx, K., and Engels, F., 1998. *The German Ideology*. Amherst, NY: Prometheus Books.

Mason, M.F., Norton, M.I., Van Horn, J.D., Wegner, D.M., Grafton, S.T., and Macrae, C.N., 2007. Wandering Minds: The Default Network and Stimulus-Independent Thought. *Science*, 315(5810): 393–95.

McCay-Peet, L. and Toms, E. G., 2010. The Process of Serendipity in Knowledge Work. *Association for Computing Machinery, Information Interaction in Context Symposium*, August.

———, 2012. The Serendipity Quotient. *Proceedings of the American Society for Information Science and Technology*.

———, 2018. Researching Serendipity in Digital Information Environments. *Synthesis Lectures on Information Concepts Retrieval and Services* 9(6): 1–91.

McCay-Peet, L., Toms, E. G., and Kelloway, E. K., 2015. Examination of Relationships Among Serendipity, the Environment and Individual Differences. *Information Processing and Management*, 51: 391–412.

McGahan, A. M., and Porter, M. E., 2002. What Do We Know About Variance in Accounting Profitability? *Management Science*, 48(7): 834–51.

Mckinney, E. H., 1966. Generalized Birthday Problem. *American Mathematical Monthly*, 73(4): 385–87.

McNally, A., Prier, C. K., and Macmillan, D. W. C., 2011. Discovery of an α-Amino C-H Arylation Reaction Using the Strategy of Accelerated Serendipity. *Science*, 334: 1114–17.

McGrath, R. G., 1999. Falling Forward: Real Options Reasoning and Entrepreneurial Failure. *Academy of Management Review*, 24(1): 13–30.

Mendoca, S., Pina e Cunha, M., and Clegg, S.R., 2008. Unsought Innovation: Serendipity in Organizations. Paper Presented at the Entrepreneurship and Innovation—Organizations, Institutions, Systems and Regions Conference, Copenhagen, June 17–20.

Merrigan, T. W., 2019. How a Global Social Network Seeks Connection in Decentralization. Stanford e-Corner, Stanford University: https://ecorner.stanford.edu/articles/how-a-global-social-network-seeks-connection-in-decentralization/.

Merton, R., 1949. *Social Theory and Social Structure*. New York: Free Press.

———, *Social Theory and Social Structure* (enlarged ed.). New York: Free Press.

Merton, R. K., and Barber, E., 2004. *The Travels and Adventures of Serendipity: A Study in Sociological Semantics and the Sociology of Science*. Princeton, NJ: Princeton University Press.

Miller, D. T., and Ross, M., 1975. Self-Serving Biases in the Attribution of Causality: Fact or Fiction? *Psychological Bulletin*, 82(2): 213–25.

Mintzberg, H., Pascale, R. T., Rumelt, R. P., and Goold, M., 1996. The "Honda Effect" Revisited. *California Management Review*, 38(4): 78–79.

Mirvis, P. H., 1998. Variations on a Theme: Practice Improvisation. *Organization Science*, 9(5): 586–92.

Mishara, A., 2010. Klaus Conrad, 1905–1961: Delusional Mood, Psychosis and Beginning Schizophrenia. *Schizophrenia Bulletin*, 36(1): 9–13.

Miyazaki, K., 1999. Building Technology Competencies in Japanese Firms. *Research Technology Management*, 42(5): 39–45.

Mulnix, J. W., 2010. Thinking Critically About Critical Thinking. *Educational Philosophy and Theory*, 44(5): 464–79.

Nambisan, S., and Baron, R. A., 2013. Entrepreneurship in Innovation Ecosystems: Entrepreneurs' Self-Regulatory Processes and Their Implications for New Venture Success. *Entrepreneurship: Theory and Practice*, 37(5): 1071–97.

Napier, N. K., and Vuong, Q.-H., 2013. Serendipity as a Strategic Advantage? In Wilkinson, T. J., and Kannan, V. R. (eds.), *Strategic Management in the 21st Century, Vol. 1: Operational Environment*, Oxford: Blackwell, 175–99.

Navas, E., Gallagher, O., and Burrough, E. (eds.), 2014. *The Routledge Companion to Remix Studies*. London: Routledge.

Nelson, R. R., 2008. Bounded Rationality, Cognitive Maps, and Trial and Error Learning. *Journal of Economic Behavior & Organization*, 67(1): 78–89.

Nonaka, I., 1991. The Knowledge-Creating Company, *Harvard Business Review*, November–December.

Owens, B., and Hekman, D., 2006. Modeling How to Grow: An Inductive Examination of Humble Leader Behaviors, Contingencies and Outcomes, *Academy of Management Journal*, 55(4): 787–818.

Pariser, E., 2012. *The Filter Bubble: What the Internet Is Hiding from You*. New York: Penguin.

Parker, S. K., Williams, H. M., and Turner, N., 2006. Modeling the Antecedents of Proactive Behavior at Work. *Journal of Applied Psychology*, 91(3): 636–62.

Pascale, R. T., 1996. Reflections on Honda. *California Management Review*, 38(4): 112–17.

Patterson, C. J., and Mischel, W., 1976. Effects of Temptation-Inhibiting and Task-Facilitating Plans on Self-Control. *Journal of Personality and Social Psychology*, 33(2): 209–17.

Pejtersen, J. H., Feveile, H., Christensen, K. B., and Burr, H., 2001. Sickness Absence Associated with Shared and Open-Plan Offices—A National Cross Sectional Questionnaire Survey. *Scandinavian Journal of Work, Environment & Health*, 37(5): 376–82.

Pelaprat, E., and Cole, M., 2011. "Minding the Gap": Imagination, Creativity and Human Cognition. *Integrative Psychological and Behavioral Science*, 45(4): 397–418.

Pentland, A., 2015. *Social Physics: How Social Networks Can Make Us Smarter*. New York: Penguin Books.

Perrow, C., 1984. *Normal Accidents: Living with High-Risk Technologies*. New York: Basic Books.

Pershing, R., 2015. Quantum Mechanics Reveals How Human Mind Can Influence the Physical World. Learning Mind: www.learning-mind.com/mind-influence-physical-world.

Pierson, K., Addona, V., and Yates, P., 2014. A Behavioural Dynamic Model of the Relative Age Effect. *Journal of Sports Sciences*, 32(8): 776–84.

Piketty, T., 2014. *Capital in the Twenty-First Century*. Cambridge, MA: Harvard University Press.

Pina e Cunha, M., 2005. Serendipity: Why Some Organizations are Luckier Than Others. *Universidade Nova de Lisboa, FEUNL Working Paper Series.*

Pina e Cunha, M., Clegg, S. R., and Mendonca, S., 2010. On Serendipity and Organizing. *European Management Journal,* 28(5): 319–30.

Pinker, S., 2017. What Scientific Term or Concept Ought to Be More Widely Known? *The Edge,* January.

Pirnot, M. T., Rankic, D. A., Martin, D. B. C., and Macmillan, D. W. C., 2013. Photoredox Activation for the Direct β-Arylation of Ketones and Aldehydes. *Science,* 339: 1593–96.

Piskorski, M., 2011. Social Strategies That Work. *Harvard Business Review,* November.

Pitsis, T. S., et al., 2003. Constructing the Olympic Dream: A Future Perfect Strategy of Project Management. *Organization Science,* 14(5): 574–90.

Plous, S., 1993. *The Psychology of Judgment and Decision Making.* New York: McGraw-Hill.

Pluchino, A., Rapisarda, A., and Garofalo, C., 2010. The Peter Principle Revisited: A Computational Study. *Physica A: Statistical Mechanics and Its Applications,* 389(3): 467–72.

Porges, S. W., 2009. The Polyvagal Theory: New Insights into Adaptive Reactions of the Autonomic Nervous System. *Cleveland Clinic Journal of Medicine,* 76: S86–S90.

———, 2011. *The Polyvagal Theory: Neurophysiological Foundations of Emotions, Attachment, Communication, and Self-Regulation.* New York: W. W. Norton.

Preethaji and Krishnaji, 2019. *The Four Sacred Secrets.* New York: Simon and Schuster.

Pritchard, D. H., and Smith, M., 2004. The Psychology and Philosophy of Luck. *New Ideas in Psychology,* 22(1): 1–28.

Pritchard, D., 2005. *Epistemic Luck.* Oxford: Oxford University Press.

———, 2006. Moral and Epistemic Luck. *Metaphilosophy,* 37(1): 1–25.

Procter, W., 2012. What is a Reboot? Pencil, Panel, Page; https://pencilpanelpage .wordpress.com/2012/10/04/what-is-a-reboot.

Race, T. M., and Makri, S. (eds.), 2016. *Accidental Information Discovery: Cultivating Serendipity in the Digital Age.* Cambridge, MA: Elsevier.

Regner, P., 2003. Strategy Creation in the Periphery: Inductive Versus Deductive Strategy Making. *Journal of Management,* 40(1): 57–82.

Ritter, S. M., and Dijksterhuis, A., 2015. Creativity—the Unconscious Foundations of the Incubation Period. *Frontiers in Human Neuroscience,* 8(215): 1–10.

Ritter, S. M., et al., 2012. Diversifying Experiences Enhance Cognitive Flexibility. *Journal of Experimental Social Psychology*, 48(4): 961–64.

Roese, N. J., and Vohs, K. D., 2012. Hindsight Bias. *Perspectives on Psychological Science*, 7: 411–26.

Root-Bernstein, R. S., 1988. Setting the Stage for Discovery. *The Sciences*, 28(3): 26–34.

Rosenzweig, P., 2007. Misunderstanding the Nature of Company Performance: The Halo Effect and Other Business Delusions. *California Management Review*, 49(4): 6–20.

Rowson, J., Broome, S., and Jones, A., 2010. Connected Communities: How Social Networks Power and Sustain the Big Society. RSA; www.thersa.org/dis cover/publications-and-articles/reports/connected-communities-how-social -networks-power-and-sustain-the-big-society.

Rumelt, R. P., 1991. How Much Does Industry Matter? *Strategic Management Journal*, 12(3): 167–85.

Runde, J., and de Rond, M., 2010. Assessing Causal Explanations of Particular Events. *Organization Studies*, 31(4): 431–50.

Russell, B., 2012. *The Problems of Philosophy*. N.P.: Createspace Independent Publishing Platform.

Ryan, R., and Deci, E., 2000. Self-Determination Theory and the Facilitation of Intrinsic Motivation, Social Development and Well-Being. *American Psychologist*, 55(1): 68–78.

Sagan, C., 1995. *The Demon-Haunted World—Science as a Candle in the Dark*. New York: Random House.

Samuelson, P. A., 1989. The Judgment of Economic Science on Rational Portfolio Management. *Journal of Portfolio Management*, 16(1): 4–12.

Sanger Institute, 2019. *Breaking the Mould—the Story of Penicillin*. Sanger Institute Blog.

Sarasvathy, S. D., 2008. *Effectuation: Elements of Entrepreneurial Expertise*. Cheltenham: Edward Elgar.

Schon, D. A., 1983. *The Reflective Practitioner: How Professionals Think in Action*. New York: Basic Books.

Schooler, J. W., and Melcher J., 1995. The Ineffability of Insight, in Smith, S. M., Ward, T. B., and Finke, R. A. (eds.), *The Creative Cognition Approach*. Cambridge, MA: MIT Press, 97–133.

Schultz, H., 1998. *Pour Your Heart into It: How Starbucks Built a Company One Cup at a Time*. New York: Hyperion.

Schwartz, S. H., 1990. Individualism-Collectivism: Critique and Proposed Refinements. *Journal of Cross-Cultural Psychology,* 21(2): 139–57.

Schwenk, C., and Thomas, H., 1983. Effects of Conflicting Analyses on Managerial Decision Making: A Laboratory Experiment. *Decision Sciences,* 14(4): 447–612.

Seckler, C., Fischer, S., and Rosing, K., 2019. Who Adopts an Error Management Mindset? Individual Differences and Its Impact on Performance in Professional Service Firms. *Professional Service Firms Annual Conference,* Boston, August 15.

Sharp, L., 2019. Leading Organizational Agility and Flow to Deliver on Organizational Purpose, in *Purpose-Driven Leadership for the 21st Century: How Corporate Purpose Is Fundamental to Reimagining Capitalism.* London: Leaders on Purpose, 49–60.

Shermer, M., 2007. The (Other) Secret. *Scientific American,* 296(6): 39.

Shklovsky, V., 2016. *A Reader* (ed. and trans. Alexandra Berlina). London: Bloomsbury.

Silverman, D., 2013. *Doing Quantitative Research.* London: Sage.

Simon, H. A., 1977. *The New Science of Management Decision.* Englewood Cliffs, NJ: Prentice-Hall.

Simonton, D. K., 2003. Scientific Creativity as Constrained Stochastic Behavior: The Integration of Product, Person and Process Perspectives. *Psychological Bulletin,* 129(4): 475–94.

———, 2004. *Creativity in Science: Chance, Logic, Genius, and Zeitgeist.* Cambridge: Cambridge University Press.

Sio, U. N., and Ormerod, T. C., 2009. Does Incubation Enhance Problem Solving? A Meta-Analytic Review. *Psychological Bulletin,* 135(1): 94–120.

Smith, R. P., and Eppinger, S. D., 1997. Identifying Controlling Features of Engineering Design Iteration. *Management Science,* 43(3): 276–93.

Sommer, T. J., 1999. "Bahramdipity" and Scientific Research. *The Scientist,* 13(3): 13.

Spradlin, W., 2012. Are You Solving the Right Problem? *Harvard Business Review,* September.

Stanek, W., Valero, A., Calvo, G., and Czarnowska, L., 2017. *Thermodynamics for Sustainable Management of Natural Resources.* New York: Springer International.

Sting, F., Fuchs, C., Schlickel, M., and Alexy, O., 2019. How to Overcome the Bias We Have Toward Our Own Ideas. *Harvard Business Review,* May.

Stock, C. A., et al., 2017. Reconciling Fisheries Catch and Ocean Productivity. *Proceedings of the National Academy of Sciences,* 114(8): E1441–E1449.

Stock, R. M., von Hippel, E., and Gillert, N. L., 2016. Impacts of Personality Traits on User Innovation Success. *Research Policy*, 45(4): 757–69.

Surowiecki, J., 2004. *The Wisdom of Crowds: Why the Many Are Smarter Than the Few and How Collective Wisdom Shapes Business, Economies, Societies, and Nations.* New York: Doubleday.

Sutton, A., et al., 2001. A Novel Form of Transcriptional Silencing by Sum1–1 Requires Hst1 and the Origin Recognition Complex. *Molecular and Cellular Biology*, 21(10): 3514–22.

Svoboda, E., 2007. Facial Recognition—Brain—Faces, Faces Everywhere. *The New York Times*, February 13; www.nytimes.com/2007/02/13/health/psychology /13face.html.

Taleb, N., 2012. *Antifragile: Things That Gain from Disorder.* New York: Random House.

Teigen, K. H., 2005. When a Small Difference Makes a Large Difference: Counterfactual Thinking and Luck, in Mandel, D., Hilton, D., and Catelani, P. (eds.), *The Psychology of Counterfactual Thinking.* London: Routledge, 130–46.

The Conversation, 2015. Stealth Attack: Infection and Disease on the Battlefield. https://theconversation.com/stealth-attack-infection-and-disease-on-the -battlefield-42541, retrieved August 2018.

The Economist Intelligence Unit, 2016. Connected Capabilities: The Asian Digital Transformation Index. London: The Economist Intelligence Unit.

Thomke, S. H., and Fujimoto, T., 2000. The Effect of "Front-Loading" Problem-Solving on Product Development Performance. *Journal of Product Innovation Management*, 17(2): 128–42.

Thompson, L., 2014. *The Mind and Heart of the Negotiator* (4th ed.). New York: Pearson.

Thorngate, W., Dawes, R., and Foddy, M., 2008. *Judging Merit.* New York: Psychology Press.

Tinsley, C. H., Dillon, R. L., and Cronin, M. A., 2012. How Near-Miss Events Amplify or Attenuate Risky Decision Making. *Management Science*, 58(9): 1596–1613.

Tjan, A., 2010. Four Lessons on Culture and Customer Service from Zappos CEO, Tony Hsieh. *Harvard Business Review*, July; https://hbr.org/2010/07/four -lessons-on-culture-and-cu.

Toms, E. G., 2000. Serendipitous Information Retrieval. *Proceedings of the 1st DELOS Network of Excellence Workshop on Information Seeking, Searching and Querying in Digital Libraries.* Sophia Antipolis, France: European Research Consortium for Informatics and Mathematics: 11–12.

Toms, E. G., McCay-Peet, L., and Mackenzie, R. T., 2009. Wikisearch: From Access to Use, in Agosti, M. et al. (eds.), *Research and Advanced Technology for Digital Libraries*. Berlin: Springer Verlag.

Topolinski, S., and Reber, R., 2010. Gaining Insight into the "Aha" Experience. *Current Directions in Psychological Science*, 19(6): 402–405.

Tsang, E. W., and Ellsaesser, F., 2011. How Contrastive Explanation Facilitates Theory Building. *Academy of Management Review*, 36(2): 404–19.

Tversky, A., and Kahneman, D., 1974. Judgment Under Uncertainty: Heuristics and Biases. *Science*, 185(4157): 1124–31.

Tyre, M., and von Hippel, E., 1997. The Situated Nature of Adaptive Learning in Organizations. *Organization Science*, 8(1): 1–107.

Van Andel, P., 1992. Serendipity; Expect Also the Unexpected. *Creativity and Innovation Management*, 1(1): 20–32.

———, 1994. Anatomy of the Unsought Finding. Serendipity: Origin, History, Domains, Traditions, Appearances, Patterns and Programmability. *British Journal for the Philosophy of Science*, 45(2): 631–48.

Van der Kolk, B., 2014. *The Body Keeps the Score: Brain, Mind, and Body in the Healing of Trauma*. New York: Viking.

Van Gaal, S., de Lange, F. P., and Cohen, M. X., 2012. The Role of Consciousness in Cognitive Control and Decision Making. *Frontiers in Human Neuroscience*, 6(121): 1–15.

Vaughan, D., 1997. *The Challenger Launch Decision: Risky Technology, Culture, and Deviance at NASA*. Chicago: University of Chicago Press.

Volkema, R. J., 1983. Problem Formulation in Planning and Design. *Management Science*, 29(6): 639–52.

Von Hippel, E., 1986. Lead Users: A Source of Novel Product Concepts, *Management Science*, 32(7): 791–805.

Von Hippel, E., and Tyre, M. J., 1996. How Learning by Doing Is Done: Problem Identification in Novel Process Equipment. *Research Policy*, 24(1): 1–12.

Von Hippel, E., and von Krogh, G., 2016. Identifying Viable "Need–Solution Pairs": Problem Solving Without Problem Formulation. *Organization Science*, 27(1): 207–21.

Voss, J. L., Federmeier, K. D., and Paller, K. A., 2012. The Potato Chip Really Does Look Like Elvis! Neural Hallmarks of Conceptual Processing Associated with Finding Novel Shapes Subjectively Meaningful. *Cerebral Cortex*, 22(10): 2354–64.

Wade, J. B., O'Reilly, C. A., and Pollock, T. G., 2006. Overpaid CEOs and Underpaid Managers: Fairness and Executive Compensation. *Organization Science*, 17(5), 527–44.

Walia, A., 2018. "Nothing Is Solid, Everything Is Energy": Scientists Explain the World of Quantum Physics. Collective Evolution; www.collective-evolution .com/2018/11/18/nothing-is-solid-everything-is-energy-scientists-explain -the-world-of-quantum-physics.

Walters, K., 1994. *Re-Thinking Reason*. Albany: The State University of New York Press.

Weick, K. E., and Sutcliffe, B. T., 2006. *Managing the Unexpected: Assuring High Performance in an Age of Complexity*. London: John Wiley.

Weiner, B., Frieze, I. H., Kukla, A., Reed, L., Rest, S., and Rosenbaum, R. M., 1971. *Perceiving the Cause of Success and Failure*. New York: General Learning Press.

Westphal, J. D., and Zajac, E. J., 1998. The Symbolic Management of Stockholders: Corporate Governance Reforms and Shareholder Reactions. *Administrative Science Quarterly*, 43(1): 127–53.

Wharton Business School, 2017. Authors@Wharton: Adam Grant in Conversation with Walter Isaacson. Wharton Business School Online: https://knowledge .wharton.upenn.edu/article/leonardo-da-vinci-steve-jobs-benefits-misfit/.

White, R. E., and Carlson, S. M., 2015. What Would Batman Do? Self-Distancing Improves Executive Function in Young Children. *Developmental Science*, 19(3): 419–26.

White, R. E., et al., 2016. The "Batman Effect": Improving Perseverance in Young Children. *Child Development*, 88(5): 1563–71.

Williams, M., Malhi, Y., Nobre, A.D., Rastetter, E.B., Grace, J., and Pereira, M. G. P., 1998. Seasonal Variation in Net Carbon Exchange and Evaportransportation in a Brazilian Rain Forest: A Modelling Analysis. *Plant, Cell and Environment*, 21(10): 953–68.

Williamson, B., 1981. *Moral Luck*. Cambridge, UK: Cambridge University Press.

Wiseman, R., 2003. *The Luck Factor*. London: Random House.

Xiao, Z., and Tsui, A. S., 2007. When Brokers May Not Work: The Cultural Contingency of Social Capital in Chinese High-Tech Firms. *Administrative Science Quarterly*, 52: 1–31.

Yaqub, O., 2018. Serendipity: Towards a Taxonomy and a Theory. *Research Policy*, 47(1): 169–79.

Yin, R. K., 2003. *Case Study Research: Design and Methods* (3rd ed.). Thousand Oaks, CA: Sage.

Young, L., Nichols, S., and Saxe, R., 2010. Investigating the Neural and Cognitive Basis of Moral Luck: It's Not What You Do but What You Know. *Review of Philosophy and Psychology*, 1(3): 333–49.

Zahra, S. A., and George, G., 2002. Absorptive Capacity: A Review, Reconcepualization and Extension. *Academy of Management Review*, 27(2): 185–203.

Zeitoun, H., Osterloh, M., and Frey, B. S., 2014. Learning from Ancient Athens: Demarchy and Corporate Governance. *Academy of Management Perspectives*, 28(1): 1–14.

Zenger, T. R., 2013. What Is the Theory of Your Firm? *Harvard Business Review*, June.

INDEX